INGENIUM

ALCHEMY OF THE MAGICAL MIND

FRATER ACHER

TaDehent Books
MMXXII

Ingenium: Alchemy of the Magical Mind
Copyright 2022 © Frater Acher.

All rights reserved.

Without limiting the rights under copyright reserved above, no part of this publication may be reproduced, stored in, or introduced into a retrieval system, or transmitted, in any form or by any means (electronic, mechanical, photocopying, recording or otherwise) without prior permission of the copyright owner and the publisher of this book.

Published by TaDehent Books 2022, Exeter UK.
Copyedited by Frater U∴D∴.
Typesetting, layout & cover design by Joseph Uccello.
All artwork by Joseph Uccello.

ISBN:
HARDBACK—9781911134640
PAPERBACK—9781911134657
EBOOK—9781911134671

contents

Preface — 7

CHAPTER I
The Way of the Adept — 11

Introduction	12
The Way of the Adept (Part 1)	15
The Uprooted Tradition:	21
❡The Four Demon Kings	24
❡The Four Kings in Ancient Practice/Catching the Wind	37
❡The Four Kings in the *HYGROMANTEIA*	43
Pragmatic Conclusions	54

CHAPTER II
Radical Otherness — 63

Breaking the idol. Raising the demon.	63
Exorcising Colonialism. Experiencing Otherness.	75
A Model of Radical Otherness	84
The Undermining Power of Pathos	94

CHAPTER III
On the Inner Tools of Magic — 105

Magic as Walking on a Tightrope	105
The Door we See in Blindness	107
Imagination, Inspiration and Inner Vision	113
Clearing the Glass of our Soul	121
Speculatio — Fantasy or Inner Vision?	129

CHAPTER IV
Paracelsian Magic — 139

You, Paracelsus — 139
Foundations of Animistic Spirit Practice: — 150
❧ The Human Constitution — 152
❧ The Inner Ascendant — 156
❧ An Ecosystem of Spirits — 163
The Plow we Pull — 168
The Planetary Cocoon — 173
The Practice of Scientia & Magica — 182
Celestial Inclinations — 187
Seeing the Light of Nature — 198

CHAPTER V
Becoming Ingenium — 205

The Book of M and the Ens Astrale — 205
Learning Demon-Language — 220
Black Fire upon White Fire — 239
The Way of the Adept (Part 2) — 242
Apodosis — 250

APPENDIX 1: *Addendum to a Model of Radical Otherness* — 256
APPENDIX 2: *Working with the Void, by Josephine McCarthy* — 258
Bibliography — 261

PREFACE

THIS is a book about human qualities. Tendering to the risk and likelihood that these do not exist in the plural, it is a book about *the* human quality.

The human being is a person composed of myriads of non-human persons. Much of this book is devoted to explaining this idea and putting it into practice. It is not a new idea but neither an old one. It is a timeless discovery. One that does not need to be handed forward in time from one human to another. Instead, it's a discovery that wants to be pulled out of your own flesh, that wants to be drunken from your own blood, inhaled from the surface of your own skin. It is a quintessentially sensual discovery. Or so I hope to show in this book.

Now, who are these non-human persons that make up the human person?

Many bees together form a hive. In a single season, thousands of bees die, thousand new ones are born, and during winter their colony is reduced to a small bundle of survivors keeping each other alive on their own body heat. Yet the hive always remains a hive. Its mutability is the source of its stability; its resistance to committing to a single form, or even to repeating itself once, is the secret of its cyclical life. As we shall see, such a mode of being cuts quite close to the *human quality*.

However, in another respect, these *persons* that constitute the human person are quite different from bees. Because they do not represent or descend from a singular species. They are legion. In this regard we will fare better by comparing humans to a *forest*, a *lake*, or a *mountainside*: That is, to a *topography* that forms the habitat for a multitude of different species, and that, by offering itself as a dwelling, becomes itself.

Some of the persons that make up the human person are tiny fragments, hardly holding a consciousness of their own. Others are rousing and unruly, fully fledged consciousness-organs in themselves, ready to pull our minds, our hearts and hands into constant assimilation. Some of these persons or consciousnesses have been with us from birth, others we have picked up along the way.

Yet, the common denominator amongst all of these persons is that they *are not us*. They are a whole world, a microcosm that has been implanted in us. Or, more correctly, I should say that we ourselves have been implanted into. But none of these persons constitute what I would like to term the *human quality*.

That is a truly marvellous thing about humans: life can cut away at them, take away from them, make them bleed, shatter them, and reduce them to fragments of what they once used to be. And yet, life cannot reduce their quality of being human. Humans have a wolf under their skin and you can kill that wolf. Humans have a hare under their skin and you can kill that hare. Humans hold dreams, bonds, vows, memories under their skin and you can take them all away. And yet, you have reduced nothing of their mysterious quality *of being human*.

Catching a glimpse of this most elusive being, the *human*, has been one of the deepest mysteries since the emergence of our species. This book is an invitation, to seek it out and see it.

It's the irony of our current civilisation that we have to come together in a book on Magic—a subject considered most peripheral to modern human society—to rediscover what might actually be at the heart of the *human quality*. Perhaps we are a species that has forgotten itself? Or perhaps we are simply gifted far beyond what we know to take responsibility for? This book aims to show pathways to discover your personal answer.

Now the journey of this book will deliberately labyrinthine. The reason being that in all things natural, the straight line is always a trap.

This journey will lead us to a new appreciation of what the path and function of the magical adept might be. It will guide us into the rough topography of *Radical Otherness*, where we will find the offer to perceive the world without value judgment, to let it come into its own and speak genuinely in its voice of otherness. For only when we have listened can we respond with purpose. From there, our journey will take us into a mystical cave where we will discover a black door, a mirrored door, one that is waiting to be unlocked. In the presence of these doors, magical tools are waiting to be touched by us and to be made our own again. And, in the midst of the depths of our expedition, we will find ourselves again in the cherished presence of Paracelsus. That man whom we have already encountered in *Holy Heretics* (SCARLET IMPRINT, 2022). He is patiently waiting on the pages of this book for us: to take us by the hand again, as Virgil took Dante by the hand, and to lead us deeper into the mystery of *being human*.

It is also from Paracelsus that I took the title of this book. The root of the word *ingenium* is taken from the Greek γίγνομαι, and the Latin *gigno*, which translates as *to bring forth as a fruit of myself*, or more generally as *born* or *begotten*. Traditionally, *ingenium* then was read as the gifts that were begotten to us from birth, the seeds that were placed inside the soil of our selves. As we will see, Paracelsus has a lot to say about these.

I place this book into your hands, therefore, steeped in Paracelsian spirit: in the hope that it will assist you in placing good seeds into yourself and in bringing forth good fruits of yourself. In the hope that it will assist you in learning how to give the wolf what is of the wolves, and the hare what is of the hares, and the human what is of the humans.

LVX,
Frater Acher

May the serpent bite its tail.

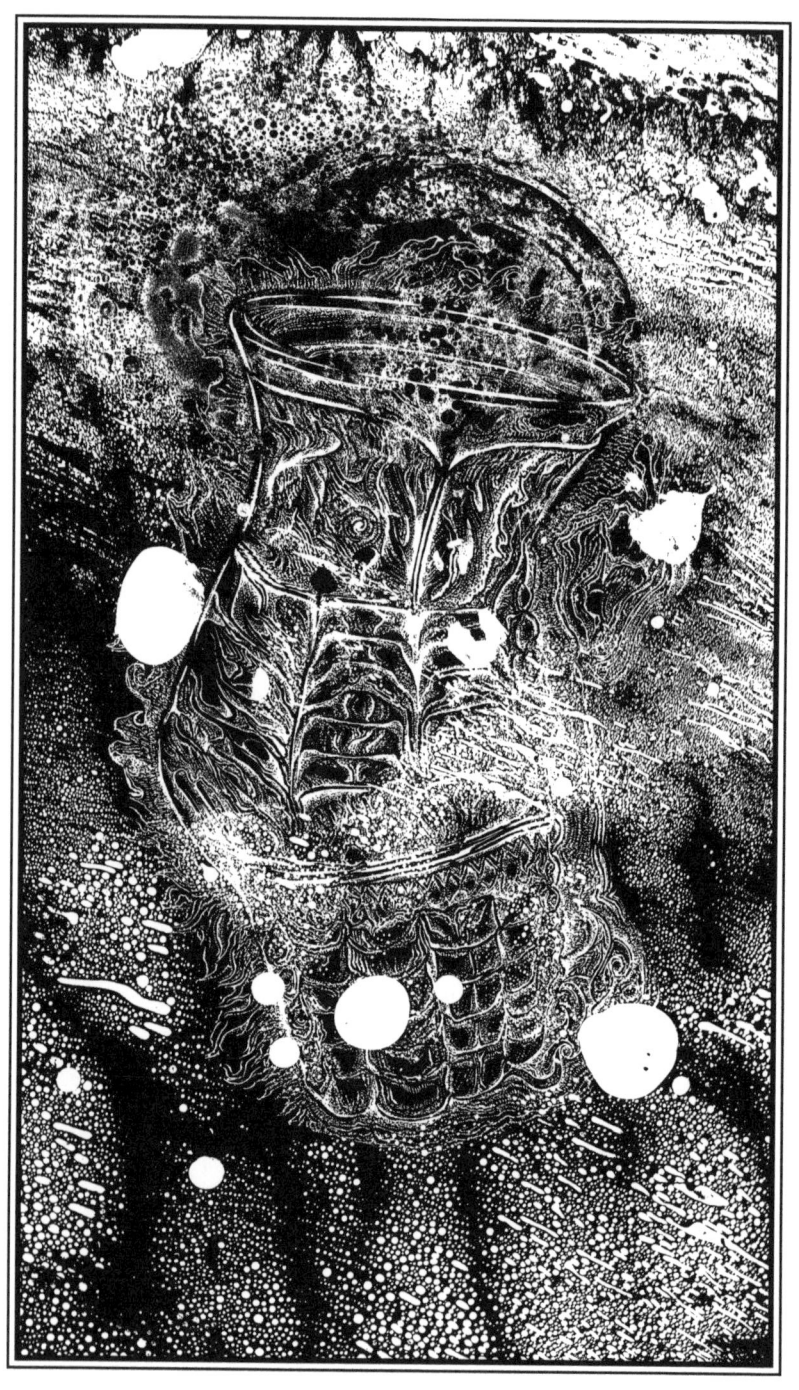

CHAPTER I

The Way of the Adept

The Glorious Wisdom [i.e. Mahakala] will display his terrifying form, extremely ferocious, eagerly wrathful, black in colour, scowling intensely and baring his fangs, and the hostile beings will be liberated. It is not meant to harm those beings, but rather to relieve them of suffering and establish them in freedom. When parents discipline their children, it is for their children's welfare, not their own. Likewise, to benefit sentient beings, you must be unblemished by the stain of self-interest, son.

Gods and demons are thus not distinguished based on their form, and it is even difficult to distinguish them based on their behaviour. There are those who behave nicely and are pleasing to behold but are demonic in harming the mind. And there are ugly, frightening, dangerous beings who act as gods in terms of benefit. Nonhuman, malicious, wicked beings, if they like us, act as gods to assist in creating conducive conditions for achieving enlightenment. Since demons act as gods, they are called god-demons. You should know that there is not a separate essence of a god or a demon—they are the same.[1]

---

1 Sarah Harding (ed.), Machik's Complete Explanation—Clarifying the Meaning of Chöd. A Complete Explanation of Casting Out the Body as Food, London: Snow Lion, 2013, p. 130

INTRODUCTION

WE NEED TO ANTHROPOLOGIZE THE WEST: SHOW HOW EXOTIC
ITS CONSTITUTION OF REALITY HAS BEEN.[2]

THE FOLLOWING is an exposition on the Way of the Adept, and how the Western Tradition of Magic has lost its roots in nature and the spirit realm.[3] We will exemplify our points by analysis of the Four Demon Kings as they appear in the tradition of Solomonic Magic.

Before we begin, however, we should clarify the position and premise that inform our approach. When writing about magic in the 21st century it is often expected to carefully consider and select a distinct audience for which the material is then arranged and presented: for historians, scientists or practitioners. Regrettably, I haven't given up the delusion yet that I might write for all three audiences. Mainly that is for two reasons: one, personally I enjoy reading, learning from and exploring all three paradigms equally; thus I am not sure why my writing should need to be more one-dimensional than my reading. Secondly, and more importantly, if the spirit realm has the same ontological reality (or lack thereof) as the human realm does, all three lenses should be able to contribute valid and mutually enriching aspects of research to our better understanding of it.

---

2 Paul Rabinow, 1986, p. 241
3 It was inspired by the wonderful chapter „The Way of the Shaman" in *Shamanism and Tantra in the Himalayas* (2002), a highly recommended parallel read to further study the similarities and differences of the Western and Eastern magical paths.

Let me expound on the second point further, as it is often not stressed enough and yet essential to understanding the nature of magic. The same scientific forces that first laid magic to rest in the evidence vault of history, have now placed the enlightened worldview of the axiomatic cause and effect dominion right next to it. Chaos theory and quantum mechanics, amongst many other young and emerging faculties, have abundantly proven that if only we zoom out far enough into either macro- or microcosm, all of our Newtonian certainties will fade away. If we follow the scientific path of logic through to the end, we suddenly see: our human, physical senses as well as our cognitive minds are the real magicians. They keep us entangled in an illusion that seems entirely self-generated, they conjure up continuous first-hand experiences that at best have brittle ontological status, and they do it in such a magical manner that exorcising i.e. banishing them, breaking away from under their spell seems absolutely impossible.

Now this is where we have to place the tip of our knife to slice through the artificial division between historic, scientific and practical perspectives on magic. Knowing that we are caught in a game doesn't make said game less relevant. A simulation remains *our reality* unless we have found a way to free ourselves from it for good. At least for the foreseeable future, no human being will free themselves from their cognitive mind and physical senses without eradicating themselves in the process as well.

Let's illustrate this by a few simple examples. Knowing that traffic rules are just standard agreements among fellow humans, without any ontological reality of their own, does not change the impact we will feel when entering the roundabout the wrong way. The crash and destruction to our car and body will still feel incredibly *ontologically relevant*. Equally, while sitting down at the dentist's for a root canal treatment, the knowledge that the signal to arrive in our brain is merely a chemical reaction will numb none of its real intensity. Virtual, abstract knowledge has incredibly little leverage over the overpowering presence of first-hand reality. Despite how hard we try to separate our lives from our physical senses by burying ourselves in artificial, virtual worlds—in the real life, mind does *not* rule over matter. And the question of what is ontologically real is only of peripheral interest compared to what holds *relevance* over the experience of our lives.

From my first twenty years of active practice in magic, this seems to be the point most often misunderstood. Magic is a science and art that operates with and through *lived reality*, not *abstract ontology*. Again, allow me to illustrate this. The fact that the sun does not revolve around the earth matters nothing to the fact that we all *see* the sun rise in the east every morning. I can *see* the sun revolve around the sky, my body experiences the change in its altitude and in intensity of its rays. Thus, astrology operates on the logic of a lived experience. The twelve houses, the decans, the head and tail of the dragon are *real* in the same way as traffic rules are. With the only difference that traffic rules represent human-to-human agreements, whereas astrology represents creation-to-human agreements. We might get lucky to evolve or change the former; we will always remain subject to the latter.

Intellectual insight, even divine gnosis—as cognitively pure and satisfying as they can be—hold very feeble power over incarnated substance. Experience is made of flesh, and bones, and blood, and kisses and cuts. The elements are the ultimate illusion, and yet they are also the ultimate womb, and we all live inside it. Quantum mechanics may prove the illusion of the lived experience. And yet, its findings change nothing in regard to the *experiential relevance* of a divorce, a dislocated back, or a disabled child.

The matrix matters; and magic offers one of the most elegant and impactful pathways for travelling within it. The inhabitants of the spirit realm—in their myriad species of deities, demons, jinns, angelic beings etc.—when viewed within such a paradigm, hold the exact same level of ontological reality as our human bodies do. They may not be entirely real, but real enough to care about.

THE WAY OF THE ADEPT

(PART I)

In helping and serving, we have the right attitude toward both the exalted beings whom we call the elder siblings and the masters of wisdom, and the lower beings in the elemental, mineral and animal kingdoms.[4]

THE way of the adept is the way of *unconditional aid*. The word "unconditional" is used here in particular in regard to incarnated ego or false empathy on the side of the adept. For the experienced magician to work as an adept they have to become a mature carrier of the divine flame. No longer under the yoke of wanting to prove their own self-efficacy, they are ready to work in service. Having learned how to balance the *triangle of healing* between its three corner-points of *creation*, *maintenance* and *destruction*, the adept turns themselves into an agent of steadfastness through work with humans, spirits, and the land.

Within the work of the adept the essential steps are no different from any mundane doctor. In a merely idealised progression, they focus on *diagnosis*, *therapy*, and *cure*. These terms are easy to voice and yet very hard to accomplish. Quite alike to Einstein's famous axiom ("If I had an hour to solve a problem I'd spend 55 minutes thinking

---

4 Bäzner, Erhard; *Die Naturgeister*, München: Drei Eichen Verlag, 1967, p. 174; (Note: all translations from the German have been done by the author unless indicated otherwise).

about the problem and five minutes thinking about solutions.") the majority of the adept's work consists in getting to know and staying in tune with the enlivened topography they are an integral part of. Knowing the lay of the land, its various realms of spirits, their intersection points with the human realm, the varying modes and methods of communication and mutual influence between the two, and then knowing how to travel, to tune and transform these marks the essence of their craft. The *art of unconditional aid* in such a sense is equally rooted in deeply pragmatic operating skills as well as in the resolute wisdom, hard-earned from first-hand experienced, when *not to apply* these.

Any adept is tasked to remain highly agile and to work upon themselves for the entire duration of their lifetime. Mostly this presents a necessity of survival in the reality they find themselves in rather than a noble gesture of elitist sublimation. Each intervention the experienced magician decides to take upon the vast weave of spirits and creation, sends ripples (or sometimes shock-waves) into many directions, and most certainly back into their own physiology and psychology.

Adepts are only human. The quality of their inner and outer disposition defines the foundations as well as the circumference of their craft and potency. Adepts get sick, stumble, fall, are surprised by fate, lose loved ones and go through divorces. And yet, when in conscious communion with the spirits they collaborate with, they have access to sources of power that are not available to humans under the circumstances of ordinary life.

Besides their magical skills, the adept's work essentially depends on a broad toolkit of robust mental skills. Understanding, diverting or disabling the venoms that impose the need for outside aid on spirits or humans, is not a job that can be done while wearing rose-coloured glasses. Rather an essential part of the adept's toolkit consists in the critical examination of uncomfortable truths, as well as the encounter with forces that operate dislocated from their intended space of agency.

Many magicians are not up to that task. Which is why the present description might read rather foreign to people who are well accustomed to the modern magical community. Instead of genuine adepts, students of Western Magic are more likely to come across egotists, narcissists, megalomaniacs, daydreamers, alcoholics, addicts, and many colourful combinations of these. The number of magicians who bluff their way through life is and always has been impressive. Such "professionals" are much better versed in taking money for nothing, than turning nothing into something.

Magic is not a profession, it does not render a regular income and by its very essence was never meant to do so. As members of Western consumer societies this is a critical paradox we have to understand. Magical skills—especially if elevated to the level of an adept—are the kind of capabilities that cost an extravagant amount of effort and energy to build up, yet are never meant to be subjected to economic restraints. The comparison to an intimate relationship might help. One can spend a lifetime of hard work on fostering and growing a vibrant relationship with a partner, they are even likely to build remarkable life-skills along the way, and yet the relationship will immediately collapse and turn into nothing if it were to be commercialised. Similarly, magical skills are often a secondary gain, a byproduct of much more intentional and important endeavours. Slowly over time, one may turn themselves into an adept by offering *unconditional aid*; one will definitely cease to be an adept by advertising it.

Most adepts are born with a strong disposition for their work and many might have preferred to be rid of it in hindsight. This complex craft requires lifelong work and dedication yet does not produce any income or livelihood. Thus, many advanced practitioners are forced to lead a double life. They are engineers, retailers, craftsmen, architects, mothers, fathers, factory workers etc. They are mundane members of their local communities; and yet, when someone comes to ask for help, they work as adepts.

This might be another modern misunderstanding. Adepts do not strut about coercing demons as if they were on a stroll through an exotic zoo, they do not abuse spirits for juvenile power-games, and neither do they mistake magic for just another way of getting their adrenaline kicks, nor as a tool for constructing a seemingly uncanny and unique identity. Adepts understand *the means of their work* as a sacred art and *the aim of their work* as a positive contribution to the world around them. In this essential sense, the idea of an adept equally describes someone with particular capabilities, as well as with a particular attitude towards life. Neither of these two aspects are more or less important than the other. Skills alone are nothing without the character carrying them, and vice versa.

The way of the adept always leads back to nature, or reversely branches out from it and retains deep roots in it. Modern academia has precious little to contribute when it comes to moving forward on one's magical path. Neither is academia known to make people street-smart and teach essential life skills (which could be the case according to e.g. an interdisciplinary or even Humboldt's ideal of education), nor is modern academia known to build character. A low level of formal education, therefore, will not get in the way of the magician, let alone the adept. Reversely, life experience as well as an intimate understanding of nature are essential requisites for the skilled handling of this craft. Understanding nature, in this context, refers to having filled one's cup of lived experience within nature. Specifically, it refers to the initiations and teachings we receive from nature through its spirits, demons, and manifold life forms.

Magic stands at the beginning of human culture. Walking the magician's way, therefore, means preserving and renewing this gift, as well as offering *unconditional aid* to the spirits who uphold it from their end.

In some parts of the world, the knowledge and practice of this craft has remained relatively intact over many centuries. For example, we find traditions of Nepalese shamans that reach back hundreds of years within the same valley and family.[5] Here, the community has integrated this craft and its practitioners into its culture,

---

5 Rätsch, 2002, p. 20.

its collective memory and active *habitus*. In such locations, while not without social tensions or deformations of practice either, we can still encounter lived and unbroken traditions. For most of the Western Hemisphere this is unfortunately not true. Two specific pitfalls therefore apply to the way of the magician *in the West*.

The first one would be to import and overlay a carbon copy of foreign practices into one's own country. I.e. a practitioner of traditional Nepalese shamanism in e.g. Switzerland or Norway, will rock up against an array of problems, unless they adopt their practices to local circumstances. This is not because said Nepalese shamanism does not operate effectively, but precisely because it does. A craft of working with living spirits needs tuning to the specific spirit-topography within which it is being brought to life. Different species and beings reside in a Norwegian fjord versus a Nepalese valley versus an African river delta. As mentioned above, the way of the magician always begins and branches out from nature. Nature in this context does not refer to a metaphor or abstract concept, but to the very land each practitioner eats, sleeps, works and dreams upon. The very words *nature* just as well as *land* in such sense include the sky above them and the chthonic depth below them; they indicate broad realms with multiple layers of reality stored within them, not a patch of soil fenced off by a garden wall.

In light of this, Western practitioners indeed can take great benefits from seeking to understand other cultures and their intact spirit traditions. In fact, the tools of intercultural and anthropological studies are among the most undervalued and underappreciated resources in regards to restoring a living spirit practice in the Western Hemisphere. However, the lessons we can take from places where the way of the adept has not been buried in the blood of two millennia of so-called Christian heretics, are precisely that: *lessons, not handbooks*. References, tips and clues can be taken aplenty from non-indigenous cults to where we live; their formulas, rituals, and bodies of orthodoxy though require severe caution before being transplanted from one continent to another.

The second pitfall unfortunately doesn't make things easier for the modern practitioner. It consists of relying blindly on the remnants of what is left in the West as an authentic spirit tradition: the Medieval and Early Modern grimoires, the restorative efforts of Johannes Trithemius and Heinrich Cornelius Agrippa, the influence of the early Rosicrucian thinkers, and then the avalanche of 17th and 18th century occult orders and lodges. With the exceptions of Agrippa and Paracelsus, few of these sources are offering a coherent and broadly anchored system of applied magic. Quite the contrary: most of them presume the operator already has strong foundations in such a coherent system of practice, and then plant themselves next to this implicitly assumed body of practical knowledge.[6]

The questionable state of the Western Magical Tradition becomes especially obvious when we examine its *non-existent relation to nature*. Western Magic's natural roots in folk magic have long been eradicated by Protestant and Catholic influences, since the early 18th century its genuine spirit has been poisoned by the twin-forces of Enlightenment and Industrialisation, while the final blow was dealt by the emergence of Psychology and its subjective internalisation of all magical forces.

It would be foolish to expect that adhering menially and uncritically to the instructions of these torn up palimpsests of what once might have been a genuine tradition of spirit-work in the West would somehow *magically* revive this now long-lost heritage. While many important lessons can be taken from the theoretical and practical study of the Late Medieval grimoires, such an approach in isolation will fail to reanimate Western Magic beyond the scenery of historic re-enactment role-plays.

The literary Ariadne thread that was supposed to guide us through this labyrinth has long since been torn. What remains as a guiding aid are the spirits themselves.

---

6 See: McCarthy, Josephine; *Quareia: The Initiate*, Exeter: Quareia Publishing, 2016, p. 341.

THE UPROOTED TRADITION

¶ The Four Demon Kings
¶ The Four Kings in Ancient Practice/Catching the Wind
¶ The Four Kings in the *Hygromanteia*

IN TIBETAN magic we encounter a class of spirits called *sadak* (*sa bdag* = earth-lord or earth-owner), powerful chthonic rulers who are identified with local areas. These beings consider the earth and ground of a specific location as their own body and self. Interferences with the natural landscape — i.e. the agricultural processes of clearing out, digging up or ploughing, just as much as the architectural processes of building shelters, houses, or temples — easily become violations of these spirits. By cutting the soil, it is the body of the *sadak* that is cut up and mutilated. Thus, they are readily incensed and known to attempt to kill or chase away their human invaders. Each *sadak* has many spirit companions who are differentiated by a lower rank and yet not by individual names, thus indicating the sadak's hive nature.[7] We also hear of the earth-lords' female counterparts (*bstan ma* = earth-women) who often appear in groups of twelve and whose character is meant to be slightly more protective and less malignant or wrathful.[8] Furthermore, we know

---

7 Harding (ed.), 2013, p. 212.
8 Hermanns, 1997, p. 37.

of *sadaks* that have formed alliances with the people living on their land. In these cases, they can even turn into household deities and accept offerings made to their dwelling place in a large stone placed behind the communal hearth.[9]

The idea of the 'genius loci', of the spirit of a particular place, is an ancient *topos* amongst most pagan traditions. Due to the spirits inhabiting them, we hear of holy and haunted places. The Greek gods dwell atop Mount Olympus, and the underworld is not an abstract idea but a reality with physical entrance points through caves, pits, and rivers. In conscious reduction one could argue that it was only the Roman temple that made the genius loci portable, mobile in a sense.

What the Western Tradition have lost since the late Graeco-Roman period is the understanding that Earth itself is the ultimate *womb* of all things created. Despite the apparent subtlety of their bodies that is also true for all sublunar species of spirits, may they be of telluric or aerial nature. Everything is incarnated through the elements, and therefore also bound into the dimensions of time and place.

Although over time the rootedness into physical locations has been lost, even today we can still witness the ancient spirits being one with mountains, rivers, plains, and deserts. For generations of spirits they have dwelled, cultivated and enlivened the same natural places. And yet, in the Western Tradition the roots of these spirits in a particular geographical site have been either forgotten or cut off long ago. Somehow spirit hierarchies in Western Magic have separated themselves from the topography of the land in which they first emerged.

Whilst the axis of *time* has been well-preserved throughout the centuries as a critical line of orientation in modern Western Magic, the same is not true for its twin-axis of *place*. Medieval grimoires provide abundant and prolific detail about the correct decan, day, hour under whose influence the time-bound "gates" to the spirit

[9] Namgail, 2020, p. 64.

realm will unlock; however, these gates themselves, just as the spirits that pass through them, seem to have turned entirely insubstantial. The spirits have become disembodied, and the Western Tradition has lost most memory of the physicality of their presence with us in the here and now.

Michael Psellus's (1017–1078) famous treatise De Operatione Daemonum[10] still provides a fading echo of such autochthonic understanding of the spirit realm. While he explains the material nature of spirits at length, he only peripherally alludes to their actual *haunts* i.e. time- and location-bound dwelling places within the actual topography of nature.[11]

The increasing alienation of spirit and land might not come as a surprise given how far our lore has travelled over the course of the last two millennia. If we were to mark the main routes of transmission on a map we would find ourselves confronted with a maze more mesmerising than the palace of the Minotaur and yet hiding a similar hybrid-hive of gods and humans. One of the more thoroughly explored routes led from the ancient Berber tribes of the North African desert into the lush gardens of Spain, further eastwards into Byzantium, and westwards again into the Late Medieval libraries of monk-magicians such as the "black abbott" Johannes Trithemius, and yet further on to the Hradčany castle district above the city of Prague at the court of Rudolf II. On and on in this way, constantly transgressing boundaries of time, culture, and language.

What is left of a living spirit tradition in the West today is a crossover between Hebrew, Demotic, Greek, Arab and Latin folklore, literary and cultural influences and has travelled extensively from the shores of Northern Africa to the rough coasts of Scotland and back into the European heartland. Many of the spirit names that survived such arduous centuries of migration are now precisely that: mere *names*. These spirits have become ghosts of what they once were. They have turned into their own distant echoes; into spectres

---

10 Skinner, Stephen (ed.), Singapore: Golden Hoard Press, 2010.
11 Psellus, after: Skinner, 2010, p. 61–64.

of what once were powerful spiritual beings, deeply rooted and sustained by an actual natural landscape.

As we will see next, the name of the Four Demon Kings in the grimoire tradition are an excellent example of such uprooting as well as the subsequent progressive fading in substance.

THE FOUR DEMON KINGS

IN Book III, Chapter XXIV of his *De Occulta Philosophia* Agrippa gives us a most succinct and yet comprehensive description not only of the four demon kings, but moreover of the magical topography within which they operate.

Opening this chapter Agrippa explains that in general the actual names of spirits are unknown to man. Rather, what the tradition has encapsulated as their titles are either descriptions of the work they are engaged in or simply denominations of rank and office in the cosmos. The personal names of the spirits can only be learned by the magician through intimate divine revelation.

This essential notion of spirits and their names is such a simple thing to assert, and yet, as history proves, so easily misunderstood. Here is a possible explanation of what went wrong. Agrippa was capturing the remnants of a Western pagan tradition, yet his readers ever since have mainly been people brought up in a Christian environment. Both the Roman Catholic and the Eastern Orthodox Church have long combated the heretic concept of *continuous revelation* i.e. the idea that divine gnosis could be achieved by any dedicated practitioner even in the present time. Rather, they enforced the viewpoint that God only revealed Himself and His secrets for a short moment in time and to a small, chosen audience: the Prophets and Apostles. Since then, no new divine revelations would or could come through. Based upon this rigid notion both Churches erected the iron dome of their right to exist. As administrators of the one, true and orthodox tradition, with all its immutable doctrines, they were the only ones to offer a universally schematic pathway towards divinity and salvation. Nor is such a subjugating and constraining viewpoint merely a thing of the distant past. Both, during the Second Vatican Council (1962–1965) and in the recent *Dominus Iesus* doctrine (2000), the Catholic Church reaffirmed their claim to sovereignty over *any* kind of divine revelations.

For centuries now not only Agrippa's work but most of the authentic documents of the Western Spirit Tradition have been read through such a monotheistic cultural lens. With an entirely inappropriate sense of Judaeo-Christian subservience, esoteric researchers and practitioners alike have aimed to excavate and restore the *correct names* of all kinds of spirits, demons and divinities. More than anything expressing the Old Testament's obsession with man's dominion over nature and thus the power inherent in the names given by the first man to all things in creation, this very idea of the *orthodoxy of spirit names* is one of the hardest misunderstandings to overcome in modern magic.

The importance to our practice of getting this point straight might become clearer if compared to the development of nomenclature in the field of biology. Because what else are spirit catalogues than an attempt to mirror naming conventions that man established in more mundane areas of their lives?

The first encyclopaedic works on plants and animals were written in the 16th century. Up until that point no general let alone standardised naming conventions existed. A loose body of diverse folk taxonomies were the common way of naming plants and animals in the vernacular, often reflecting their visible properties and aspects of human utility. Surprisingly to some, such non-scientific approach of identifying plants and animals led to a relative high degree of biological accuracy.[12]

---

12 Berlin, 1966, p. 273.

However, one of the key problems with folk taxonomies is their innate tendency to increase in complexity as ever more species are discovered. Thus, the description of any particular specimen over time "is made more and more special—hence specific—and [thus equipped] with the highest possible predictive value with respect to the operations for which it is employed."[13] This, in return, explains the many deviations and variations in descriptions of plants or animals according to folk taxonomies. They evade standardisation and proliferate in increasing levels of detail.

Here is a famous example. Still in 1718, the botanist Johann Jacob Dillen described a type of moss as "Bryum aureum capitulis reflexis piriformibus, calyptra quadrangulari, foliis in bulbi formam congestis,"[14] while his contemporary Rupp called the same moss in the same year "Muscus capillaceus folio rotundiore, capsula oblonga, incurva."[15] Today, it is simply called Funaria hygrometrica, *bonfire moss*.

At the end of the day, most historic attempts to simplify and standardise nomenclature of biological (or spirit) species have the tendency to tell us more about the observer than the observed. Or, as the scientists in the above quoted Nature article put it, any system of classification tells "us nothing about the structure of nature itself, but a great deal about our own view of this structure."[16] Already in 1903 the early anthropologists Emile Durkheim and Marcel Mauss had asserted the same notion, coining the now famous dictum that "the classification of things reproduces the classification of men."[17]

Returning to our analysis of the Four Demon Kings, we find Agrippa, already in the early 16th century, pointing out this precise problem regarding its implication for the names of *any kind of spirit* species:

13 Berlin, 1966, p. 275.
14 Latin, translates as: *Golden pear moss with recurved pear-shaped heads, quadrangular cover, with leaves compressed into bulbous shape.*
15 Latin, translates as: *Hair moss with round leaf, long and curved capsule.*
16 Berlin, 1966, p. 275.
17 Durkheim, Mauss, 1903, p. 7.

Many and diverse are the names of good spirits, and bad: but their proper, and true names, as those of the stars, are known to God alone, who only numbers the multitude of stars, and calls them all by their names, whereof none can be known by us but by divine revelation, and very few are expressed to us in the sacred writ.

[...]

But because a name that may express the nature of divinity, or the whole virtue of angelical essences cannot be made by any human voice, therefore names for the most part are put upon them from their works, signifying some certain office, or effect, which is required by the quire of spirits: which names then no otherwise than oblations, and sacrifices offered to the gods, obtain efficacy and virtue to draw any spiritual substance from above or beneath, for to make any desired effect.

[...]

Of this kind are the names of those angels, Raziel, Gabriel, Michael, Raphael, Haniel, which is as much as the vision of God, the virtue of God, the strength of God, the medicine of God, the glory of God. In like manner in the offices of evil demons are read their names, a player, deceiver, a dreamer, fornicator, and many such like.[18]

We can now see the predicament the modern practitioner finds themselves in: the nomenclatures of deities, spirits and demons in the Western Tradition has deep historic roots which often reach back more than two millennia and which grew from a highly syncretic and cross-cultural soil. They obviously stem from a time long before luminaries like Carl Linnaeus (1707–1778) introduced the first kind of standardised system for botanical species. Understanding, therefore, how recent the idea of a *universally applicable classification of names* is in general helps us grasp the exact nature of the problem

---

18 Agrippa, quoted after: Tyson (ed.), 1992, p. 532.

we are confronted with. Western spirit names (as far as we may even use this term legitimately, given many of their North African and Middle Eastern origins) are mostly distant echoes of ancient folk taxonomies, not relaying the divine, secret names these enlivened forces go by, but rather man-made labels that intended to describe *what they do, where to encounter them or how they appeared.*

The facing table on the Four Kings (a.k.a. the *Four Heads, Four Helpers* or *Four Elders* as they are called in the Arabic Tradition[19]) illustrates this notion very well. Over the relatively short period of roughly 500 years from the 13th to the 18th century we encounter a wealth of variants in both names and attributed cardinal points to this simple group of spirits.[20]

Obviously, referring to their most common and widespread appellation, we could settle on an average value or alleged "consensus pattern".[21] Which is precisely what many magicians since the Late Middle Ages chose to do — and still do today. Pursuing such an approach, the names given in Agrippa's table of the number four[22] would most likely be our best bet: *Oriens* (East), *Amaymon* (South), *Paymon* (West), and *Egyn* (North).

And yet, from a goêtic — or generally speaking from an animistic — perspective, this is not only a careless way of approaching one's magic, but precisely the wrong one. Let's examine why.

It's Agrippa himself, in his section describing these demons, who emphasises the ambiguity of their names. In particular regarding the demon ruler of the North he advises against blindly following the common naming convention.

> *Now every one of these spirits is a great prince, and hath much power and freedom in the dominion of his own planets, and signs, and in their times, years, months, days, and hours, and in their elements, and parts of the world, and winds. And every one of them rules over many legions.*

19 Canaan, 1937, p. 84–85/Shadrach, Harrison, 2005, p. 76.
20 also see: Skinner, 2015, p. 137.
21 Skinner, 2015, p. 13.
22 *De Occulta Philosophia*, Book 2, Chapter VII.

SOURCE	AUTHOR OR COMPILER	SOURCE DATE	EAST	SOUTH	WEST	NORTH	QUOTED AFTER
["The Four Heads" in Arabic Magic]	Anonymous	—	Māgar	Quasurāh	Kamtam	Taykal	Canaan, p. 84–85
Sworn Book of Honorius	Anonymous	14th century	Barthan	Maymon	Harthan	Iammax	Peterson (ed.), 2016, p. 227–233
The Book of Abramelin	Abraham of Worms	between 1387–1458	Oriens	Amaimon	Paimon	Ariton	Dehn (ed.), p. 148–149
The Magical Treatise of Solomon or Hygromanteia	Anonymous	15th century	Loutzipher	Bergeboul	Astaroth	Asmodai	Marathakis (ed.), p. 101–106
Testament of Solomon, RECENSION C	Anonymous	15th century	Oriens	Amemon	Boul	Eltzen	Johnson (ed.), p. 51–52
Livre des Esperitz	Anonymous	15th or 16th century	Orient	Amoymon	Poymon	Equi	Stratton-Kent (ed.), 2016, xvii
De Occulta Philosophia, BOOK 2, CHAPTER VII	Agrippa von Nettesheim	1533	Oriens	Amaymon	Paymon	Egyn	Tyson (ed.), p. 259
De Occulta Philosophia, BOOK 3, CHAPTER XXIV	Agrippa von Nettesheim	1533	Urieus	Amaymon	Paymon	Egin (Samuel, Azazel, Azael, Mahazael)	Tyson (ed.), p. 533
Pseudomonarchia Daemonum	Johannes Weyer	1563	Amaymon	Ziminar	Corson	Goap	Skinner, Rankine (ed.), 2009, p. 23
A Book of the Offices of Spirits	Anonymous	1583 or later	Oriens	Amaymon	Paymon	Egin	Harms, Clark, Peterson (ed.), p. 208–215
Grimoire of Pope Honorius III	Anonymous	17th or 18th century	Magoa	Amaymon	Baymon	Egym	Tyson (ed.), p. 536
Grimoire of Pope Honorius III VARIANT EDITION	Anonymous	17th or 18th century	Maimon	Amaymon	Paymon	Egin	Skinner, Rankine (ed.), 2009, p. 23
Clavis Inferni	Anonymous	18th century	Urieus/Oraeus	Maymon	Paymon	Egyn	Skinner, Rankine (ed.), 2009, p. 23

THE FOUR KINGS: THE FOUR HEADS, FOUR HELPERS, OR FOUR ELDERS.

> *And after the same manner amongst evil spirits, there are four which as most potent kings are set over the rest, according to the four parts of the world, whose names are these, viz. Urieus, king of the east; Amaymon, king of the south; Paymon, king of the west; Egin, king of the north: which the Hebrew doctors perhaps call more rightly thus, Samuel, Azazel, Azael, Mahazuel, under whom many other rule as princes of legions, and rulers; also there are innumerable demons of private offices.*[23]

We could now delve into a detailed analysis of the rich legacy inherent to each of the four alternative names provided for *Egin*: *Samuel*, *Azazel*, *Azael*, and *Mahazuel*. However, for a better understanding of all four demon kings the fact that Agrippa only mentions variants for the North might be a more promising lead. Because finding a broader set of demons specifically attributed to the Northern region is a pattern that we also discover with the Sābians of Harran whose celestial star lore played an influential role in shaping Arabic Magic since the 9th and 10th century.[24]

While Sābian cosmology and magical practice was decisively focussed on the planets and their celestial rulers, they also worshipped a "mysterious deity" which they simply called the "North" and which was considered to be the "Chief of the Jinn, who is the Greatest Divinity."[25] This spirit stood out from the rest of their celestial pantheon in being much less transcendent, more telluric in nature, actively directing the planetary spheres in the sublunar realm and residing over the jinns. Rites were performed on fixed days in order to "win the assistance of the North to take control of the jinn and devils, who served the North."[26] The adoration of the North went so far that even during rituals in honour of the planetary ruler of the Sun in February the Sābians would not turn directly to the Sun, but instead "they prayed to the North, the jinns and demons."[27] The

---

23 Agrippa, quoted after: Tyson (ed.), 1992, p. 533.
24 Lorry, 2006, p. 529.
25 Lebling, 2011, p. 131.
26 Lebling, 2011, p. 132.
27 Lebling, 2011, p. 133.

being called North thus seems to have taken not only a gatekeeping function for other planetary influences but also a ruling function over many tribes or hierarchies of jinns associated with it.

Obviously, such mysteriously titled Sābian spirit could be related to the North Star or Pole Star, Polaris. This would blend well into the Sābian pantheon of celestial rulers. However, it would not explain its distinct quality of residing closer to the sublunar realm of creation and acting as intermediary to the other stars. Instead, the correlation to the wind of the northern realm, Borealis, offers a link that takes us to the heart of our investigation into the emergence of the four demon kings.

One of our earliest sources on the four kings, the *Sworn Book of Honorius* from the 14th century, is very explicit in introducing the kings as spirits of the air and of the winds. We will quote the related passage in full, not only because of its importance, but also to illustrate how easily such critical context can get lost in the magical tradition.

> *Therefore we now will prepare a treatise concerning the nature of the air and all the spirits residing in it. The air is a corruptible element, fluid, and subtle, capable of receiving qualities from the others, and is plainly invisible, but it is seen to be composed of parts of itself. In which are spirits, which the holy mother church calls damned, but they themselves assert the opposite to be true, and therefore we prefer to call them neither good nor evil. And those spirits that are governed by air act according to the nature of air itself, and therefore we can understand their nature.*
>
> *The air therefore, insofar as an element, is governed by the influences of the planets. It therefore readily takes on diverse combinations, which we will now describe, for there are certain daemons established for the disturbance of the air, which Solomon has called winds, because they raise up the winds, and behind which the air is moved. And a spirit of that part may be compelled to serve, hence each one should consider which wind is suitable for the operation, because the daemons of that part are awakened then. But the wind for the invocation is not always easily discovered. Therefore we*

order them to be raised up, which «then» are indiscriminately called calm air [aere sereno].[28]

Peter Greenfield, Pablo A. Torijano, Jake Stratton-Kent and Joseph Peterson unambiguously identify the four kings as "demons of the four winds" which sometimes even "become solidified into distinct geographies."[29] Jake Stratton-Kent then goes on to provide a masterful exegesis of the four kings and their diverse network of roots into Western magical tradition.[30] He truly exemplifies a goêtic approach to understanding these spirits. Weaving their echoes through both volumes of The Testament of Cyprian the Mage,[31] returning to them frequently and yet each time through a unique lens, Stratton-Kent manages to draw the reader closer to the effervescent character and history of these spirits. At no point does Stratton-Kent attempt to ring-fence their meaning, their names or appearances into stalled orthodoxy. We, as his readers, do not encounter *one correct way* of reading these spirits, of connecting with them; instead, we are encouraged to follow them into a mythological landscape, a living topography from which they emerged in various disguises.

After more than 400 pages, Stratton-Kent leaves us with a straightforward conclusion, as it relates to the Four Kings.

It is shown that the Four relate as much to points of the solar cycle, daily and annual, as to the winds or elements as things in themselves. That solar decans and lunar mansions played a major formative role in the shaping of grimoire spirit hierarchies is established. The formative influence of pagan theurgy on shaping magical thought, both pro and anti, is beyond doubt. The implications of this, in regard to use of physical materials in magic,

---

28 Peterson, 2016, p. 227.
29 Peterson, 2016, v, also see: Greenfield, pp. 225–233/Torijano, 2002, p. 214.
30 Stratton-Kent, Vol.1, 2014, pp. 64–70 / Stratton-Kent, Vol. 2, 2014, pp. 24–33, pp. 159–163 / Stratton-Kent, 2016, pp. 45–50.
31 Scarlet Imprint, 2014.

and recourse to hermetic god making technology, must impact any serious approach to Solomonic magic.[32]

The diametrically opposite approach in analysing the Four Kings is taken by the grimoire-purist Stephen Skinner. In his book with the orthodoxy-evoking title *Techniques of Solomonic Magic: The Origins and Methods of Solomonic Magic*,[33] he dedicates a full chapter to the Four Kings. While he calls out various mythical connections of the many names attributed to the Four, his main focus firmly resides in deciphering the exact correlation of names and cardinal points. As part of his overview on the topic we can pick up a lot of valuable information, meticulously annotated, because Skinner's historic erudition is as unquestionable as his precision in nailing down the details.

However, from the perspective of an explicitly goêtic approach Skinner is missing the most essential point. Almost casually he remarks at the beginning of his analysis of the Four Kings that "originally these may have been demons of the four winds, but later they became associated with the direction rather than the wind."[34] In a footnote on the same page, he still calls out that the Ancient Greek were "preoccupied" with the winds and that in both Greek and Hebrew languages the word for *wind* is semantically related to the word for *spirit* (pneuma in Greek, respectively ruach in Hebrew). From there onwards, the chapter is entirely focussed on deciphering the correct attribution of naming variants and their correct cardinal direction. Finally he concludes:

> The technique identified in this chapter is the appeal to the Demon Kings of the four quarters for authority to command spirits of their legions. This developed into a system of evocation which was direction dependent.[35]

---

32 Stratton-Kent, Vol. 2, 2014, p. 200.
33 Golden Hoard, 2015.
34 Skinner, 2015, p. 128.
35 Skinner, 2015, p. 140.

From the technocratic perspective of Early Modern Solomonic Magic Skinner, of course, made no mistake. A group of four living spirits, that once had been known to be the four winds, over time became truncated into their specific function of ruling over the cardinal directions. According to such a one dimensional approach to *who these spirits truly are,* no cognitive dissonance has to be experienced when later on they are first placed under, and then fully replace the senior hierarchy of Judaeo-Christian hell. As long as the practitioner holds control over the respective thwarting angel ruling over each of them, there is no reason to fear the Four Kings.[36]

We deliberately titled this chapter "The Uprooted Tradition" and now we can see the precise location where the roots are being cut. As orthodox and correct as the above ritual procedure might be from a Solomonic perspective, it is little more than static that jams actual spirit contact from a goêtic perspective. Correct names, titles, directional alignment and correct timings are the locks and keys according to Solomonic orthodoxy. For a goêtic practitioner, all of these *might* become relevant at a later point in time, but initially all that matters is understanding *the actual being* we are attempting to commune with. For a wind is a wind is a wind.

We all can choose how we want to look at the world: through a lens of encountering beings in their own ontological reality, or through a lens of human utilisation or even exploitation. According to the former a donkey is a donkey. According to the latter it's much more accurately described in its function as a four-legged mill-wheel-engine or load-carrier. Equally, according to the former worldview a prison inmate is still a human being with all its mesmerising depth, whereas to the latter they will be much more efficiently described by their cell number. In our practice as Western magicians we have to make an essential choice; the antagonistic traditions of goêtic and Solomonic magic illustrate this tension extremely well. Either we can choose to approach magic as an optimisation engine for our own needs, or we can approach it as gate that

---

36 Skinner, 2015, pp. 210–211.

leads into an otherworldly realm, populated by species essentially different from the human, a world in which *we* are the exotic foreigners, and mythologies become the interfaces through which we encounter life and otherness.

Whichever choice you choose to make, provided you have laid the right foundations your magic will work. Yes, the grimoire-purist approach of coercing demons will work, just like donkeys for centuries have done outstanding service by pulling the stone wheels for grinding grain. However, the question in the end will be on which side of the circle stands the donkey and on which one the engineer? In most advanced ritual operations the risk rarely is that there won't be a magical effect. The risk rather is that the impact might be created by something entirely unintended, both in nature and consequence.

The term *parasite* only holds a negative connotation when applied from the host's perspective; from the parasite's viewpoint it's all about the pragmatic balance of remaining hidden inside the host's ecosystem for as long as possible, while simultaneously extracting as many resources as possible. This notion translates extremely well to modern ritual magic. An operator invoking barbaric names and truncated spirit-titles which even five-hundred years ago nobody would have understood makes for a wonderful host to all sorts of parasitical spirits. The host-human's vital energy, combined with their naive faith in the protective shield of orthodoxy and the unconscious desire for success—all of them single-pointedly funnelled and folded into a ritual act—shine bright like a beacon in the inner realm. A flame attracts moths; a magician attracts parasites. Even the early Golden Dawn adepts knew that much, and yet deviated into a host of banishing rituals and techniques. As Gustav Meyrink reminded us in his initiatory novel *The White Dominican*,[37] the challenge in magic is not necessarily to learn how to release the arrow from one's bow (i.e. how to invoke a spirit), but how to ensure the arrow's flight ends in its intended target. For *something*

---

37 Gustav Meyrink, *Der Weiße Dominikaner*, Vienna: Rikola Verlag, 1921.

will always be hit by an arrow in the end; and there are many eager, hungry mouths on the other side of the circle, waiting for humans to become their hosts.

Ask yourself: how well can any magical ecosystem be protected against parasites if it includes names whose actual nature you don't understand? Also consider this. The more you expand and diversify your ecosystem of magical artefacts, the easier it becomes for unintended guests to intrude. Magical lamen, swords, wands, robes, chalices—all of which inscribed with allegedly orthodox spirit names that you were handed over by tradition, but of which you have no first-hand knowledge: how safe is such an ecosystem, if for a moment you could convince yourself to consider the spirits were just as smart as you are? Or maybe even smarter.—Yes, *something will be conjured*. Something, in the end, will dwell in the engraved letters on your dagger, something will sleep on the altar you erected, and something will nest as close as possible to you i.e. the battery that keeps this whole ecosystem powered. Reading the diaries of John Dee is a sharp reminder that this reality is not only a pitfall to novices but remains acute and relevant all the way through our magical journeys.

In the following we will portray outlines of a magical path that is designed to avoid such pitfalls. It does not start with tradition but with what is present right now, right here. It does not aim to reenact or retrace rituals performed hundreds of years ago but to generate lived experience with spirits that are as old as the earth. For this, we need to stop romanticising the ancient past as a locus of greater wisdom than what the *Book of Nature* can teach us in this very moment. And, most essentially, we need to understand spirits, demons, and deities as peers on eye level, entangled with us in a constant process of co-creation.

The Path of Darkness is not a brief excursion, prior to having a flashlight stuffed up your blindfold, and called Initiation. Nor is this darkness the ooky-spooky world of anti-cosmic poseurs playing at occultism. It is not an adolescent turning off the light—hand nervously hovering thereafter on the switch. Both the play acting pseudo-dark and the light — whereby acknowledgement of danger, death and disease are kept at bay — are equally alien to Goetia. Our magic is sprung from plant, stone and creature, from the earth and the sea, the forest, the cemetery and the street, how then to eschew the cosmos? We are exorcists and healers of the Nocturnal Sect, how — indeed why — are we to quit the night and seek the day![38]

THE FOUR KINGS in Ancient Practice
Catching the Wind

FOR a moment, sit back and in your mind's eye begin to see what it must mean to be wind?

You are roaming free now, from the highest point in the sky to the damp depths of the caves. Nothing holds you back. You swell into a storm, overthrowing towers, then you gently kneel to cradle the grain in waves. Your centre is everywhere and nowhere is your periphery. You are yourself in all places; eager to touch it all, you hold on to nothing. You are silent, without utterance, until you meet resistance, on the edge of which your clarion call arises. You roam deserts and oceans, fly over mountains, disappear in darkness and goad the clouds. Nothing means anything to you, for you are essentially free. In a moment's instance you shift from being the great enabler to becoming the great destroyer. You are eternally volatile, bowing to no one, a tool in its own hand, a force that is its own master.

38 Stratton-Kent, Vol.2, 2014, p. 206.

The ancient Babylonian creation myth, the Enūma Eliš is one of the oldest written records we know of. Some elements of its mythological cosmology date back to 1894–1595 BCE. Its tale begins in the time before creation, where we encounter the primordial gods. On its first tablet we witness the father of Ea, Anu creating the four winds. On its fourth tablet, a generation of gods later, we witness the enthronement of the king of creation, Marduk. When he gets ready to fight the primordial chaos, Tiamat, he is donned with the weapons of the god: a bow, a quiver, a mace, as well as bolts of lightning, together with the most "irresistible weapon," the four winds — then he fills his body with a flame.

Let's read the original section to highlight how essential the role of the winds in the fight against chaos were:

> They rejoiced and offered congratulation: "Marduk is the king!" They added to him a mace, a throne, and a rod. They gave him an irresistible weapon that overwhelms the foe: (They said,) "Go, cut Tia-mat's throat, and let the winds bear up her blood to give the news."
>
> The gods, his fathers, decreed the destiny of Be-l, and set him on the road, the way of prosperity and success. He fashioned a bow and made it his weapon, he set an arrow in place, put the bow string on. He took up his club and held it in his right hand, his bow and quiver he hung at his side. He placed lightning before him, and filled his body with tongues of flame.
>
> He made a net to enmesh the entrails of Tia-mat, and stationed the four winds that no part of her escape. The South Wind, the North Wind, the East Wind, the West Wind, he put beside his net, winds given by his father, Anu. He fashioned the Evil Wind, the Dust Storm, Tempest, the Four-fold Wind, the Seven-fold Wind, the Chaos-spreading Wind, the...Wind. He sent out the seven winds that he had fashioned, and they took their stand behind him to harass Tia-mat's entrails.[39]

---

39 Lambert, W. G., "Mesopotamian Creation Stories" in: Geller, M. J., Schipper, M. (ed.); *Imagining Creation*, IJS Studies in Judaica 5, Leiden: Brill Academic Publishers, 2007, pp. 15–59, quoted after: http://www.etana.org/node/581.

As so often, we see fire being fought with fire. The most powerful weapon in the process of taming the primordial chaos are the most rebellious spirits themselves: the four and seven winds. Equally, in one of the earliest written accounts of a magical battle, we encounter the winds as the ultimate magical tools of the mythical hero.

The winds feature in many of the primordial battles of the Enūma Eliš. Their mastery underlines the mightiness of Marduk both in combat and as a spiritual being in general. For the winds hold the power to terrorise the land and to churn the sea. Equally, they are the living forces that can inflict confusion and madness on the enemy they are called upon.

Critically for a proper understanding of these essential raw forces, is the fact that Marduk does not conquer or coerce the winds himself, but instead is initiated into their knowledge and handling by his father, Anu, the original creator of the winds.

> *Anu formed and gave birth to the four winds. He delivered them to him [Marduk], "My son, let them whirl!" He formed dust and set a hurricane to drive it, he made a wave to bring consternation on Tia-mat. Tia-mat was confounded; day and night she was frantic.*

A striking parallel to the four winds in Babylonian cosmology is found in Ancient Egyptian myths. Here the four winds are already adorned with specific names, they are also placed under the aegis of a specific deity in each case and we hear of four consecrated chambers in the section of the sky known as QEBHU where they can be withdrawn to or released from. The role of Marduk, the deity to whom their taming and control was entrusted, is assumed here by none other than Thoth.

> *The Four Winds. These were supposed to be stored in the QEBIU, i.e. "the Cooler" or North wind, belonging to OSIRIS, SHEHEBUI, i.e. "the Heater" or South wind, belonging to RĀ. HENKHISESUI, the East wind, belonging to ISIS. HEDJIUI, the West wind, belonging to Nephtys. The*

four winds were kept by THOTH *in four chambers of the sky, and he kept shut or opened the doors at will.*⁴⁰

In the Graeco-Roman period we also begin to see personifications of the four winds. Amongst a variety of composite shapes, we most often encounter the southern and northern winds as double-winged rams, the eastern wind as a winged scarab and the western wind as a falcon. In cases where all four winds come together we see them being arranged facing each other (South facing North, East facing West and vice versa), indicating their dominion over the cardinal directions.⁴¹

Meanwhile, 700 miles or 1000 kilometres further north in the Mediterranean, the Ancient Greeks held a similar view, which should prove to shape much of the Western Medieval collective memory of the nature of the winds. Here they were called the four *Anemoi*,⁴² offspring from the Titaness Eos, the divine persona of dawn, and *Astraeus*, a celestial Titan, an early astrological deity and ruler of dusk. Homer is one of the earliest sources to tell us about their progeny: *Boreas* the rough north wind and bringer of winter; *Eurus* the wind of the east (according to some sources of the south-east), the only one not associated with a season and to be mentioned in the Orphic Hymns, the cruel *Notus*, ruler of the South and bringer of autumn storms, and the poetic *Zephyrus*, ruler of the West, bringer of spring and summer breezes.

In the Greek pantheon the role of Marduk and Thoth as the ruler over the winds is taken by *Aeolus*.⁴³ Instead of being kept in chambers in the sky, we encounter the four winds often represented as wild horses kept in a divine stable under Aeolus' charge.

From Homer's epics we also learn much about their applied function. They determined the weather at any time of the year, they crucially impacted the harvest, the single most important source of

---

40 Budge, 1934, p. 239–240.
41 Kitat, 2016, p. 47.
42 Greek: Ἄνεμοι, „winds".
43 Greek: Αἴολος, „quick-moving, nimble".

food (and wine!), they affected the mood of people and entire nations and even abducted Oreithyia, daughter of the Athenian king. Critically, they ruled over maritime warfare and destroyed or made victorious entire fleets. Unsurprisingly, we see the Ancient Greeks working magically with the individual Anemoi, attempting to appease, control, banish or evoke them. Our earliest evidence of a "Priestess of the Winds" hails back as far as the Mycenaean period (1600–1100 BC) and later sources frequently attest animal sacrifices to either of the four winds.[44] In Antiquity the winds were known to live in caves or on mountain tops where they were summoned from or sent back to. From Aristotle onwards and into Medieval times we find them in increasingly abstract or *uprooted* representations, most commonly arranged in a naturalistic scheme as a double axis on the circle of the horizon, facing each other.[45]

However, despite this process of seeming domestication of the primordial winds, they never truly fitted into the all-pervasive Aristotelian scheme of the cosmos. Speculations about what precisely caused, raised or tamed the winds remained abundant and their spirited, unruly, free and yet occult nature often led to association with the demonic realm.

> But winds always remained a problem with respect to the order of nature and had, as it were, a basic dual character and role. Mainly because of their irregular and violent movements, winds could not be completely integrated into the general explanatory schemes—a fact revealed by the very proliferation of theories on the genesis of winds and the diversity of their representations. Aristotle therefore states the subordinate position of winds in the cosmic scale of perfection when, at the beginning of the Meteorologica, he emphasizes that the movement of winds is less regular than that of the elements which, in turn, is less regular and perfect than the spherical rotations. Throughout Western cosmology, irregularity was associated with ir-

---

44 Burkert, 1985, p. 175 / Obrist, 1977, p. 38.
45 Obrist, 1977, p. 42.

rationality and violence, and accordingly winds were sometimes correlated with evil in the hierarchy of moral values.

Their negative aspect also has to do with the fact that their location was never an entirely fixed one. While texts on natural philosophy and handbook summaries tend to press them into a rigid scheme of distribution in the sky or on the horizon and to give a neutral account of winds, ancient poetic texts convey a vivid picture of the constant threat of their breaking free.

[...]

However, the four major winds also appear in the opposite role of guarantors of cosmic order by being associated with the cardinal axes, the other winds being reduced to the subordinate position of potential troublemakers. Pictorial representations of winds constitute a main source of information on the view of winds as maintaining the stability of the cosmos, while textual evidence, ancient and medieval, of some sustained kind is scarce for the period preceding the twelfth century.[46]

In this short historic exposition we have learned a few things about the "Four Kings" that remained surprisingly constant for almost four thousand years of human interaction with them. From Babylonian to Egyptian to Greek and Medieval times they were always understood as unruly, untamed, somewhat demonic, and yet essential in their function to uphold the natural tides of time and creation. If the celestial stars represent the sublime weavers of creation and fate, then the winds (or storms) are their dirty hands on the ground that get the job done. Mastering the winds was never regarded as a foundational practice to "open the quarters" before one would proceed to the "main conjuration." Instead, consciously interacting and partially directing the four winds was a privilege reserved for mythical heroes and gods, often imparted upon them by nature and blood, not even via their own accomplishments or

---

46 Obrist, 1977, p. 37f.

deeds. It was the gift they were given by their ancestors. Even then, however, the winds needed to be stored in safe locations—removed in celestial chambers, divine stables or chthonic caves—and the function of the mythical hero was to responsibly oversee their summoning and banishing, not in order to cater to their own pleasure but with the purpose to keep the lands fertile, the season rolling, and the constant threat of primordial chaos at bay.

The FOUR KINGS IN THE Hygromanteia

And Rehoboam asked: "Father, in which things does the virtue of things reside?" And Solomon replied: "In herbs, in words and in stones."[47]

WITH such rich historic context in mind, let's immerse ourselves into one of the source-texts of Solomonic Magic and examine what became of this mythical heritage. The *Magical Treatise of Solomon* or *Hygromanteia* emerged in its current form in the late 14th or early 15th century. Despite its fragmentary nature, it is seen as an important stepping stone in the timeline of Solomonic Magic, bridging the early textual forms such as the *Testament of Solomon* and *Sepher Raziel* towards its Late Medieval expressions in the *Claviculae* and Solomonic grimoires.[48]

Combined from earlier fragments the text that emerged under this name "is apparently a fusion of various magical techniques,

---

[47] Hygromanteia, after: Marathakis (ed.), 2011, p. 33.
[48] Greenfield, 1988, pp. 160 and 269–270.

primarily for controlling demons, which rely most often on celestial and angelic assistance."[49] The text presents itself in the classical shape of divine instructions handed down from teacher to student and father to son, unsurprisingly epitomised in this case by King Solomon and his son Rehoboam. Although described as a "muddled and confused" text,[50] the Hygromanteia is an important artefact of the Western Magical tradition, providing Late Medieval evidence of the depiction of Solomon the King as a Hermetic sage,[51] as well as for its technical instructions providing echoes of the much older, highly syncretic Greek Magical Papyri.[52]

As A. D. Nock pointed out most succinctly, the very history of the origins of the grimoires contradicts any kind of orthodoxy.

> *Working copies have a history which is quite different from that of ordinary literature. In literature the form is essential; one may insert glosses, and one makes errors of transcription, but one seeks to preserve its shape. A working copy has to be useful, and so one modifies it and incorporates suggestions from other sources.*[53]

Therefore, by its genre-definition the Hygromanteia and its later offspring grimoires which make up much of the material of the Solomonic Tradition as hybrid working manuals, were "prone to corruption or manipulation" and "not protected as canonical or aesthetical significant compositions."[54]

As we delve into a specific section of the Hygromanteia, this context has to inform how we approach the text as modern practitioners. We should not at all expect to receive coherently polished techniques that have stood the test of time. Rather, we should prepare ourselves for a mosaic of fragments, reflecting diverse elements and

---

49 Greenfield, 1988, pp. 159–160.
50 Greenfield, 1988, p. 161. *See also*: Torijano, 2002, p. 155.
51 Torijano, 2002, p. 151.
52 Greenfield, 1988, p. 161.
53 Nock, p. 220.
54 Torijano, 2002, p. 155.

preferences of our ancestors which were then fused into a single text. This process of re-compilation and re-fusing obviously occurred over a protracted period of time and was often repeated, each instance including additional nuances and ideas of the practitioners through which hands these copies travelled. Thus, a grimoire like the Hygromanteia needs to be approached with great care, a great deal of critical thinking on the reader's side, and not at all driven by an attitude of discovering *Ancient Truth* on its pages. Genuine grimoires are meant to spur our own practice, invariably under the premise that any risk we run is ours alone. They are not at all meant to provide recipes for safe and automatic repetition.

So what is it that we can learn from the Hygromanteia about the Four Kings?

We receive our answer by jumping right into the main conjuration of the text. Here, we are instructed to slowly enter the circle of the art, to face east, and then to direct a prayer to "Lord Sabaōth" for His grace to "subdue the spirits of the demons and to make them fall before my feet." In a next step, the Lord is evoked and called upon in a long litany of 122 variations of orthodox as well as barbaric divine names. Immediately, and in striking generality, the main conjuration follows.

> *I conjure you spirits, by God who is seated upon the Cherubim, to whom the whole world visible and invisible, obeys. I conjure you, demons, come before me. Wherever you may be, whether on a mountain, on a hill, at a plain, at a grove, in a cave, in a river or anywhere else, I conjure you to come quickly, at once, outside this circle. I coerce you and command you by God, whom the Angels, Archangels, Principalities, Thrones, Dominations, the Cherubim and the full of eyes Seraphim, Virtues and Powers are serving and not ceasing to cry and say: 'Holy, holy, holy Lord Sabaōth, the heaven and the earth are full of thy glory, hosanna in the highest, blessed is he that cometh in the name of the Lord,' in order to appear before me at once, in a beautiful human form, wherever you may be, without harming my soul or my body and without doing any evil.*

> *I conjure you, demons Kontostor, Tzizaniel, Khalekiel, Rhampael, Loutzipher, Beelzeboul, Asmedai, Orniel, Pagareth, Garpazeki, Dasmatar, Mastraoth, wherever you may be, come here quickly, at once, eagerly and indefatigably; because I conjure you, spirits, by the heaven, by the earth and by the holy mysteries of God.*
>
> *I conjure you, spirits, by the seven planets of heaven, wherever you may be, come to me at once, without delay or tardiness. I conjure you by the air, by the fire, by the water, by the earth, by the sea and by the rivers, wherever you may be, whether in heaven or in earth, in a mountain, a hill, a plain, an open sea, a lake, far or close; wherever you may be and wherever you may dwell, come here without delay.*
>
> *I conjure you by the great commander-in-chief Mikhael; I conjure you by the great commander-in-chief Barkhiel; I conjure you by the great commander-in-chief Pharmouthiel; I conjure you by the great angel Ourouēl; I conjure you, spirits, by the two great archangels Gabriēl and Rhaphaēl, come here eagerly, quickly, immediately.*[55]

Now there are two ways we can read such an approach to conjuring spirits. Option 1 is that the person undertaking this working is desperately lost. Instead of knowing precisely whom they are attempting to contact and commune with, they choose to approach their work in an essentially scatter-gun-manner and simply conjure *everything*. On the divine side they call for patronage of more than a hundred different divine names and thus over a hundred distinct appearances of divinity. Similarly, on the demonic side they initially seem to think that "you, demons" is an appropriate appellation to spirits, only to become slightly more specific by directing their call towards twelve demonic spirits subsequently. However, even in this latter instance they seem entirely oblivious as to where these spirits may currently dwell, what might keep them from showing up or whatever element or realm of creation they stand in general resonance with.

---

55 Marathakis (ed.), 2011, p. 171f.

It would not be unfair to compare such an approach to ritual magic to someone who spends the entire night cold calling random numbers in a telephone book, demanding that the other person immediately appear on their doorstep. While most people will simply hang up on them, some actually might decide to come by, and unsurprisingly these nightly visitors will be quite upset or angry about the stupid person creating all the commotion. Reversely, the caller themselves will come out of this night feeling completely exhausted. They will report back to others that "magic" is incredibly draining, hard work, and that the "spirits" that will appear on one's doorstep are frightening and very dangerous. What they really will have accomplished by the end of the night is to fully exhaust themselves, to broadcast an incredible amount of static and noise into the spiritual realm, and to make themselves visible to all the spirits who were just lingering around anyway, waiting for a stranger to ask for trouble.

I guess the takeaway is a testament to what we found above. Just because a grimoire is historically accurate, does not at all mean that its methods have to be valid. This might hold an essential life-lesson in store for some of us, namely to begin acting like a grown up, irrespective of the source of information we are presented with, we must *not* presume that all necessary critical thinking has been conducted already. In other words, let's take nobody's word at face value but only rely on common sense and the practical correlation to our own first-hand knowledge. If we we are lacking in first-hand knowledge in the arena we are about to step into, that is an excellent warning sign to not run into it wildly scatter-gun style, throwing about conjurations left, right and centre, but to tread carefully, with respect for what we are about to encounter, calmly, silently—like an animal exploring unknown territories.

Of course, there is also Option 2 to read the above in an alternative light. In magic we know of so-called "general conjurations" or, as I prefer to term them, a *call to the cosmos*. My book Holy Heretics builds up over many chapters to introduce us to such a ritual at the very end. Putting such operation into practice is the work of a lifetime and will leave us changed forever. Possibly, the above section of the Treatise of Magic once was part of such an operation. If this should be the case, what has come upon us in the actual text is a strongly truncated and deformed version. Rather than showing the elegance of a call to all beings in the cosmos around us to honour us with their presence and awareness in the ritual about to unfold, it reads like someone whose magical senses have gone entirely numb, needing an army of spirits to feel anything at all. So if this section was meant to attune, align and activate the magician and their position in the cosmos of spirits, its has adopted a rather garbled and helpless form. — I am quite positive: once we understand the underlying dynamics and purpose of such work, we all can write a much more fitting and elegant form of such a ritual for our own practice. Indeed, yes, we can pen *our own grimoire*.

What follows in the operational workflow of the *Treatise of Magic* is another random fail-safe measure. Just in case nothing at all happens, the text informs us, conjure this list of 84 apocryphal angelic names.

Now it's unclear if the following section establishes the next part of the operation, or if it is still an extended element of the fail-safe option in case the initial general conjuration didn't work. However, it's here that we encounter the call for the appearance of the "King of the East, first among and ruler of the four kings."[56] A few lines later then, the call broadens and the fellow three demon kings are conjured as well:

> '*I conjure you who fell from heaven. I conjure you first, Asmedai; I seal you and coerce you by Him who shall come to judge the living and dead, whose appearance shall change the heavens and make the stars fall. I conjure you by the trumpet that the angel of resurrection shall sound. I conjure you, Loutzipher, I conjure you Astaroth, I conjure you Beelzeboul, I conjure you Asmedai, the ones who have the first thrones among the demons, come from the four parts of the world, wherever you may dwell and wherever you may*

---

56 Marathakis (ed.), 2011, p. 172.

be; come before me pleasantly and calmly, without scaring me or maltreating me, without striking or harming my soul and my body. Be meek, calm, truthful, agreeable, gentle, kind and truthful, in human form, and do at once, indefatigably and eagerly, what I want, for this is the reason I came here and evoked you.'

When you say the above, you will see that something like a regiment or gathering is coming. Remain within the circle and they will come close to it at once, but they will not be able to enter. Do not move from your place, but remain there courageously and bravely, and command them to do what you want. At first ask them to tell you who their master is. And when they show and reveal him to you, tell them to take an oath on his head. Then tell them to take an oath on his royal garb, on the office of his kingship and on his head, together with all the officers, so that they will be submissive to you and to your will.

Now you know the procedure of calling the spirits before the aforementioned circle and of speaking with them.[57]

This section makes it entirely clear why Solomonic magic is called just that. In a highly condensed form we are encountering an attempt to replicate the coercive subjugation King Solomon allegedly undertook according to the *Testament of Solomon*[58]. As Peter Busch has shown, such line of tradition remains inherently fragile and inconsistent if not misleading. Although the ToS is often referred to as the earliest source of the correspondent magical tradition, it actually stands in open tension with it. The figure of Solomon we encounter in the ToS explicitly is not portrayed as a ritual or grimoire magician but rather as a pious praying man devoted to God. Nowhere in the ToS are any ritual instructions to be found. Solomon derives his power over the demons he evokes, coerces and then commands entirely through the grace of God and the seal imprinted on his magical ring. Equally, this ring itself was not crafted

---

57 Marathakis (ed.), 2011, p. 173.
58 Abbreviated as *ToS*, written during fourth century CE.

by means of occult knowledge of a secret magical craft. Instead, it was given to Solomon directly by God.

> *When I, King Solomon, heard this, I went into the sanctuary of God and prayed with all my soul, praising him night and day, that the demon might be given into my hands and that I might control him. And it came to pass, as I was praying* TO THE GOD OF HEAVEN AND EARTH, *a ring was given to me by the Lord Zebaot through Michael the archangel, having a seal cut in precious stone. And he said to me: Take, Solomon, son of David, the gift sent to you by the Lord, the supreme God Zebaot, and you will imprison everything demonic, female or male, and with its help you will build Jerusalem—bearing this seal of God.*[59]

For the Jewish and Christian traditions respectively, Flavius Josephus (37–100) as well as Origen (184–253) provide the earliest evidence for an emergent grimoire tradition under the nominal patronage of Solomon. Origen specifically speaks of „conjurations, written by Solomon"[60]. The earliest textual evidence of such a ritual handbook is the *Sepher Ha-Razim*[61] in which we encounter the figure of King Solomon as a *magical teacher*, imparting technical magical methods and knowledge to his son Rehobam.[62]—The *Testament of Solomon*, however, is not part of such tradition of practical textbooks or grimoires, intending to impart ritual techniques and methods. Instead, the ToS portrays a human-demonic encounter mediated and empowered through direct Divine grace, not magical craft.

In contrast to the narrative of the ToS, the entire Solomonic grimoire tradition is based upon the implicit premise that magical craft cannot perhaps *replace* but at least *rival* the grace of God. This dichotomy of approaches is still apparent in the above quoted section of the *Hygromanteia*. The direct, mystical dialogue, which we encounter in the ToS between Solomon and Divinity has become

---

59 Busch, 2006, p.86, translation by author.
60 *a Salomone scriptis adjurationibus*, Busch, 2006, p. 5.
61 Compiled during the early fourth century CE.
62 Busch, 2006, p. 42.

mantled in an orthodoxy of recipe-like prescriptions. Knowledge of seemingly occult words, their correct sequencing and utterance while turning into a specific direction, knowledge of drawing a circle with the consecrated sword, and the safety of fall-back options made up of further litanies of occult angelic names: all of this has replaced the *Living Thou*, the *Divine Other* whom Solomon communed with through nothing but prayer in a sacred place.

Accordingly, the Four Kings of the *Hygromanteia* have degenerated into dim dignitaries. No other individual traits or characteristics of theirs are mentioned except for their functional formula in the ritual i.e. that they are the "ones who have the first thrones among the demons." They no longer hold any kind of individuality, let alone differentiation from each other, but appear in a collective "regiment," require to be "commanded" and coerced to reaffirm their loyalty to their "master" by following essentially human courtly protocol.

The tendency to project human officialism into the spirit realm (or vice versa) is a common formula since the early Christian period. We already encounter such mundane-divine parallelism in the writing of Athenagoras of Athens (133–190) and since Pseudo-Dionysius the Areopagite (5–6th century CE) it turned into a common topos.[63] However, such recession of living, individual spirits behind their official function in the cosmos should not be read as a degenerative expression in and of itself. As we found above, actual spirit names are incredibly hard to come by and often only valid in a one-to-one relationship between operator and spirit. Thus, the attempt to pass on specific knowledge about any particular spirit must revert to other aspects of their presence than a singular label. Traditionally, this would have been accomplished through the above mentioned folk taxonomies which describe spirits[64] according to their appearance, where they are encountered and what actions they perform.

---

63 Agamben, 2007, p. 53.
64 Just as such man-made taxonomies exist for any species within fauna and flora yet discovered.

And this is where the Christian spirit taxonomy according to courtly officialism is falling short. It does not tell us anything about these spirits' visual appearances, preferences, tempers, dwelling places, ancestry, or original myths of emergence. Instead, it reduces everything to a denomination of power-hierarchy.

After these reflections on who the Four Kings might be and how they are presented to us in the *Hygromanteia*, it is time to turn the tables. It is equally, if not more important, to examine *who you are*. And while not expounding the operator's identity explicitly, the *Hygromanteia* gives us plentiful implicit clues on the place and position it presumes for humans in its micro-cosmology.

To examine this, we encourage a re-reading of the above quoted sections of the *Hygromanteia* and then to look back at yourself through the lens of the Four Kings: *Who and what do you see?*

Here is what the Four Kings might tell us. We see a human who has no understanding of natural human-spirit cohabitation. Rather, this magician seems to be looking at the world in a distorted manner. Instead of perceiving creation as an enlivened ecology with interdependent purposes and functions, in their mind the web of creation has fallen apart into singular strands which remain dormant unless awoken by human attention and dominion. Equally, this magician sees him- or herself not only as superior to everything else but as uniquely worthy to act on behalf of our common Creator. Expressly, they seem to have very little interest to comprehend our, the demons' side of things. Instead of attempting to understand us, they coerce us. If they didn't appear to be so naive and yet driven by so much aggression, they'd be rather wretched. Somehow they managed to trap themselves in a paradigm that is marked by isolation, antagonism, and dissociation considerably more than connectedness, exploration, and respect.

Being the raw and untamed forces of the four winds that they are, it is highly unlikely the Four Kings would ever actually reflect in such terms about us. The point I am trying to make with such inversion of perspective is a different one. I am trying to help raise our awareness how much is at stake for us, the humans, if we approach magic through such a degenerated lens as is represented in Solomonic grimoire magic. What comes into play here really is an issue of sociology, whether applied to our relationships to spirits, fellow humans or the environment we live in. People who comfortably assert themselves towards spirits in such a manner gamble away their integrity to engage in e.g. ecological or social movements that aim for more respect, equality, inclusion, diversity and compassionate long-term thinking for future generations. For how could our attitude towards spirits be any different from our attitude towards nature as such? The values we exemplify in our magic are also the values that will come to mark our lives.

I am not at all advocating that all spirits should or even could be approached in a careless or even fraternal manner. Quite the opposite. The rewilding of wolves and bears in the European Alps presents a wonderful parallel for the complexities and paradoxes we also encounter when engaging with spirits through a lens of respect and concern for ecology. Solomonic Magic has turned itself into the antagonism of an integrated path of magical practice because it optimises for one single species alone because its premises are based on a monotheistic mentality of exploitation, megalomania and human self-centredness.

Irrespectively of how well we have forged our consecrated sword, we will actually *never be kings and queens*. Neither in mundane life nor in the circle of the art. For bears and wolves, and spirits alike, do not submit to kings and queens. Granted, unless you get killed in the process, you might be able to trap them, bind them and lead them through a painful process of degeneration until they or their offspring wither away in zoos. But they will never obey a king. — The historic evolution of the ritual approach to the Four Kings, these ancient autochthonic aerial spirits of the land and sky, presents a striking example of this paradox. Verily, the Four Kings are unruly primordial beings, necessary to maintain fertile lands, and yet demonic and destructive when entering the human realm wild and unbound by purpose. It could not matter less to them how humans' associations of them changed over time,⁶⁵ just like a wolf remains a wolf and could not care less which mythological framings humans may project upon their species.

Sartre once famously wrote "hell is other people." In the same vein, we can conclude that according to Solomonic Magic, "the demon is the other." In the following we will provide both hands-on examples of how to engage with spirits through a much more ecologically conscious lens. Additionally, and maybe more uniquely to this book, we will also offer a cognitive framework to encounter *otherness* through a lens of authentic contact, exploration and respect.

> Then the Spirit of God was taken from me, and I became weak, and from that day on my words were empty talk.⁶⁶

Pragmatic
CONCLUSIONS

So what are we taking home from this for our own practice?

ONE conclusion would be to inverse the utilitarian logic of Solomonic Magic. Rather than choosing the spirits to work with according to their power hierarchy and respectively assigned office from a grimoire, choose the spirits who are already present with you at this very moment. After all, we are living on a planet that is saturated with spirit consciousness in every blade of

---

65   Skinner, 2015, p. 128.
66   Busch, 2006, p. 274, translation by author.

grass and crack in the pavement. If we were willing to give up our human agenda of agency, we could begin to work with those spirits who are already calling for our attention and service right around us.

Doing this in practice could not be simpler. Next time you encounter the wind in your area, slow down and take time to observe it. See how it moves through the trees and bushes and how it interacts with the land. Lift your view and regard how it weaves and drives the clouds high up in the sky. Now consider the immense scale and dimension of its ephemeral body, stretching all the way from above the clouds to right above the ground. Consider how it has mastered to balance its forces, here sweeping the sky, there touching the leaves of a tree without harming them. See what else you can observe in the wind...

Then maybe begin to speak to it. This might be easier than you think, for wind by its very nature is resonant with utterance and breath. If you hold some skill in visionary magic, conduct a simple exercise. Close your eyes, calm yourself, then lift your consciousness out of your body above your head and rise upwards vertically. Allow your consciousness to rise high, see how it leaves the house you are in, how it lifts above tree crowns or skyscrapers, and begin to observe the unfolding diorama of a miniature world below you. Don't things tend to seem really small, once you behold them from above? When your consciousness is somewhere below the point where the wind meets the clouds, slow down and hover in place. Now feel the wind around you. Realise how it craves contact and yet does not hold on to anything. Grasp the qualities of the wind you are working with. Is there curiosity or anger, playfulness or petulance? Is it dry or moist? From which direction is it coming and where is it headed? Can you begin to extend your consciousness and come to feel its periphery? You might want to speak to it again while residing so close to it. What does it want? Where does it come from? Is there something you can do for it? Would it be willing to do you a favour and if so, feel free to ask it for help. In the end, it might even offer you up a key of utterance, a name by which you can call it in future.

Once you have begun to experience the wind in your area through such direct, unmediated contact, you might be surprised how often you'll realise its presence going forward. Your senses are now awake to see a being that has always been there, hiding in plain sight, in-between all the physical forms surrounding you. Your ecosystem of spirits is now enriched by one important species. Over time you'll realise all sorts of interdependencies between yourself, the land, the animals, the plants and tides of time with the wind.

Now, if you wanted to take this into a context of ritual magic, the approach remains the same, but we are moving to a new stage setting. From the natural environment of the land and sky we are shifting into the idealised power-grid of sacred architecture, the temple. We could also say that we are moving from the frontend of creation to its backend, or from its user-interface to its code. We are going one layer deeper. Here we are working in a four-fold pattern with a gate to each quarter as well as with a fifth-central gate in the centre. Immediately we have created two spaces: an inside of the circle and an outside, as well as five places of immense importance: the five *thresholds*.

What is critical to understand here is that a temple is merely a condensed and idealised setting of an underlying core-pattern that manifests everywhere in life. The magical thresholds of the four quarters in a temple-circle are indeed unique and they lead to very specific locations that have been travelled from both sides for many millennia. However, the logic that applies to the magic contained in these thresholds is the exact same dynamic that we would encounter on any other mundane threshold i.e. place of entering and exiting, of transition, on the original liminal sphere. To highlight this more vividly, let's read the following illustrations of the importance of the threshold in a Berber tent, taken from Edward Westermarck famous work *Ritual and Belief in Morocco*.[67]

---

[67] Westermarck, Edward, *Ritual and Belief in Morocco*, in Two Volumes, London: MacMillan and Co., 1926.

Besides the fire-place there is another haunted place in the house, namely the threshold. Nobody is allowed to sit down on the threshold of a house or at the entrance of a tent; should a person do so, he would become ill himself or give "bas"[68] to the dwelling. So also it would be unlucky for the house and its inhabitants if anybody should pull up the backs of his slippers on the threshold. A bride is carried across it; Chenier says that when the bride enters the bridegroom's house, her relatives carefully observe that "she shall not touch the threshold of the door." The "masters of the house" are walking in and out over the threshold. Every house, and indeed every place, has its jinn owners. These spirits are called "the masters of the place," "the men," "the people of the place." If the masters of the house are good the inhabitants will prosper, if bad they will have misfortune or soon die.[69]

A very frequent and powerful method of making 'ār[70] is to sacrifice an animal on the threshold of the house or at the entrance of the tent of the person from whom a benefit is asked. If he steps over the blood or only catches a glimpse of it, he is, for his own sake, obliged to grant the request made by the person who killed the animal. If he has previously heard that 'ār sacrifice has been made outside his dwelling and he is unwilling to do what is asked of him, he tells his servants to remove the dead body and to wash away the blood carefully, and in this case, when he has not seen the blood at all, the danger is lessened. On the other hand, if he fulfils the wish of the supplicant, he need not be afraid of stepping over the blood, since the curse it carries is only conditional. If a person who has been thus appealed to is unable to give the assistance required, he may be obliged to provide another animal to be killed as 'ār on somebody else.[71]

The Ait Wāryager put tar on the threshold of the house and at the place on the floor where they sleep, as a protection both against jnūn and snakes.[72]

---

68 *l-bas*, "that which is bad," an impersonal force of evil, differentiated from *jinn*, see Westermarck, Vol. I, 1926, p. 26.
69 Westermarck, Vol. I, 1926, pp. 295–296, note: unmarked omission of Arabic and Berber expressions from original.
70 i.e. transference of conditional curses.
71 Westermarck, Vol. I, 1926, p. 527.
72 Westermarck, Vol. I, 1926, p. 307.

In Andjra a sheep, goat, or cock is killed on the spot where the house will have its entrance, to prevent its being haunted. When the threshold has been made, some salt is buried underneath it.[73]

If anybody sits down on the threshold of the house, Šîtan will sit down by his side.[74]

The threshold is the prime example of an interspace. Neither part of the inside nor the outside, it is the demarcation line that separates both. The threshold is the crack, the fine line that divides what becomes two sides of one coin. In a magical setting it is not only the place where one room is differentiated from another, it is where one *realm borders onto another*.

Obviously, when considered as part of a tent, a house or any other structure of fortification meant to offer safety[75], the threshold is also the most vulnerable space of the architecture. It is the point that is meant to open and therefore cannot be permanently sealed.

The uninvited transgression of a threshold, therefore, is a primal act of aggression towards the inhabitants of the space it was meant to secure. More uncanny than transgression, however, is the pure lingering, the dwelling, the living on the threshold itself. It marks the being who is neither at home here nor there, who is part of two worlds, who is the eldritch nomad between two realms or more. The threshold is the place of *the other*.

Accordingly, in a temple setting the thresholds marks the most important points of active work. Here the adept regulates what comes in and goes out; through the thresholds they participate in the dynamics of time and creation and interact with the living powers that flow from each quarter, as well as the central pole or flame of the work.

As we have seen, overlaying the winds of the quarters on this fourfold pattern is an obvious and ancient choice made by many ad-

---

73 Westermarck, Vol. I, 1926, p. 315.
74 Westermarck, Vol. I, 1926, p. 410.
75 Peterson, 2016, p. 29.

epts before us. Yet, just because it makes logical sense does not mean we have understood anything about its inherent power dynamics. Remember, working in a temple setting means we are attempting to operate on the backend of creation. To accomplish this, minute knowledge of and personal familiarity with the forces we are calling over the four thresholds is required. Invoking any ancient name or formula, embroidered in a prayer steeped in Christian delusions of power, simply won't cut it.

Let's return to the exercise we recommended at the beginning of this chapter: to encounter the local wind in your area. If you have practiced this work, you will have gained a much better understanding by now for what kind of operations or acts of service you can collaborate with such a powerful being. If you are a farmer, then their rulership over the seasons and the climate ecosystem is a critical angle. As a fisherman or sailor you will know their importance in determining weather patterns and tides of the sea. If you are a pilot, then the same is true for the skies. However, chances are high you are neither of the above. So why work with the wind?

Now we come full circle to our temple setting. Here we are no longer dabbling with the frontend of creation where we can allow ourselves to be playful, curious and maybe just go for a ride on the wings of the wind. Each decision taken in the circle of the art carries significance. Depending on your talent and skill it might have an irreversible impact on your life, the lives of your loved ones or an even greater community. It might change the pattern of the land you live on for a split-second or for generations to come. Who knows? Well, frankly speaking, *you should* know if you desire to take such decisions.

Can you now see—if at all you were able to pull it off—how delusional an isolated run through of the main conjuration of the *Hygromanteia* would be? As we pointed out above, *something* will always be conjured. In magic thresholds rarely ever remain vacant and unoccupied. Chances are you will definitely *get a kick* from performing such a fragmentary ancient rite. Chances also are that so will a host of parasites who have been waiting for another dabbling magician trying to access the engine room of creation armed with a handkerchief and a toothpick.

Nevertheless, if for whatever reason the spirits of the Four Demon Kings i.e. the four winds of the quarters truly appear, are you ready to actually interact with them? These are the very beings who Thoth needed to guard in designated chambers in the sky, who Marduk held in his hand fighting primordial chaos. Again, such responsibilities and dangers only present themselves when working with these raw spirits ritually in a temple setting, not at all when working with their mediated forms on the physical plane.—So once you stand face to face with the beings we have come to call *Oriens, Amaymon, Paymon,* and *Egyn* (or was it *Barthan, Maymon, Harthan,* and *Iammax*?), and endless time is echoing through the forms in which they appear, and the power that holds together the four quarters of the world is beginning to form cracks on the surface of your mind, do you know who you are, why you have come here, who they are and why you dared to summon them?

To be clear, I am not advocating *not* to practice magic at such a deep and powerful level. I am merely suggesting two simple things. First, to acquire the necessary knowledge, skills and competence required for the operation at hand. And secondly, to anchor ourselves in the precise knowledge of *why we are willing to take such a risk*. Most adepts who I know would agree that for every rite they performed they chose to *not* perform a thousand others.

Josephine McCarthy in her QUAREIA course offers a calm, precise and non-orthodox approach to working with the four winds in a ritual setting. It is embedded in the middle section of the *Initiate* course, under the heading of "Deities and the Magician."[76] It is impossible to practice the given instructions without completing the *Apprentice* course first; this means there is an automatic protection lock over these materials that will take any student at least one to two years of solid practice before they can access it.

---

76 Josephine McCarthy, *Quareia: The Initiate*, Exeter: Quareia Publishing, 2016.

Here then, after careful preparation for many months, we finally encounter Tefnut, Shu and Atum, as well as the *Vision of the Cave of the Four Winds*. Our spiritual bodies are permanently altered by the hands of chthonic demons, and only then do we begin to practice the pattern of *The Ritual of the Four Winds*. In all of this, we will not be asking for anything other than gaining experience and a broader understanding of the ecology of creation. We will learn to show respect and humility as travellers into realms that we don't belong to. And maybe, slowly over time, we will gain access to power that can break us in an instance; yet also, if applied wisely, create changes of significance.

In the end though, even more importantly than striving to master such adept level of magic, is something else. Something much more simple and straight forward: when we enter the circle of creation, life leaves no blank canvas around us. Immediately, everywhere, we are surrounded by spirits. The land speaks, the sky speaks, the wind travels between them and knows their stories. All we need to do is listen.

CHAPTER II

Radical Otherness

/

Breaking the idol. Raising the demon.

One with a great deal of merit need recite the mantra here only 10,000 times; one with medium merit should recite it 100,000 times; and one whose merit is small should recite it 10,000,000 times [...] Moreover, he says, the following numbers of recitations must be subtracted from the total number: for falling asleep, fifteen; for sneezing, ten; for breaking wind, seven; for stumbling, five; for coughing, five; for yawning, three; and for spitting saliva or mucus, ten.[1]

IT IS THE sad reality of magical traditions in both the East and the West that the few people who actually knew what they were doing either disappeared without a trace or, in rare cases, left some

[1] 17th century mantra meditation instructions, from: Stephan Beyer; *Magic and Ritual in Tibet: The Cult of Tara*, Delhi: Motilal Banarsidass, 1988, p. 244.

evidence of their practice which then was turned into literary works that became quickly misunderstood, reinterpreted and dogmatised. To make matters worse, such rare literary treasures—today often obscured by time and orthodoxy—rest at the bottom of an ocean of mostly useless literary works on magic, produced, copied and recompiled by an army of so-called practitioners and officials. These, in turn, were usually distinguished by the fact that they had no first-hand experience whatsoever with the subject they were writing about or editing, or else, they considered their audience to be so stupid that what they spoon-fed them lacked not only elegance and cohesion but, above all, practicability and effectiveness.

Matters of magic are incredibly difficult to capture in writing. We will explore some of the reasons why that is the case in this chapter. Suffice to say for now that despite the uninterrupted efforts made over the last four millennia, so far magic has successfully withstood the human desire to codify and control it. It seems that one of the most prominent characteristics of the elusive, often heretic currents of practices and premises loosely assembled under the term of magic is its ability to avoid the trap mounted between the covers of a book—where paper and ink, like the needle piercing a beetle in a biological collection, are ever ready to turn living spirit relationships into mediocre and misunderstood recipes for power acquisition.

Stating this in such obvious terms, while writing a book about magic myself, evidences both my own averageness as well as the inherent paradox all practitioners of magic have to wrestle with: if we choose to read up on the history of Magic in East and West not through the lens of an *occult practice*, but through the lens of any other common craft, we'd be shocked to find how little reliable *craftsmanship* we will actually encounter.

If any genuine artisan had built houses, cobbled shoes, blown glass, hammered iron or ploughed their fields in the same trial and error way in which still today we endeavour to raise spirits after centuries of alleged "practice," they would not only have long gone out of business but also be much more prone to attracting angry customers than powerful deities. It might be fair to assume that had our ancestors not been burned as heretics, even more of them would have been chased out of their cities as quacks and charlatans. Medieval fantasies in both East and West of what magicians were able to do not only by far exceed the tight perimeter of their actual agency. Unintentionally, these fantasies also coloured a playground of dabblers in the luminous splendour of adepthood which should have been reserved for masters of the art who truly deserved the title. Nobody we know of seems to have ever practiced magic with the same level of perfection with which Michelangelo controlled his chisel, with which da Vinci guided his feather, or with which Dürer carved his plates. While all of these masters of the liberal arts might have been inspired by spirits, the actual art and science of *engaging with these entities directly* has eluded the cultivating rigour, training and codification that the other liberal arts experienced over the last millennia.

What might read as a polemic rant for magical practitioners is an obvious stereotype to anybody who never attempted to practice magic. As Gustav Friedrich Hartlaub (1884–1963) put it in his introduction to Arthur Schopenhauer's *An Enquiry concerning Ghost-seeing, and what is connected therewith*, at least since the Enlightenment magic has always been deemed an "anus-science."[2]

Rather than proving such derogative denunciation wrong through clean spirit-practice and self-critical examination of the tradition's past, the cultural strata of Eastern and Western Magic continued to leaf-gild over elements of fair criticism mainly by projecting dreams of grandiosity and mighty magical ancestors into their own past and present. From Milarepa to Dr. Faustus, despite all differences in cultural milieus and time, it seems to be a common trope of magical traditions that the mythical far too often supplants the realistic, wishful thinking substituting for clean practice, and the hedonistic lust for story-telling ousts the painful precision of honest truth-telling.

---

2 German: *Afterwissenschaft*, quoted after: Schopenhauer, 1922.

Of course I invite you to disagree with such broad sweeping statements and examine the situation for yourself. While in the West we have seen a fair amount of critical thinking when it comes to the figure of the Medieval Mage, especially Western practitioners still like to look to the East with rose-coloured glasses. The gaze looking for lineage, tradition and orthodoxy in the Eastern currents of Magic easily falls into the age-old trap of mistaking a path well trodden with a path that empowers.[3]

For your own reflections on how myth is balanced with reality and philosophical speculation with practice, I can offer the following framework (see pages 68–69). It consists of two dimensions that can help us step back from magical texts and look at their genuine value with regard to our own practical path. If we overlay these dimension on top of each other, we arrive at the classical four quadrant scheme and can easily assign the genres of written and oral magical traditions to each of them. Whether you are reading Homer's epics, Medieval grimoires, the Northern Treasures of the Nyingmapa school, or an 18th century Masonic initiatory text, this model might assist you in your exploration. It can help strip back man-made layers of dogma, story-telling and lineage—and to help you see whether what you have in front of you is a trustworthy source to lean your own practice against, or just another possible case of the Emperor's new clothes.

Wouldn't it be nice to go for a long walk now together? I'd love to hear what you found out about the texts of your magical studies with this simple framework...Regrettably, as I cannot offer you an actual joint walk, let me at least offer my own reflections from applying this model to several of the source-texts I am currently working with.

Having looked at these literary artefacts through the hard lens of both of the above dimensions, here are the facts I needed to concede to myself again.

---

[3] e.g. "The literature on the [Northern] treasure revealers is almost as extensive as the Treasures themselves [...]", Fitzgerald, 2019, p. 49.

As lone practitioners we need to own the hard truth that there will never be a path paved for us by others. By the very nature of our work we walk alone, we learn and take from everything that is useful, and yet we don't allow ourselves to be taken by the hand for more than a few steps. We will never feel the oozing social warmth of being fully embedded into a spiritual community of equals, let alone of handing over the map of our journey to a saint, a guru or a perfected master.

We are *goês*[4] wherever we go, be it in Tibetan mountains or on Mediterranean shores. We work and learn from the spirits themselves, not from man-made tradition. The scaffold of ascent that organised religion is to many, is a fence to us. With this in mind, we do not accept any kind of human power hierarchies. We challenge ourselves to look at everyone as an equal or a role model at best—from Enoch all the way to Padmasambhāva. We don't *pray* to humans, deceased or alive, however deified they might have become. Instead, we *work* with them and follow their path in our own footsteps.

Not because we want to, but because our work requires us to, we embody the unruly, comfortably walking on the edge of waywardness, driven by the pursuit of clean practice and first-hand experience. We allow the doors of temples to close behind us as we walk out into the wild. We are the stone fallen from the altar, never compromising freedom for comfort or critical thinking for social cohesion.

Where others seek a sound place of arrival, we seek the tension of possibly failing all by ourselves. Where others strive for gnostic ascent or enlightenment, we strive to become one with the inhabitants of the sky and the land. Where others aspire ethereal ness, we embrace all things created as divine. And where others idolise joy

---

4 For an in-depth exploration of the term *goês* see José Gabriel Alegría Sabogal's and my book *Clavis Goêtica: Keys to Chthonic Sorcery* (Hadean Press, 2021). Alternatively, you can read a free introduction on my webpage theomagica.com in the Essay section: *Goêteia—explorations in chthonic sorcery*.

FIGURE 1

WHEN WORKING WITH SPIRITUAL TEXTS, CONSIDER TWO DIMENSIONS TO DEFINE YOUR APPROACH.

MYTHICAL

- Very high risks.
- Only to be overcome by mythical heroes.
- Everything is exaggerated, enjoyable and satisfying to read.
- A far cry from what we can aspire to do ourselves.

Is it an entertaining read, or is it safe to trial?

REALISTIC

- Acceptable risks.
- Experience made by a real person.
- Genuine experience shines through narrative.
- Challenging but possible if pursued with sufficient persistence and humility.

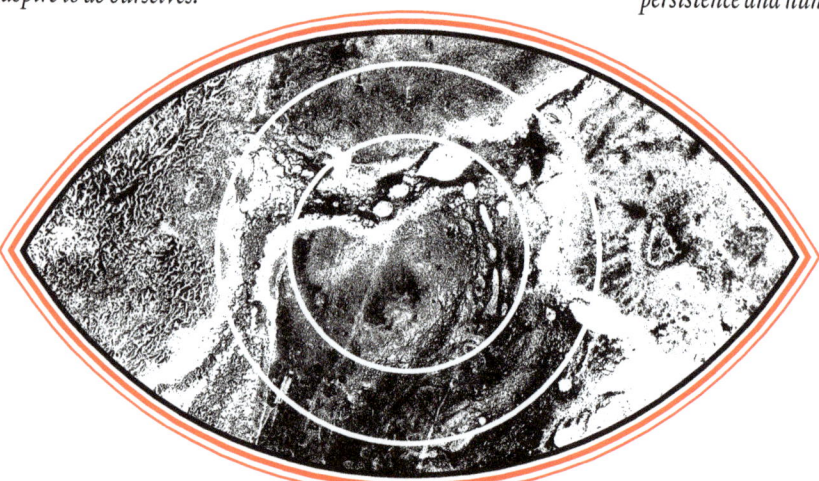

CLEAR THINKING

- Pivots on conceptual thinking.
- Consists of skilfully analyzing, assessing, dismantling and reconstructing an object of reflection.
- Aims to create a sharp, agile and integrated thought process.

Is it aimed to help you think clearly, or practice cleanly?

CLEAN PRACTICE

- Pivots on lived experience.
- Consists of skilfully approaching, encountering, engaging and withdrawing from an object of experience.
- Aims to create prudence and agility in interacting with an ecosystem.

FIGURE 2

HOW WILL THIS TEXT HELP ME FURTHER MY PATH?

REALISTIC
- Acceptable risks.
- Experience made by a real person.
- Genuine experience shines through narrative.
- Challenging but possible if pursued with sufficient persistence and humility.

Orthodox Education

Oral Traditions

CLEAR THINKING
- Pivots on conceptual thinking.
- Consists of skillfully analyzing, assessing, dismantling and reconstructing an object of reflection.
- Aims to create a sharp, agile and integrated thought process.

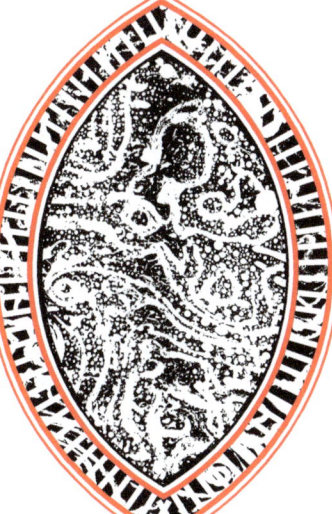

CLEAN PRACTICE
- Pivots on lived experience.
- Consists of skilfully approaching, encountering, engaging and withdrawing from an object of experience.
- Aims to create prudence and agility in interacting with an ecosystem.

Philosophical Texts

MYTHICAL
- Very high risks.
- Only to be overcome by mythical heroes.
- Everything is exaggerated, enjoyable and satisfying to read.
- A far cry from what we can aspire to do ourselves.

Ancient Myths

and happiness, we understand that a muscle that isn't ready to be strained is a muscle vanishing.

Now while they might sound condescending to some, these reflections on the path of the lone practitioner do not entail any sort of judgement. A *scaffold* or a *fence*, *enlightenment* or *ecosystem* — natural objects do not carry any intrinsic value judgment; it's the human desire to categorise and to control that adds the judgmental component.

When I contrast spiritual pathways in the above manner, it is precisely to highlight the diversity and richness of choice that we all have. Walking all by yourself bears the risk that you won't make it very far; walking in the footsteps of others bears the risk of running in circles. Both risks are real, and the one isn't any better than the other. But it is my sincere desire with this book to expand your choice. There is a lone practitioner's path that doesn't even need a name. It only takes *you* to walk it. You can take inspiration freely from all traditions of this planet, dead and prosperous ones, orthodox religions and heretic fringe cults, left-hand and right-hand, celestial and chthonic. And yet nothing should escape the probing hammer blow on the anvil of your own practice. Our concern is not syncretism versus purity of man-made traditions, our concern is the reality and first-hand understanding of the magical realm.

This is an important point that needs to be emphasized again and again. Scholars of comparative religion, especially in the last sixty years, have spent an enormous amount of time and paper trying to categorize and map various "traditional" paths of ascent up the mountain of magic. For the purposes of their studies, such "traditions" must be pinned down as much as possible and stripped of ambiguity and fluidity so that they can be (ab)used as personal battlegrounds over interpretive sovereignties and master narratives. In fairness, however, it must be conceded to the oft-maligned researchers of academia that these same battlefields existed long before their arrival, except that they were populated by religious and spiritual functionaries who, for millennia, sought to confine and secure the same paths of ascent up the mountain of magic (i.e. esoteric traditions) with the barbed wire of dogma and capital-T-truth.

From our, the lone practitioner's point of view this is obviously missing the point entirely. For the mountain of magic does not want to be ascended, it wants *to be lived with*. The very notion of an "ascent" is underpinned by implicitly colonialist undertones of conquest, competition, and human takeover. The topography loses its ontological reality, its integrity as an ecosystem of itself, and is turned into a narcissistic mirror of human agendas. As a *goês* we could not care less about the purported orthodoxy of pathways of ascent, the comparison of this path versus the other, nor about coming first or last. We care about the mountain, we live with the mountain, we aspire to become one with it. For that we walk slowly, we speak to blades of grass and listen carefully to what will answer us. Our true ancestors have lived on the mountain of magic for centuries, and yet never attempted to "ascend" it. Unfortunately, that also implies most of them never attempted to write books about what to them simply was the reality of their existence. Magic from such a vantage point is not a tradition, it is not a craft and neither a discipline. It is the furthest thing removed from another spear hurled onto the battleground of orthodoxy.

If you commit to encountering magic in such a way, you will quickly realise how much hard work comes with it. A single paragraph in a book might take you several months, if not years, to put into practice and to probe against through your first-hand experience. The name of a spirit, a deity, a natural force, dropped in passing in a book on an entirely different subject, can become the work of a decade. If—and that is the essential point—we truly have the courage to not accept anything unless it has passed through the needle eye of our own practice.

Earlier above we touched upon magic's strained relationship with natural sciences, and it is worthwhile returning to this point before we begin to look at things through a more practical ocular. I mentioned that rather than accepting the gauntlet the sciences had thrown at the magical tradition, we turned to seek refuge in glorifying our past or leaf-gilding foreign traditions we hardly understood.

Now, picking up this gauntlet, in my humble opinion, does not at all mean attempting to apply the paradigm and methodology of modern natural science to magic. Obviously this can be done, and Dean Radin's *Real Magic*[5] is one of the latest and very thought provoking books that attempt to do precisely that. Personally, though, I see a third way that can lead us past the extremes of either hiding in mystery or dismantling it. To me, such a third way of overcoming the lack of reliability and validity much of the magical tradition holds both in the East and West, lies in radically redefining what the term magic really describes.

Most often in the pertinent literature we find magic described as a spiritual technology, often alluded to as a *craft* in a traditional sense i.e. an either inborn or/and learned activity involving skill in making things by hand which in return bestows the practitioner with access to certain amounts of power. As stated above, if this was the bar for excellence for the magical tradition both East and West, it has miserably failed to live up to the common standards of functionality, reliability, and utility of other traditional crafts.

Considering that at least some of our ancestors were actually quite good at what they did—and yet still, our tradition cannot live up to the standards of any other common mundane craft—we might want to consider if we have actually chosen the correct benchmark? Are the standards of a *craft* really the adequate measure for assessing the elegance and impact of one's magic? I want to suggest that they are not. For whatever it is worth, from my own experience as a practicing magician there is something else magic holds much more in common with than *artisanry, liberal arts* or *modern sciences*, even though it freely borrows from all of the three. Magic, I want to suggest, is not a craft, but a *relationship*.

Let's zoom out and reflect on this idea for a moment...

---

5 Dean Radin's *Real Magic*, New York: Harmony Books, 2018.

As the species of Homo sapiens, we look back upon millennia of attempting to lead a happy life with other people around us—and yet what is the state of the world we live in today? Speaking more personally, we look back upon centuries of an ideal of romantic love and spending longer periods of time with another being as an intimate partner. And yet, in 2020 in the European Union divorce rates were as high as never before.[6]

Now, does this failure of becoming better at loving, of becoming better at being social take away any of our intrinsic desire to love and to be social? Not at all. Generation upon generation is throwing themselves into the storm of *mastering relationships*. Few of us ever come out of it fully successful; and still, we would never give up as a species. Call it foolish, ignorant or biologically conditioned—whatever creates the urge to love and to be social, these drives are at the heart of what actually make us human.

Now, judging our *progress in loving* through the standards of a *craft* would be missing the point entirely. Of course there is an aspect of art and science in building relationships as well as in leading a long and happy life with another partner. However, the way Peter and Paul achieved decades as a happy gay couple might be entirely different from how Jill and Tom created their own fulfilled relationship. This is because Peter, Paul, Jill and Tom are not the same human being; they are just as similar as they are also different. Suggesting that alternatively Jill and Peter could have become just as happy as Jill and Tom would sound crazy to each of them—and yet that is what we would expect *if loving was a craft*. As an artisan we want to produce reliable, repeatable results, taking into account the uniqueness of our raw materials, true, but ultimately bending them into a state of perfection according to the codified rules of our craft. Well, having been married quite happily for several decades, this is certainly not how maintaining *a living relationship* has worked for me and my partner.

---

6 Eurostat, 2020.

See, if magic was defined as a relationship, it would immediately become obvious why each magician will need to walk their own path, why traditional rules will apply only with some vague sense of reliability (like your aunt's great sure-fire advice on finding the „right" partner), and why the measure of our success can never be judged by anyone, except for the very people (or spirits) with whom we lived in a relationship with. Each life is a genuine and new adventure, often a struggle, a Promethean ordeal in learning how to love and how to be social. In building the right relationship between oneself and the world. And so it is with magic.

I suggest, we look back for a moment to most of the magical source-texts of the Eastern and Western traditions, and ask ourselves how helpful their instructions are in terms of conscious *relationship building*? I'd argue most of this material isn't even as refined and sophisticated as what I once read on a tea mug: "Be friendly if you want to fuck."

> *But if they delay to approach you, put your right hand on the lamen, your left hand pointing to the place where the disturbance of the spirits is heard, and say these names:*
>
> Mparakiel, Damariel, Parariel, Bedariel, Okhthriel, Bathykariel, Noramiel, Alphiel, Rhompilem, Rheraphimil, Ampouna, Rhaniel, Stephanael, Adoukin, Donaliel, Morkilen, Patsaralim, Douralee, Elmee, Ieth, Daririn, Rhasael, Eleroim, Aphai, Tai, Areniel, Emael, Mporkeo, Rheilen, Anael, Ismeel, Rhasiel, Sadiel, Rhadenabil, Mperasam, Almeraki, Danatan, Mpeniel, Kerampiel, Anabliel, Permpael, Alananael, Amenim, Bathykim, Mpeliroua, Myrak, Arinephael, Rham, Rhamael, Kaidarakhy Mperael, Amiel, Mephioran, Kananan, Mparaniel, Karenabiel, Ietaiel, Askhiel, Alamiel, Karamiel, Anphiiel, TakhU, Ieliel, Martae, Oukhai, Anaranare, Zeseme, Zeagourdeel, Aoule, Alempae, Konariel, Oudotiel, Elmei, Aoura, At, Iaphil, Anariel, Rhamiel, Tzarael, Aiphiel, On, Kesmpanole, Metareel, Obel, Moulomeel.[7]

---

7 Hygromanteia, after: Marathakis (ed.), 2011, p. 172.

Exorcising Colonialism. Experiencing Otherness.

Let's start with what happened at the beginning. After having completed the necessary preparatory stages of meditation, reflection, note-taking and reference reading, I was about to start writing this chapter on *Otherness*. It was a warm evening in a rental home in Croatia we had frequented for several years. A remote villa in central Istria, surrounded by nothing but vineyards, rolling hills, deep forests and plenty of open sky. The swallows were cutting down from the roof of the villa onto the shimmering surface of the salt-water pool and disappearing into the lush green of the valley beyond. We were sitting in the shadow on the porch, my wife, my daughter and I, enjoying a self-cooked dinner and preparing for an evening of cardboard games and watching 101 *Dalmatians*. It was one of these rare moments in the year when life was calm and perfect.

In that moment an exhausted young man of Southern looks turned around the corner of the villa, holding a phone and a charging cable in his hands. I got up, slipped into my sandals and walked towards him over the gravel path. It quickly turned out he was a refugee, allegedly all by himself, and needed to charge his phone. It also turned out he neither spoke English nor German, so we had little chance of communicating meaningfully.

I realised that, in that very moment, through the presence of this foreigner, *Otherness* had intruded our little bubble of perfection and entirely changed the situation. With the young man a dozen questions had arrived that required addressing without delay. Whether he presented any kind of danger to my daughter and wife, whether he was alone or if there were more refugees waiting in the forest on the hillside above us? Simply put: whether to invite him in and provide shelter, or whether doing that would compromise the shelter we ourselves had found in this place. How much could, how much should be shared? How much of our *own* should be given up to accommodate for the needs of this *other*? At least for me, there were no social rules or reference points for such a situation. In hindsight, offering hospitality could prove to be dangerous naivety, whereas excluding him and sending him away unaided would definitely result in a violation of the ethics I live by.

Intuitively I made my choices. I plugged in his phone, seated him on one of the sun chairs on the porch, got him some dinner and water. I learned, he was originally from Algeria, had arrived somewhere in Croatia by boat, where water had damaged his battery powerpack, and probably taken all of his other belongings from him, leaving him with nothing but the clothes on his body and his now empty phone. He was on his way to France, he explained in broken English and with multiple attempts, intending to walk from here into Slovenia, then towards Trieste, from there to Genoa and further West until he'd arrive in Southern France which seemed to be the destination of his journey. That evening I swung between intimate father-son moments with my daughter, playing cardboard games, watching a movie together, and checking on the stranger on our porch. I fed him, gave him cigarettes and 100 EUR, some provisions for the journey, a sport vest against the cold and a warm blanket to sleep on the sun lounger until his phone had fully charged.

I did not invite him into the house, I did not offer him to shower, I did not offer to drive him closer to the border the next morning — all these choices I could have easily made.

In the previous chapter we proposed to define magic as relationship; now we must come to terms with the fact that there is no relationship more difficult to define and pin down than the uncanny tension that fills the space between the self and the Other.

In the example above, despite all the challenges of communication, it was only a brief moment before the "it" of the man who had intruded on our family evening turned into a "you." Positive intent and a gentle measure of risk-taking to trust from both sides were enough to bridge the initial distance of foreignness. In our magical work with spirits, however, this distance will never dissolve and this tension will never subside. At least insofar as we decide to do our work carefully and with the necessary integrity.

To illustrate the kind of Otherness we are exposed to when working with spirits, allow me to introduce a few personal examples. If you are reading this as a practicing magician, I am sure you'll have plenty of your own experiences to offer. If, however, you hold no or little first-hand experience in this field, it might be helpful to establish the following explorations as some common ground. I am deliberately offering these examples without elaborate context but will instead cut to the actual experience of Otherness directly. Obviously, I am intentionally offering these examples to illustrate that *there is nothing remarkable about them at all*; but that they are the kind of experiences we should be prepared to make frequently when setting out on a magical path. Finally, they also will help to contrast a *goêtic approach to spirit contact* with the highly problematic Solomonic techniques we expounded upon above.

EXAMPLE #1 — The Dream Witch

After a series of magical workings I encountered the following being in a dream.

> *I dreamed of a witch tonight. Her skin was white like her hair, she was old and made only of bones and skin. She held in her hands the upturned skull of a goat or a big bird. In this skull she put a bundle of herbs and said, this is your brain. Then she took a small tied up bag and said, these are your intestines.*
>
> *She ground the herbs in the bowl. Then she put the bone and the bag in a big brass kettle. She instructed me to lie down under the cauldron, which was suspended above me in a kind of covered wagon. I lay down on the hard wooden floor and waited to fall asleep. Directly above me in the darkness I*

saw the heavy brass kettle glowing, big as a belly. Was I the fire that fuelled it? Was my sleep the embers that would bring the water to a boil...?

I knew that at the stroke of midnight I would have to get up, carry the kettle to the field and drink of the brew. I was afraid, I felt alone, and I did not know whether to obey or to flee... Drinking from the witch's potion would mean many things and the future was as uncertain as the darkness around me.

Then I slept all night, woke up in the morning and wondered. The witch was gone and the power of the potion was gone. Had I overslept out of fear or had fate come to my aid?

I remember the witch very well. She was neither good nor evil, neither peaceful nor hostile to me. She was the guardian of a threshold, on both sides at the same time. She did her job and showed me the way. Whether it was sweet or torturous meant nothing to her...[8]

❧ EXAMPLE #2 — The Telluric Familiar

At this time I was working with a familiar of the Bavarian land. This spirit was as much an aid to the seasons, tides and dynamics of the land I lived upon as it had volunteered to work with me in partnership. It was of tall and rough stature, and covered in long fur. I never saw its face, let alone its eyes. It had the tendency to lie down in the ground and merge with the earth at once; strangely it never made a difference whether it stood before me in physical form or whether it was working from within the ground. I could always sense and follow its consciousness quite easily; it probably did a lot from its end to uphold the bond between us. Our interactions were rarely longer than a few minutes. I would come and visit it at a shrine in an old barn at the back of our garden. Lighting a candle, stepping through the flame, and coming out on the other side in vision was entirely enough to connect with it. Some days the being was absent, working at a deeper level than I could follow, or more closely merged

---

8 Frater Acher, *Magical Diary*, June 2012, (unpublished).

with a power I had no access to. The below two incidents when I was sick were the only examples where the being ever entered our house and came to my bedside.

> *I am quite fed up with being sick now. My body seems so fragile — or maybe my schedule and life are much more brutal/ungentle than I realise? Clearly it will take more exploration and it shouldn't go on like this: a sickness, a cold every three months, intersected by my regular cancer scans and follow-up.*
>
> *I asked N.N. for help this morning. He came to my bed, then worked to cover my body in thick honey, put on an additional layer of earth and wrapped everything into dried leaves. Then he bound me up with the long hair from his fur. A hair tied around every limb, fingers, head, toes, etc...— My body turned very weak and exhausted after that and still feels like that.*[9]
>
> *Finally, this was a really restful night. Before falling asleep, I called out to N.N. again. Instead of working on my body, he just laid himself into me. He enclosed all of my body like a big brown coffin of spirit and hair. It was such a wonderful feeling of closeness and togetherness. So still and deep. Why didn't I think of this much earlier — after all, he is always lying down in the earth and becoming one with it, and coming out of it stronger...*[10]

❡ EXAMPLE #3 — Rah Omir Quintscher's Magical Contact

This example goes back to to the early days of my goêtic work in the cave in the Bavarian mountains. I have shared more about this work in my book *Clavis Goêtica*.[11] As part of this endeavour, I inquired into the work German magicians had previously performed with this land. In particular, I was interested to learn more about the roots and origins of the magic practiced by Rah Omir Quintscher, a.k.a. Friedrich Wilhelm Quintscher (1893–1945).

---

9 Frater Acher, *Magical Diary*, March 2016, (unpublished).
10 Frater Acher, *Magical Diary*, January 2017, (unpublished).
11 Hadean Press, 2021.

Today I went back to the temple. My concern was to find out about the magical current that was initiated or taken up by Quintscher.

I went to the Temple, meditated, ignited the central candle, then the incense of my angel and went into the Void. There I began the Merkaba meditation and extended the Merkaba to the floor plan of the entire house. Then I called my angel and let him receive me. As soon as we were one, I jumped into the shaft in front of me and began to fall...

[...]

Upon entering the Inner Library, no contact appeared to me. I descended the ladder to the ground floor and looked around. A jellyfish-like creature was hanging in the air in front of me. I examined it and then decided to follow it. It floated to the right and up, I climbed a ladder and followed it further behind an arch of stone. There, on a shelf on the wall it stopped in front of a small golden booklet. I grabbed the book and the contact disappeared. Above the shelf, embedded in a stone burrow, was a holder into which I inserted the booklet. It flew open and the pages fluttered through the air.

I recognized images of war, cracks in a vessel and new forces entering through those cracks. At the same time I saw the ghosts of Sättler and Quintscher, unable to absorb these forces for what they were. Like hot lead in contact with water, these forces coagulated in their spirits to structures and formulas which let the essence behind them disappear into forgetfulness. What was alive and wanted to be, died in the imprint it left in the spirits of the people.

Then a man appeared on my left. He was slim and tall, wore a long coat and had black hair. He seemed to be the figure of one of the invisibles that Quintscher had seen. He indicated to me that this was not his true form but merely a dress so that I could see him. He took my arms and rubbed them with a sticky, honey-like liquid. The left arm seemed yellow, my right one reddish. Then he turned me back to the little golden book in the wall and made me drink from it. A blue drop as of oil flowed from the book into my mouth... I knew what to do.[12]

12 Frater Acher, *Magical Diary*, December 2012, (unpublished).

From these exemplary spotlights we immediately comprehend a few things. As peripheral as these common characteristics might seem to the experiences themselves, they become essential when we investigate the attitude and stance with which the goês engages with spirits in general.

(A) For what we can tell, neither of the spirits encountered belonged to or associated themselves with any particular man-made *tradition*. Instead, they embody generative conscious forces of a particular kind bound into a pattern that chose to appear as a witch, a fur being, or a cloaked man. The spirits themselves are not a witch, a fur-being or a cloaked man, they simply offered me these forms as interfaces of interaction.

(B) Once in their presence, there is no space for a human's sense of *normality*. Not even repeated exposure to them results in a slow process of cumulative normalisation. Instead, the way these spirits comport themselves, the fluidity of their actual appearance and the oscillation of their presence contradict a human's sense of normality as primed by the physical realm of creation. Communing with these spirits means entering an interspace that defies the norm and the habitual and requires us to live in a field of constant contingency.

(C) Bonds formed with such kind of spirits centre essentially not on proximity and alikeness but on *contrariness* and *paradox*. For example, my collaboration with the telluric familiar was precisely not defined by how similar we were and what we had in common (because that would have been very little). The telluric spirit did not search out other telluric spirits like him to conduct the work at hand but the exact opposite. It was open to our collaboration because to him I represented the other, missing side of the coin. My (limited) capabilities were the mirror image of his own. Where he could move vast amounts of force and substance in the inner realm, I could e.g. light a physical candle or move a physical stone in the outer realm.

Such spirit bonds, therefore, centre on the notion of Otherness. What forms the basis for the decision to form a mutual bond is precisely the difference between us. The Other is an extension into a realm we have no access to ourselves. However, it is precisely *not* an extension of ourselves.

The witch's familiar, in such a context, is only *familiar* on the outside, on the inside it is a bridge that leads directly into Otherness. Living with such spirit contacts means we always have an interface open into Otherness. The refugee is always in the background waiting to step forward, and vice versa we ourselves adopt the role of the refugee on the edge of two worlds for the rest of our lives...

To approach the spirits with such an open yet intentional stance requires the practitioner to invert the notion of *colonisation* that still runs so deep in many magical traditions today.

The term *colony* is derived from the Latin word *colere*, which translates as *cultivate*. Central to the term, then, is the idea of encountering a *terra incognita*, an uncultivated wilderness that becomes an extension of one's domain and sphere of influence through civilisational as well as economic exploitation (in German: *Nutzbarmachung*). The colony itself is thus perceived as virgin soil, often wild and unruly by nature, to be tamed and subordinated to an agenda determined by human utility. It is often assumed that the history of the colony begins only with the arrival of the new usurper, that it suddenly leaps into existence from the unchartered black territory of a map; everything that happened before the usurper's arrival is derivatively relegated to primitive barbarism.[13]

Once the process of colonisation is achieved, the topography of the colony will be considered to be appropriately tamed and made accessible to exploitation. The once foreign land might maintain a superficial sheen of exoticism; however, underneath this surface the same economic forces are now put to work that are known from the

---

13 Thus, America and its native peoples are finally "discovered," regardless of the fact that they have actually been living there for tens of thousands of years—demonstrating the conquerors' hubris, pure and unadulterated.

soil and land at home. Yet in the colony they can be applied in an unmoderated and brutal *modus operandi*, as here in the distance and far away from one's homeland neither ethics nor nostalgia need to constrain the full force of resource extraction and exploitation.

Unfortunately, such historic realities also depict a rather accurate picture of the state of magic in the East and West since the slow demise of animism and the increasing dominion of orthodox belief systems. When examined through this lens, the histories of our economic and spiritual past reveal a common essential driver: *the spirit of annexation of Otherness*.

Either this drive originated from a motive of resource expansion and power acquisition, or (and!) it took its roots in a deep seated sense of uncertainty and fear with regards to what constitutes one's own identity. Because such primitive depreciation of Otherness can only be deemed logical if otherness is necessarily perceived as an instantaneous threat to whatever is defined as one's own. If I run the risk that everything I built up for myself as identity, culture, or resource crumbles into nothingness simply by standing in the face of Otherness, of course I will find myself caught in the either-or decision of defeat or attack. In other words: we will only be able to encounter Otherness free of any colonising intuition if we know ourselves to be safely grounded and cared for in what is our own.

To approach spirits in such a manner postulates a mature human being who is capable of and committed to an ethic that requires them to approach all of their life in such a manner. There is nothing that speeds up the harvest of turning ourselves into such beings—not even the right book at the right time. But it remains to be hoped that the latter at least can render the right impulse at the right time.

A MODEL OF
Radical Otherness

> High towers and the metaphysical great men similar to them, around which there is commonly much wind, are not for me. My place is the fertile bathos of experience.[14]

IF we aim to extract the notion of colonisation from our magic, we have to become capable of holding the tension of living a life in contact with radical Otherness. The aspect of *radicalness* in this context is a pure concession to our long history of exploitation and usurpation of Otherness. In reality the following framework and considerations should not at all be considered *radical* but rather trivial and obvious. At least it is my hope that they will be recognised as such in the future of our tradition of building healthy spirit-relationships.

In the following we are grounding ourselves in a field-model of consciousness that will help us understand the realities, dynamics and ongoing demands upon us as practitioners that we have to be willing to face up to.

> The challenge of a radical Other that we are confronted with means that there is no world in which we are completely at home, and that there is no subject that is master in its own house.[15]

As we defined magic at its most essential level as a *relationship*, a phenomenology of radical Otherness has to make a statement about

---

14 "Hohe Türme und die ihnen ähnlichen metaphysisch-großen Männer, um welche gemeiniglich viel Wind ist, sind nicht vor mich. Mein Platz ist das fruchtbare Bathos der Erfahrung." (Kant, *Prolegomena* A 204).
15 Waldenfels, 2020 (1997), p. 17.

the kind of relationship (or lack thereof) we have with this Other. In order to delve into this thought to the appropriate depth, we'll solicit the help of two modern researchers who spent the better part of their careers studying precisely that, Self and Otherness.

The first one is Karl Bühler (1879–1963), a German psychologist and linguist, who made significant contributions to gestalt psychology and who was the dissertation advisor of Karl Popper. The other is Bernhard Waldenfels (born 1934), who to this date remains one of the most important thinkers of contemporary German-language phenomenology, and whose research is focussed specifically on Otherness.[16]

In his synoptic 2006 release, *Grundmotive einer Phänomenologie des Fremden*,[17] Waldenfels takes up Bühler's central motif, the I-Here-Now system, and reinterprets it as the central element not of a theoretical model but of a field of consciousness.[18]

The following double page illustrates the way in which I recommend to leverage Bühler's and Waldenfels's work,[19] in order to step back and free ourselves from the dysfunctional dynamics that at least for the past millennium have been at the heart of practiced magic in both East and West. It's only from such a vantage point, I will aim to show, that we can reconcile with the mistakes of our past and begin to see the practical path ahead.

Let's examine some of the key points of figures 3 and 4 on the following pages (87–88).

Following on from the central origin point of I-Here-Now, we can identify a second field of consciousness of relative familiarity which is best described as the *You-There-Then* field. This field is not

---

16 German: *Fremdheit*.
17 Suhrkamp, 2006.
18 Waldenfels, 2006, p. 37.
19 Furthermore, we will be integrating several foundational aspects of what is known as *deictic frames* research. As a further reading on this subject we point to the field of Relational Frame Theory and the rather dry literature that comes with it. E.g. Symon Dymond (ed.); *Advances in Relational Frame Theory: Research and Application*, Oakland/CA: Context Press, 2013.

FIGURE 3

FIGURE 4

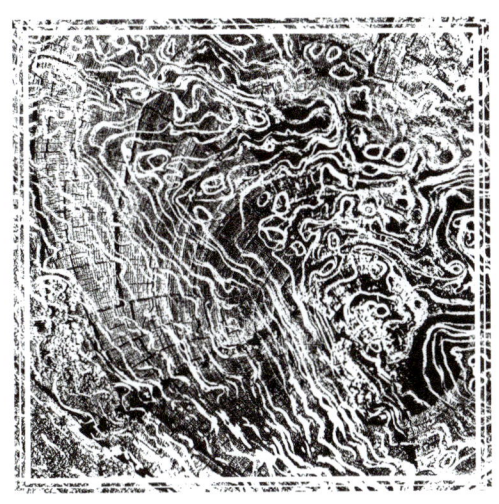

  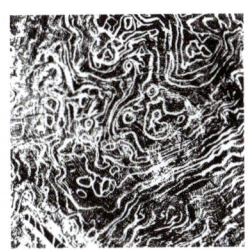

I	You	It
Here	There	Where
Now	Then	When

| THE REALM OF ORIGIN | THE REALM OF EXPERIENCE | THE REALM OF OTHERNESS |

as intimately known to the "I" as its own realm of origin. However, through the threefold lens of *gestalt-locality-time* it is *still known well enough* to be encountered as a "You" i.e. as a living point of reference who deserves addressing, respect and the effort of interacting with it on relative eye level.

This field in itself fans out into a multi-facetted dimension that spans from *intimacy* all the way to *foreignness*. I.e. a life-long partner will still remain in the You-There-Then field; however, in close physical proximity they will interface directly into one's I-Here-Now field. On the other hand, a foreigner in a foreign land met by a chance encounter also remains part of the You-There-Then field for as long as they are recognised as a fellow human being in a somewhat familiar physical environment.[20]

Next to these two fields, we encounter a third and significantly larger sphere (figure 4) within the topography of experience, the It-Where-When field. This is the field within which we are exposed to the experience of radical Otherness. In its most simplistic form this field describes a *terra incognita*, a space of radical exposure that bears too little resemblance to our own realm of origin for us to intuitively and constructively relate to it. This sphere is so removed from our normalised field of experience that we cannot even with certainty locate it in time and space. At the same time this field is ubiquitous and everywhere around us. Like a ghost or the reverse side of seemingly familiar objects, this realm is at the same time hauntingly present with us and yet only visible in the periphery of our sight before it gets mantled again under the presence of the realms of "I" and "You." Under normal conditions the It-Where-When field is avoided by most human and only experienced in the

---

20 Further below we will show why the idea of a *You-Here-Now* field in practical magic is quite different from what one would read about this notion in Relational Frame Theory. For our exploration here, any other person, irrespectively how intimately we might have bonded with them, will always remain and be part of the You-There-Then field. Even if e.g. they are naked next to us in bed. At its most essential level, the border between *Here* and *There* in our model is formed by human skin.

form of a befalling, an infliction or intrusion into one's regulated world of norms and habits. We will examine its interface into the human realm in the next chapter.

Ultimately, however, the essence of the It-Where-When field is to elude all human attempts of definition, control and confinement.[21] The realm of dreams is a classical example of exposure to radical Otherness we all encounter occasionally. As we have seen above, expeditions into unknown territories are historic examples of sought out exposure to radical Otherness, ones that normally resulted in catastrophe one way or the other.

> *Attention is awakened, or it falls asleep. Like waking up and going to sleep, we cross a threshold that separates the familiar from the foreign, the visible from the invisible, the audible from the inaudible, the touchable from the untouchable. What emerges beyond the threshold, that is, where I am not and cannot be without becoming another, proves to be enticing, frightening, stimulating.*[22]

What this model helps to illustrate is that magic, as we are exploring it here, is best understood as the paradoxical art and skill of *cultivating relationships of radical Otherness*. To comprehend what this means in practice, we have to understand the organic dynamics that enact between and even within the three fields of I-Here-Now, You-There-Then and It-Where-When.

First, as shown in figure 4 above, we must understand the three fields as distinct yet interpenetrating areas within a broader topography. As the image shows, the I-Here-Now field has by far the smallest circumference and scope; it is followed by still a relatively thin field of You-There-Then. Both of these, are then embedded into a vast topography of It-Where-When, i.e. the field of radical Otherness.

---

21 See Appendix 1 in this book for an abbreviated summary of how the *It-Where-When* field can manifest itself in the human experience, which is entirely indirectly through *our reaction to it*.
22 Waldenfels, 2018 (2006), p. 99, translation by author.

These proportions establish the critical importance of learning *how to positively relate to Otherness*. This is the essential skill that allows the I-Here-Now field to objectively engage with and orientate itself within the broader topography it forms a tiny fraction of. Without this skill, we are confined to our small subjective realm of origin.

Secondly, it is important to grasp that human beings, consciously or not, are constantly engaged in a three-fold process of *coherence creation* that could rather awkwardly but still accurately be described as *selving, thouing* and *othering*. Each of these three modes serve an individual's inborn need to categorise, order and label the world of their experience, and thus to foster their subjective sense of control and cohesion.

Whether it takes place within the realm of I, Thou or It, this process is enabled by two essentially opposed forces that can appear in the various forms of *attraction and repulsion, absorption and expulsion, construction and destruction,* etc. This means they can be leveraged to either expand and enrich or reduce and diminish the respective realm. The following table (facing page) provides an abbreviated overview of the inherent interdependencies and complexities of this dynamic.

Simply put, the growth of "I" can just as much indicate a genuine growth of self as well as an exploitation of resources originally belonging to "You." Similarly, an expansion of the realm of "You" could be nothing but a dressing up of Otherness into a form more comfortable for us to experience. A simple example might be of help here. The process of *Disneyfication*[23] of nature and animal life is a wonderful example of artificially *reducing Otherness* into compromised shapes of "You." These shapes are being bent and broken from their original forms in order to allow humans to relate to them without too much exposure to the untamed and uncanny. Just compare a villain in any Disney or Marvel movie to the characters e.g. in a David Lynch movie, where anybody is granted

---

23 For further reading on the subject I recommend Bryman, Alan E; *The Disneyization of Society*, London: Sage Publishers, 2004

	ATTRACTION- ABSORPTION- CONSTRUCTION	REPULSION- EXPULSION- DESTRUCTION
Selving	¶ The Process of expanding the Realm of Origin. ¶ New ways of being, resources, or capabilities are integrated into the I-Here-Now field. CRITICAL QUESTION: Is the expansion of «I» leading to a depletion of «Thou» or «It»?	¶ The Process of reducing the Realm of Origin. ¶ Ways of being are recognised as not belonging to the I-Here-Now field and demarcated from it. CRITICAL QUESTION: Upon which criteria are such decisions taken and by whom?
Thouing	¶ The Process of expanding the Realm of Experience. ¶ New ways of being, resources, or capabilities are integrated into the You-There-Then field. CRITICAL QUESTION: Whom does this serve? Is this a projection, or genuine enrichment of the field of You-There-Then?	¶ The Process of reducing the Realm of Experience. ¶ Ways of being are denied the status of You and expulsed into Otherness or appropriated into Selfness. CRITICAL QUESTION: Whom does this serve? Who took this decision, how and why?
Othering	¶ The Process of expanding the Realm of Otherness. ¶ New ways of being, resources, or capabilities are recognised to be part of the It-There-Then field. CRITICAL QUESTION: Have we explored a new part of the topography, or withheld the status of «You» from another being?	¶ The Process of reducing the Realm of Otherness. ¶ Ways of being are expelled from Otherness and either tabooed or integrated into «I» or «You». CRITICAL QUESTION: Are we clothing Otherness in a projected «You» because we can't stand not knowing it well enough?

sufficient Otherness to suddenly surprise us as a villain or, even worse, as something entirely unknown.

Such theoretic grounding is leading us straight back to our subject of inquiry. One could argue that magical currents such as Solomonic Magic are prime examples of the Disneyfication of spiritual Otherness. Rather than challenging as well as guiding the magician to develop living relationships into a liminal sphere that escapes the standards and norms of common "I-Thou" relationships, it attempts to turn magic into a theme park of sanitised, codified and unilaterally controlled rituals. Practitioners are invited to enter the theme park, go through several stages of preparatory works, and then to freely choose the "ride" they want to go on at any particular day. The demons or spirits are thus commoditised, extrapolated from their original topography and offered in canned versions, always available at the magician's disposal. In a similar turn, humans have tried to commercialise love and invented brothels long ago where (mainly female) bodies are offered up for the satisfaction of (mainly male) customers' needs, in exchange for currency. At least, one could argue, a client in a brothel accepts that they will need to pay for the service and (in cases where governments constructively regulate such exchanges) a sex-worker can earn a living from it. Many modern magicians don't even understand that they will have to pay for their experiences.

Such human dreams of omnipotence, to break the unruly spirit of real relationships in order to turn their dynamics into fuel for spiritual technologies and economies, have never fared very well in the long run. Despite the plain ethics illustrated in the many versions of the legend of Dr. Faust, the illusion of a magical technocracy from Sigil magic to Grimoire rituals is still thriving.

Rather than condemning such approaches because they won't fit an animistic paradigm, we want to shine a light on the natural force, the raw disruptive experience that is undermining them from the inside. For why is it, one should ask, that no magician ever arrived at a fully shielded, sanitised and tamed version of "their craft"? Why can't we lock ourselves up in a domesticated realm of Magician-I and Demon-You? How is it that Otherness rocks up against our orderly realms of human rituals and knocks our sense of self, the world and normality off centre, again and again? Essentially, after several millennia of trying hard, why do we still fail to turn both magic and our world of experience into a theme park of our own making?

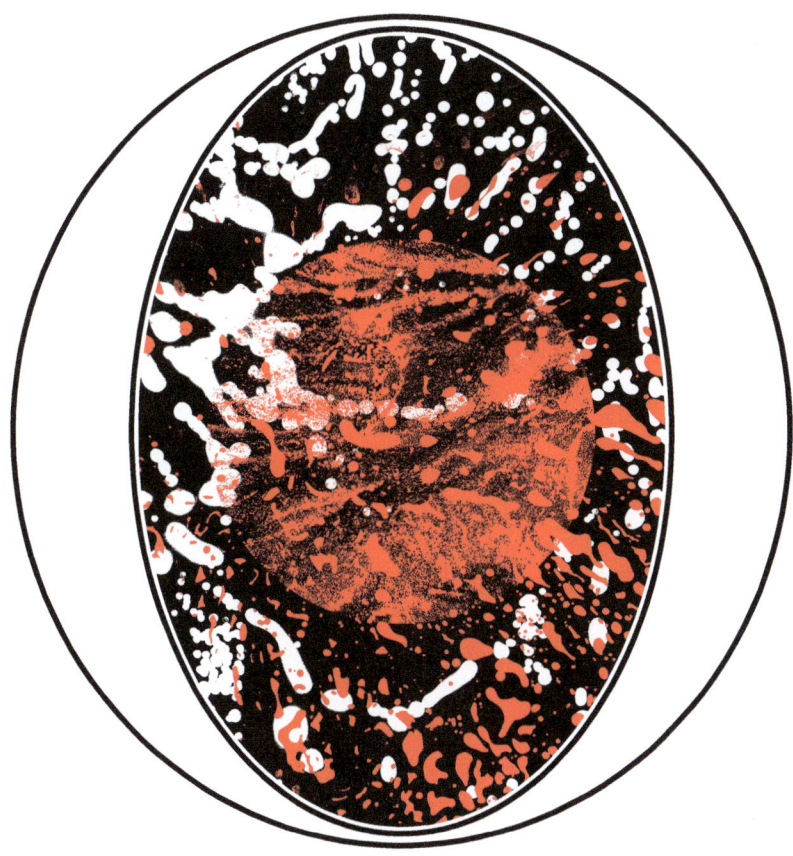

THE Undermining Power of Pathos

THE majority of magical literature in East and West is an attempt to rationalise the numinous experience, the experience of spiritual Otherness. While triggered by human encounters that all disrupted the common and expected, these books take it upon themselves to close the circuit of sense-making again,[24] to heal the wound that was inflicted by the unexpected. In such a way the term *magic* itself becomes a *gate*. What is anticipated on the other side of the term is an inherently foreign, disruptive and yet powerful vigour. By channeling it through the *gate of magic* we attempt to inscribe order, control and meaning into it. Magical literature, thus, is the attempt to codify the very forces that escape or even break the code. It is a genre of curative treatment for everyday order, norms and commonness, by attempting to expand human sovereignty into territories that otherwise would be characterised as exactly violating all of the above. *Something* is constantly tearing at the garment of man-made order. Magic is the restorative effort of humans to knit together again those threads that have been torn from the fabric of the anticipated. The common understanding of the *gate of magic*—and this is in theory only—holds the promise of boundless resilience against the demonic forces of Otherness.

Accordingly, it is only logical that traditional magical literature is rather averse to objectively examining and giving space to its seemingly untamed antagonistic force, Otherness. Or more specifically, viewed through a phenomenological lens: to the forces that break the circuit of our sense-making, the forces that befall us, and

---

[24] Waldenfels, 2018 (2006), p. 42

which in equal measure can inflict surprise, shock and suffering[25].

It's important to stress that on the other side of *the gate of magic* we encounter an entire world of its own. Thus, to speak in general terms of the dynamics, the topography and species of this world would be reckless. However, we can indeed speak in general terms of the *instinctive human reaction* caused by encounters with such unexpected and often disruptive forces. This would be the field of magical phenomenology, if it actually existed. And, as we will see, in our initial attempt to explore this field we will be offered the key to overcoming the visceral human reaction of wanting to colonise Otherness as a means of reestablishing security and control.

Bernhard Waldenfels in his decades of research on Otherness has equipped us with a most precise term for the general experience inflicted upon humans by *things that befall them*. The Ancient Greek term of *pathos* (πάθος) describes precisely that, and expands into a field of words that include *suffering, experience, something that one undergoes*, or *something that happens to one*. Essential to its meaning is the unintentional nature of the kind of experience it defines; the fact that the one encountering pathos is thrown into an experience of exposure and vulnerability that is accompanied by the feelings of surprise, shock and suffering.[26] Pathos thus defines the antagonistic human experience to *apathy* as a state of indifference and freedom from suffering and even sensation.

The most foundational reality of the human encounter of magical Otherness is that it collapses indifference and catapults even the most disengaged spectator into the exposed position of a sensually befallen or attacked.

---

25 As Waldenfels highlights, the original meaning of the term *pathos* does not indicate an experience of "learning to suffer," but the idea of "learning through suffering." Thus, the original use of the term should not be confused with the modern English use of the word *pathetic*. (Waldenfels, 2018 [2006], p. 42).

26 The German triad of *Erstaunen, Erschrecken, Erleiden* seems even more coherent.

*Pathos [...] as a foreign body that tears open existing fabrics of meaning.*²⁷

*Pathos means that we are hit by something, in such a way that this Whereof is neither founded in a preceding What, nor is it cancelled out in a subsequently achieved Wherefore. Different forms of pathos can be distinguished, episodic and chronic ones, those that work in a "volcanic" way and those that work in a "neptunian" way. In addition, there are different degrees of intensity; as passion, pathos reaches a form of intensification that affects everything. [...] The pathos in which something happens to us throws a series of all too common distinctions off the track. [...] The pathos is an event, but an event of a special kind that happens to someone. The person affected occurs in the dative case, in an "address-dative," as Bühler calls this case, but not in the nominative of the perpetrator.*²⁸

Where vulnerability is the foundational motive in human's experience of pathos²⁹, traditional magic is mostly geared towards releasing humans from the surprise, shock and suffering of the personally affected witness of an event that is happening to them. Traditional magic aims to catapult the human befallen back into the role of the active perpetrator, or as it is more often called in traditional literature, the *operator*.

In many forms of overly codified ritual magic we still find a distant echo of the experience of pathos. Obviously, it presents itself in a sanitised, tamed, or one could say Disneyfied form. In an illusionary trick it is attempting to use the force of pathos not to disrupt but to stimulate, to tickle and turn the operator in a state of consciousness that is aroused with a comfortable pinch of Otherness: *voces magicae* or *Barbaric names* are the peacock feather of magic with which one tries to tickle the numb ritualist into the voluptuous experience of tamed Otherness.

---

27 Waldenfels, 2018 (2006), pp. 52–53, translation by author.
28 Waldenfels, 2018 (2006), pp. 43–44, translation by author.
29 Robert, Stöhr; *Zwischen Pathos und Response. Bernhard Waldenfels über Verletzlichkeit als Grundmoment der Erfahrung*, in: Stöhr et al. (ed.) Schlüsselwerke der Vulnerabilitätsforschung, Springer Link, 2019, pp. 145–167.

Irrespective of their linguistic histories, in ritual practice barbaric names are intended to function as a liturgic device to transport the principles of classical dialogue—the rule-bound, logos-oriented interplay of speech, of question and answer—into the realm of Otherness. By calling in *an othering way*, the practitioner is attempting to open themselves to the broad horizon of the experience that resides beyond the realm of You and I. Barbaric names are proclamations of Otherness, intended to invoke a related experience in the operator without giving up control of the process as such. They are a ritualist's attempt to work around the seismic immediacy of the direct experience of Otherness, to loosen the harrowing grip of one's exposure to the vastness of the unknown topography around oneself. They are the attempt to uphold human agency and the principles of classical dialogue when actually radical Otherness is precisely defying these human aspirations and norms.

Unmasking feeble historic attempts of co-existing with Otherness is not good enough, of course. The actual question buried in the dysfunctional approaches of the past is how we will do better in the future of our own magical practice?

The answer we suggest starts out by creating space for the experience of pathos as such. That means returning to the original idea of *magic as a venture*: as an activity of risking a loss. Thus, we'll need to relinquish not common sense but a lot of the ossified safety-making mechanisms offered in the magical traditions of East and West. Instead, we'll need to find appropriate ways for deciding and regulating *how much we are willing to lose* as part of our exposure to Otherness. Rather than trying to control the topography of It-Where-When, we should begin to control our movement within it.

To understand the significance of such considerations, it is important to comprehend *the act of communing with spirits as a penetrating experience* on a physical, spiritual and mental level. The notion of penetration in this context is not meant to evoke phallic or vaginal connotations but rather implies natural processes such as osmosis. Communing with a spirit is a process that cannot take place without the human *becoming vulnerable* to the respective spirit. Its nature is deeply aligned to Waldenfels's description of the human experience of pathos. Being momentarily bound into the same realm of presence as a spirit means we give permission to the Other, as embodied by the spirit, to puncture our realm of I-Here-Now, to open a penetrating wound and to infuse Otherness within us.[30] In this experience we become foreigners to ourselves in order to create space underneath our own skin, within our minds and in the circumference of our hearts to kindle a spark from the other side of the gate that is magic.

Such essential premise of an organic compound formed between practitioner and spirit immediately reveals the fallacy behind much of the Medieval grimoires. The related practical tradition falls into the age-old trap of attempting to *wear a crutch as a crown*.

Of course we all depend on crutches when we are young or injured and attempt to (re)gain certain capabilities. Knowing when and how to apply *crutches* to all kinds of learning processes is a solid measure of civilisation and commoditising access to cultural techniques. However, it's also obvious that a literal "Grimoire Tradition" can hardly be more than a "Tradition of Crutches:" a wonderful school to stay in for one's entire life if one doesn't aspire to walk freely and unconstrained. As so often in nature, there is zero judgement in the decision to use a crutch or not to—but judgement only follows one's explicit intent and purpose.

The first step, then, on a path of magic without crutches, is to leave the Other its inexplicability. It means interacting with the mystery without wanting to unmask it. For what might appear to us as camouflage, as a shadow, as a hiding place is in fact the necessary self-entanglement,[31] the introversion of radical Otherness so that in the intimate moment of the subjective encounter it can temporarily reveal itself in a fluctuating, yet deeply personalised form.

---

30 I am grateful to Frater U∴D∴ pointing out in a personal conversation that a further exploration of this idea can be found in Peter Sloterdijk's concept of "spheres." See his books *Sphären, Volumes I to III*, Frankfurt am Main: Suhrkamp, 1998, 1999, 2004.

31 In German: *Selbstverschränkung*.

In these moments of communion, we still feel the radical rupture with our mundane reality, but we sense a tightrope now stretched under our feet on which we can balance for a short time out into this Otherness. As soon as we begin to explain, to interpret, to make sense of it, we step back from the rope onto solid ground and exchange the foreign with our own again. We return our gaze from Otherness back into the confined familiarity of the mirror.

So the next question is, how do we teach ourselves to walk out on this tightrope a little further? Or maybe just as far, as we are willing to loose ourselves?

To illustrate the deeply telluric reality of this consideration in applied magic, allow me to share another personal example. Again I am not offering snippets of my own magical biography here because they are in any way extraordinary, but precisely because they are not. Instead, I would like to claim that they illustrate relatively common experiences amongst practitioners of "magic without crutches."

❰BECOMING A MASK OF SEKHMET

This was 2013; a close relative had very suddenly fallen very sick. Their family had returned from holidays in Egypt and the young daughter of less than 6 years had contracted an aggressive viral infection that was recognised too late. Once the doctors began to identify and treat it her organs had been severely affected. I was told the virus had the tendency to attack the outside of the inner organs and to dissolve it. When I met her crying parents in the yard of the hospital where she was tendered to at the intensive care unit, both of her kidneys had already stopped working. The doctors said there probably was a 48 hours window; should her kidneys not begin to work again, she would loose both of them. Because of her young age and still-growing body, an organ transplant would be highly unlikely to work out. The alternative consequences were patently clear.

I remember being very calm. I remember sitting down on a park bench once everyone had left. I went into vision, crossed through the Void and emerged back in the yard of the hospital, only now in vision. My visionary body walked towards the hospital. While I had not been able to visit her inside the hospital in person, I knew roughly where she was kept in the ICU. I floated through walls, hallways and along hospital doors, until I found her room. I saw her lying in the bed, her small body outsized by the bed frame and white linen, fragile, connected to tubes, and sleeping numbly under heavy sedation.

I stood to her right side, my back towards the windows, and called for Sekhmet. The fierce majestic goddess had offered her help when I had contacted her in the preparatory stages of this intervention. I remember wondering how a goddess of such fierce warrior power and majestic stature was able to slip into my own body so smoothly? She had approached me from behind, walked towards my back out of the desert that was her home, into the hospital room where the three of us were suddenly present. It was as if a mountain of power merged herself with me. My body became a mask she wore, my hands gloves she sported, my eyes keyholes through which she gazed.

Then we got to work on the body of the young girl in front of us. It was a relatively simple process. In the course of my preparation for this moment, Josephine McCarthy had helped me to clearly see the various stages I had to go through in order to pull out the illness from her body. I followed this process carefully and then in truth I really didn't do much. It was rather like climbing the stairway in an endless tower: one step after the other, with consciousness not to exhaust yourself too early, knowing how high up (or deep down?) you were supposed to still go. Once we had pulled out the illness into an orb above the body of the girl, we buried it deep underground in the earth outside the hospital. It was mind-bending to see how effortlessly Sekhmet moved from one place to another, both holding on to the interface of my body, as well as the cumulated illness in the orb. We repeated this process another time; maybe a third, which I am not sure about anymore in retrospect.

I remember looking at my young relative in the white hospital bed before leaving the room. She slept as if nothing had happened. I wondered what exactly had taken place. Sekhmet had pulled free of me and disappeared right after the work had been accomplished. I floated back through hallways and ceilings, emerged from the hospital in the yard again and entered back into my physical body.

Josephine had advised me about the potential impact of this work upon my own body. How careful I needed to be in vision to ensure the illness would not remain in contact with my own body, but Sekhmet scraped it off cleanly and buried all of it in the earth. Josephine had also cautioned me to not repeat this process too often. I was 36 at the time, so the worst I imagined would happen if I depleted my own powers too much was another heavy migraine attack or a few weeks of severe flu...—I repeated the process multiple times over the next few days; sometimes twice per day. I remember once doing it in the moments before I went to bed. Going into vision, checking on my relative, standing at her bedside, then being lifted up like a twig in a sandstorm by the approaching deity behind me. Once Sekhmet had merged into me, power seemed an endless resource and going through the steps of the intervention of pulling out the disease was effortless; purely a matter of calm and concentration.

On the third day, the doctors spoke to my relative. They said they had never seen something like this. Their prior diagnose that it was "unlikely" for the kidneys to recover had been a strong positive exaggeration in order not to devastate my relatives when there was still so much time to do that later. They now said that they had never seen two kidneys springing back into functioning after being affected so heavily in such a young body and after such a long period of having completely ceased to operate. One of the kidneys seemed to have lost some of its vitality, but both were working again. I don't recall whether I held my crying relative in my arms while she told me this or whether it happened on the phone. Sometimes you can feel so close to people that physical distance doesn't matter that much. At least we get to tell ourselves such things in retrospect.

Shortly after that moment in 2013, as the doctors told me later, my own cancer must have begun to grow. When it was finally diagnosed in early 2014, several of the medics rebuked me: why had I not come earlier? My right testicle had basically been concaved and completely replaced by the tumor; it had also grown significantly in size. At this point, anything that would have put pressure on the testicle such as a long bike-ride, could have burst the thin protective layer of the tumour and would have spread its cancer cells into the entire body. From first diagnosis to surgery less than 24 hours passed. During my first doctor visit afterwards, my GP told me this was my very lucky day as his best friend died of the same cancer diagnosis only ten years ago, when treatment had not yet advanced that much. What followed I have described elsewhere to illustrate the forward-looking impact of significant illnesses on one's process of magical maturation. What I haven't spoken about yet is the backward-looking clarity I had in the moment of hearing my diagnosis.

I had been giving some health, and some health had been taken from me. The scales of Ma'at were even again; the deal was settled.

See, in many myths it is part of the hero's journey to lose their virile potency in exchange for access to (underworld) contacts and experiences they otherwise would not have had. There are threads of this weave running deep in Egyptian culture—unsurprisingly as I had been working with Sekhmet—but also in other times and narrative universes. However, the reason why I am sharing this personal story here is to make the point that exegesis, interpretation, and personal sense-making of such myths is secondary; as a magician what matters most *is living the myth*. Over the years of my recovery I did climb through a maze of underground tunnels of mythical research. I did come across fascinating insights on the fierce underworld goddess taking its male allies' testicles as a pledge. But all of this is secondary to the actual, unfiltered experience of Otherness: Sekhmet in the moment of healing through me, then Sekhmet again in the moment of taking from me. She herself draped in a metaphorical form that my visionary mind could make sense of, behind that form an underworld of female consciousness and power.

I promised myself I will not turn the moment of her presence into a palimpsest of my own writing. I will not force the immense foreignness of Sekhmet's It-Where-When into a narrow frame of my own understanding, into a You-There-Then. Rather, for the last eight years since I encountered her first, I enjoy the continued, peripheral presence of her uncanny Otherness. The radiating beauty and cognitive dissonance of her blinding immanence. Every time I reach for her, she is still there—reminding me of how far I once walked out on that rope towards her.

Working magic without crutches, up on that tightrope, is a most worthwhile venture. Call it a science or art, a skill or a craft, whatever you like. The simple truth is: for every step you make your blood is changed and yet you will pay for it in blood. Echoes return immediately or never, tomorrow or in your past; for time is of no concern in the moments when we are with the spirits. What each of these encounters, however, teach us is that our human world has not only internal borders, but swims within an ocean of external ones. The world we know of is anything but all-encompassing. In fact, it is only held in place through its many border-spheres to Otherness, which both elude integration and yet hold the promise of a beyond.

What at first may seem to be such an insignificant realization, turns into a fundamental challenge of human safety once we acknowledge that with the omnipresence of Otherness, everything within the human realm is turned *relative*. The experience of Otherness breaks the dictate of explicability and objectivity. To accept a realm that exists beyond sense-making, beyond myth, beyond a storyline with purpose, confronts us with our own conditionality; it forces us to awaken from the dream of human sovereignty.

The illusion of the Ancient Greek was to think of their well ordered cosmos of creation as a place of only relative Otherness. Their greatest fear was that of *radical Otherness*, of the black space beyond, which, like a constantly moving blind spot, eluded their relentless efforts of mythological mapping.[32]

---

32 Waldenfels, 2018 (2006), p. 17.

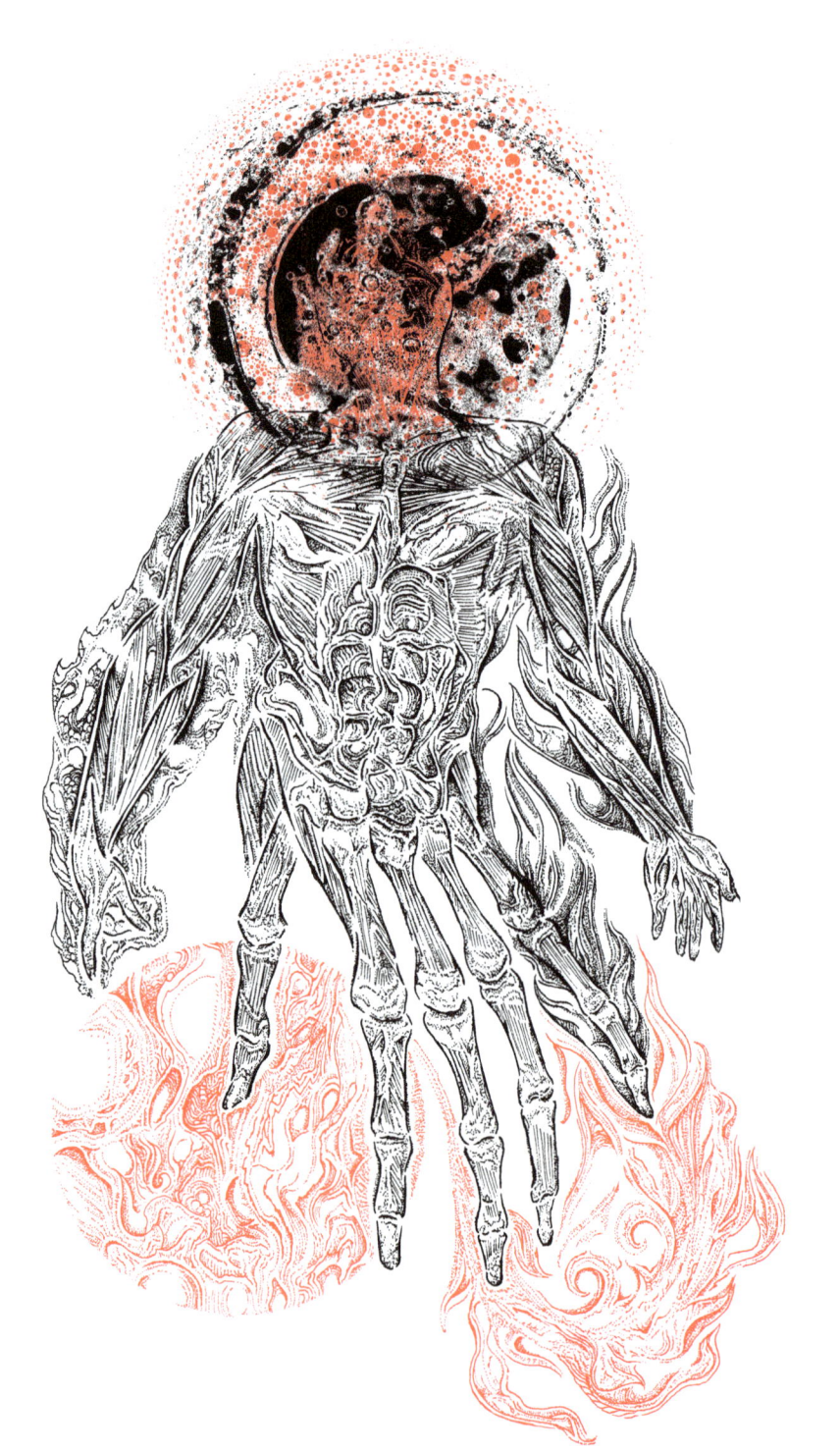

CHAPTER III

On the Inner Tools of Magic

/

MAGIC *as Walking on a Tightrope*

> To otherness which we experience as pathos one can only respond, one cannot answer it like a question or solve it like a problem.[1]

To recapitulate our stance on Pathos and Otherness in mundane simplicity, we could summarise the following: Otherness unsettles all aspects of normality. It will never be experienced in HD or

---

1 Waldenfels, 2020 (1997), p. 100, translation by author.

4k signal, but comes in the form of a disruptive factor. Otherness appears as an artefact, as noise, as a disturbing signal towards our mainstream cosmology of sense-making. Otherness is a pirate signal not towards the mainstream collective, thus stabilizing our own sense of identity as being counter-culture, unique and in a positively reaffirming sense outside the norm; Otherness is a pirate signal against our very idea of selfhood. It is the essence of the uncanny, allowing the circuit of sense to be broken.

A positive relationship to Otherness thus does not aim to resolve its mystery and its immanent field of tension. Instead, it focusses on responding to Otherness by leaning in, by widening our contact to it, by opening our senses further to the surprise, shock, or even suffering it initially presents itself in. All with the aim of turning the contact between Otherness and us *from noise to signal*.

Our response to Otherness, therefore, is a gentle drawing out of the actual underlying question it posits. We do not ask concluding or definite questions such as "Who are you?" but questions that open a pathway for further probing such as "What does your and my encounter want from me right now?" A constructive response to Otherness is an invitation for further mutual examination, a careful sensing if another step on the tightrope can be taken.

If approached in such a manner, we might be able to bear the tension of the It-Where-When experience always remaining eldritch with regards to its impossible fixation in the Form-Location-Time field. We no longer have to mask and pin it down with an artificial You-There-Then definition and destination. Instead of attempting to stare the Other right into its absent face, we are directing our view at its periphery—at the place where we discover and also regulate our contact to and relationship with it.

We walk safely in the unknown because we are content with making only a very small piece of it known to us. We are guided, one could say, by the Unknown, seeing nothing but the shadow of a hand it stretches out to us. Walking in such a way, we can participate in and experience far more spaces than we will ever be able to understand and appropriate.

In order to engage positively with radical Otherness we have to learn to cancel out the human reflex of cognitive sense-making so as not to artificially constrain our realm of participation with Otherness. It takes several things to achieve this, in many instances most essentially amongst them a life-time of trying and training. Walking out on the tightrope into Otherness is not a capability that we "unlock" but an attitude towards the world—underpinned and supported by several key skills—that we have to earn each day anew. The weave made of a desire for comfort, an aversion to fear and the obsession with I, Me and Mine is contracting around us constantly. This weave reduces the realm in which we can roam freely. It is not doing this to hinder us but to stabilise the organic system that we are. Our bodily and psychological functions are geared first and foremost towards self-maintenance, not towards explorations into Otherness. If we want to change or enhance their function we cannot cut through this weave, but we have to teach it to become more *elastic*. This is what most magical training is about in its first decade: turning our mind and senses more elastic, resilient and ready to expand.

Luckily we are not doing this in isolation. In an animistic paradigm nobody is ever alone or by themselves. Instead, we have spirits touching our mind and senses from the other end, welcoming us to engage with them and ready to interact with us.

THE DOOR WE SEE IN BLINDNESS

HERE is a thought experiment that helps us to understand how these two perspectives come together: Think of your mind not as a generative but as a *receiving faculty*. Consider the possibility that at the other end of your thought resides a living being trying to communicate with you. In fact, go one step further even and consider your thoughts *utterances*: In this scenario your mind is but an ear pressed to a door behind which these words were spoken. This brings a whole lot of questions to bear: How did you arrive at this particular door and not at the one next to it? How did this exact thought capture you and not the one behind the other door?

The goal is not to try to take control of this entire scenario and to usurp such multilayered dynamic under our human will. Humans were neither designed nor meant to control such levels of complexity. Rather, the point is to begin to see how vast the world extends behind *that door through which we hear our thoughts*. And how much accepting this fact, by its very nature, fragments any sense of I, Me and Mine.

How then do we work with this door? Well, in principle our mind has three different perceptive modes to interact with it. In the following we are familiarising ourselves with each of these three modes. It is worthwhile slowing down to examine every one of them in detail. Of course, over the course of your practice you will find that these three modes are not fully mutually exclusive and can blend into one another at times. However, such blending equally can be an alert for lazy practice or simply confusion of paradigms under which we choose to operate. As there is no hard and fast rule, it is even more important to understand each mode by itself and to recognise it from within our own practice.

Let us stress again that all three of these modes take place while our physical eyes are closed. That is, we are aiming to illustrate how we work with our mind on *the inner realm*, or put even more simply, in *magic*.

☾ 1. THE BLACKED-OUT DOOR

The door can be *painted black*. Looking at it in this way entrenches our mind in silence and an absence of new sensations. This is the mode of deep meditation as taught in particular in the Eastern schools. Such state cuts out all signals—messages and static noise alike—which normally seem to emerge from this door. The reality is, however, that only a small part of this noise emerges from the room behind it while the bulk of it echoes back from the door after our own minds projected it.

So the *black door* is a door of expansion into annihilation: the world disappears in the moment our mind lets go of it and stands quietly in moments of presence upon presence following each other in an endless sequence. Few people these days invest the proper amount of time and training to gain significant skills in *painting the door black*. We live in a world of distraction, drowning ourselves out in noise; accordingly it takes unusual amounts of effort and discipline to master this faculty of our mind.

In order to become proficient in magic we do *not* need to become masters of deep meditation. A small dose of this capability already goes a long way. As magicians we do not use this mode of cutting out the signal as a silver bullet to enlightenment but as a failsafe switch when it is urgently needed or—in some cases of more significant operations—as a preparatory stage to opening the door.

❦ 2. THE MIRRORED DOOR

The surface of the door can be *metallized* and *turned into a mirror*. Looking at it in this way offers a wealth of wonderful introspective methods to learn about ourselves. Standing with a naked mind in front of it, what we see in this magical mirror is not simply a plain reflection of the architecture of our mind. Don't we wish anything was that simple! Instead, what we observe are fragments of a complex *entity*, unfolding and contracting itself before our mind's eye.

Think of what you see in this mirror as a stack of photos of yourself. A photo was taken each day of your life and placed on top of each other. However, these are magical photos: they capture not only how you looked on the outside on that day, but also on the inside. So within each photo we see all your feelings, desires and fears, all sensual impressions, real-live and imagined encounters that were present with you in that specific moment of your life: one photo for each day and night.

Now it gets more complex: The photos are not made up of colour pigments fixed on paper; these magical photos of yourself are made up of elementary (and other) beings in their own right, arranged in a particular pattern and frozen in time. Each photo is showing us a slightly different pattern and a different moment of *you* in time. Thus, the closer we look at any particular photo on this stack, the less we see of *you* and the more we discover a microscopic realm of Otherness. See how the maze of our mind likes to play tricks on us? Upon close examination the "particles" that make up *you* in each of these photos reveal themselves as doors behind which we again encounter spirits of Otherness. In this manner, with our eyes closed sitting in silence, we can transcend from the I-Here-Now field (our mind looking at the metallized door), to the You-There-Then realm (the stack of photos we see reflected), to the It-Where-When realm of Otherness (the elementary and spirit patterns constructing us in each of these photos.)

All forms of psychology—from Psychoanalysis to modern CBT[2]—help us to look into this metallized door and to make sense of what we perceive in it. They offer powerful tools of sense-making for working with the stack of photos we find reflected in it. Modern, especially more clinical forms of psychology, furthermore focus on enhancing our freedom of putting new photos on top of this stack that follow patterns of our own purpose and intent, not habitual dynamics of the images of us we accumulated and piled up already.

Psychologised forms of modern magic such as *kabbalistic pathworking*, *tattwa travels* or some forms of *dreamwork* are equally significant tools to engage with and travel through the entity we encounter in that magical mirror. However, what they all have in common is that they are looking into the *metallized door* i.e. they lead us into explorations of the realm that is ultimately held together by the horizon of

---

[2] Cognitive Behavioural Therapy.

our own being, presence and mind.³ This does not at all take away from the powerful growth and healing capabilities such tools hold in store for us, quite the opposite. Equally, the related techniques are extraordinarily well positioned to gently guide us closer towards actual magical work; for they all help us in the essential endeavour of *turning our minds more elastic*.

❡ 3. THE OPENED DOOR

Lastly, and as an act most rarely performed by most humans, one can treat the door for what it is. Instead of painting it black or metallising it, one can open the door and venture through it.

This unlocking of the domestic perimeter of our mind and slipping over its threshold into the realm of It-Where-When is a most simple practice once we have learned how to pursue it. Unfortunately, through the advent of the monotheistic religions, then enlightenment and eventually modern psychology the process has become widely misunderstood and often misinterpreted both in the East and West.

In a worldview where many of us attempt to transcend directly from our mind's quiet reflection (the mirrored door) into *samādhi* (the blacked-out door), there is no longer a domain for an actual, independent spirit world. In the artificially reduced topography created by our Western world, our minds are believed to border directly onto the Divine and vast realms of creation are either excised or faded out. The world of the spirits has been rendered into an actual *hinterland* of our spiritual pathfinding, at best promising un-

---

3 This realm in itself is vast beyond the apparent boundaries of the biography contained in the stack of photos. For as we explained, each photo is made up of fragments of spiritual beings in its own right. Thus these tools have the power of gently familiarising us with the border-territory between the You-There-Then and the It-Where-When realms. I highly recommend them at one's earlier stages on the path as they perform their work in a relatively safe and protected environment.

necessary detours, and more commonly perceived to be a maze of spiritual entanglement and affliction.

To regain the ability to slip through this door we essentially have to redefine or just give up on terms such as *meditation, visualisation,* and *imagination*. Despite their young age at least in the West, these terms have come to dominate and usurp our inner terrain of practice. What else could you possibly do when sitting in silence, eyes closed and calm breathing, than to meditate? Oh yes, maybe you are visualising a river and allowing your thoughts to pass by? Or maybe you are imagining a god-form rotating above your cranium and allowing yourself to bathe in its divine light. Yet, whatever it is that happens, because we have closed our physical eyes, it is perceived to be *in our minds*.[4]

So our mind can stare at a black door and sit in enlightened silence. Our mind can also look at the mirrored door and examine layers of itself which ultimately lead out into the world again. Or, as we pointed out, we can open the door and see what lies behind it. The aspect of permanence in all three operative modes is that our mind will be *looking at something*. The inner capacity to see, to hear, to smell, to taste, even to feel while our physical senses are blinded out is the key criterion for our magical work. In the first scenario these inner senses are calmed and temporarily put to rest, in the second they are turned inwardly to interact with the entity that we are. Only in the last scenario, the one of walking through the door, are they assuming the same function again as their outer, physical senses do in the world of material creation: Our inner senses are

---

4 While this should seem to be an obvious misperception at least to practicing magicians today, even within our own modern magical tradition the same confusion is ubiquitous: *Meditation* is seen as a preparatory stage to the actual, physical work in the magical circle, and *imagination* is a faculty that requires development because it is perceived as a supporting function when we are standing robed in the ritual. Maybe this is part of what creates the attraction of grimoire magic in the early 21st century—that their practice is so effervescently physical and bound into the realm of substance? May that be as it is, we hope the metaphor of our mind and the door might help overcome this grave misperception.

processing impulses and impressions that are not generated but *received* by them. It is in this sense that passing through this door precisely is not an act of *meditation* (i.e. reflecting on something) or *imagination* (i.e. manipulating an image) but one of acquiring new first-hand experience in a vast topography that is entirely invisible to the physical realm and yet holding the same ontological reality and ligation to its inherent own laws.

IMAGINATION, Inspiration and Inner Vision

OUR hand has the capability to hold a fountain-pen and just as easily write lies or truths. It does not cost the hand more effort to write truth rather than lies; the quill will stroke the paper with the same ease and smoothness whatever the hand desires to write. What determines whether lies or truth are landing on the page does not reside within the hand itself but within the mind that guides it. If we were to look within this mind, we would be perplexed by how complex the processes are that have to be consummated to distinguish lies from truths. Yet all of this complexity is invisible and irrelevant to the hand that holds the fountain pen.

Man's capability to see in their mind's eye, to use their imagination is nothing but an invisible fountain pen, set at the rim of the fountainhead of inspiration, always ready to ink the paper of our minds.

Now, which *hand* will get to guide this pen that makes for the mystery of *imagination* in magic? Wherever a human mind is setting its hand on the fountain pen of imagination, the results will be confined by that human's desires, dreams and dreads. Whatever the pen of imagination will write or draw while in the hand of a human mind, it will speak about the hand that guides it first and foremost.⁵

> For our speculation ascends in the imagination, just as theirs [i.e. the imagination of the stars] descends. If we step so deeply into imagining, our curses become true, but their poisoning is our disease.⁶
>
> Now be that as it may, as a final decision and reason, know that the imagination makes a spirit, which is the carpenter, and accordingly the spirit is as spirit are, and has the power of spirits, therefore it has the colours, the brushes, the instruments of a spirit.⁷

If we know how to do so, passing through the door in our mind, into the inner realm or the realm of It-Where-When allows us to temporarily place the fountain pen into the hand of the spirit of our choice.

What we will see, hear, taste, perceive under such circumstances will still be coloured by the limitations of our humanness. For even

---

5 We like to recall the observation we made in the First Chapter as part of our exploration on the *Four Demon Kings*. At the end of the day, most historic attempts to simplify and standardise nomenclature of biological (or spirit) species have the tendency to tell us more about the observer than the observed. Or, as the scientists in the *Nature* article quoted above chose to put it, any system of classification tells "us nothing about the structure of nature itself, but a great deal about our own view of this structure" (Berlin, 1966, p. 275). Already in 1903, the early anthropologists Emile Durkheim and Marcel Mauss had asserted the same notion, coining the now famous dictum that "the classification of things reproduces the classification of men" (Durkheim, Mauss, 1903, p. 7).

6 *Denn unsere Speculatio geht im Imaginieren hinauf, wie jene [der Sterne] herab. So wir uns dermassen in das Imaginieren begeben, so werden unsere Flüche wahr, aber ihre Vergiftung ist unsere Krankheit.*

— Paracelsus, *Fragmentum libri: De virtute imaginativa*, in: Sudhoff, Karl (ed.); *Paracelsus Sämtliche Werke*, Band XIV, München und Berlin: Verlag R. Oldenbourg, 1933, p. 316.

7 *Nun aber wie dem allen sei, so wisse als letzter Beschluss und Grund, dass die Imaginatio einen Geist macht, welcher der Zimmermann ist, und dementsprechend ist der Geist, als ein Geist [ist], und hat die Macht der Geister, darum so hat er die Farben, die Pinsel, die Instrumente als ein Geist.*

— Paracelsus, *Fragmentum libri: De virtute imaginativa*, in: Sudhoff, Karl (ed.); *Paracelsus Sämtliche Werke*, Band XIV, München und Berlin: Verlag R. Oldenbourg, 1933, p. 318.

if Divinity holds the fountain pen of our Imagination, S/He has to write on the human paper of our mind's limited ability to receive and perceive. However, the source of inspiration guiding our perceptions will no longer reside in ourselves nor be confined by our own human agenda. We are now ready to *see* or to work magic *in vision*.

Let's look at a few examples of how incredibly clear this point has been articulated by our magical ancestors in the past. It is important to pause on the longer quotes, to truly inhale their meaning as they hold the power to cut through the ambiguity that has been cast over the subject of *imagination* and *visualisation* in modern magic. Like the sun burns off the morning haze, so Jakob Böhme's and Paracelsus's words hold the radiating force to burn through our confusion of these topics and to nourish us with bone-deep clarity.

In particular what has to be *burned off* is the confusion that resulted from Eliphas Lévi's elucidations on what he termed the *Astral light*.[8] Originally thought of as a planetary aether, in Lévi's writings it turned into the causal source and trigger for a vast array of heavily

---

8 As very much en vogue in the 19th century, Lévi describes the astral light as a "fluidum," a "world-soul," a "universal agent," a "ray," an "electromagnetical aether," and a "living heat- and light-being," all in one. So you can take your pick with regards to its specific nature (Eliphas Lévi, *Transzendentale Magie—Dogma und Ritual*, Basel: Sphinx Verlag, 1995, p. 106). Essentially, however, his theory was heavily inspired by Paracelsus and Jakob Böhme and then amalgamated with ideas and terminologies hailing from Mesmerism and the emerging electro-magnetic sciences. The 112th initiation letter he wrote to Baron Spedalieri gives evidence of this when Lévi explains: "*The immersed [spirits] communicate with us through the astral light to try to live at our expense, since we attract them by our imprudences, and the controllers of chaos would manifest themselves to us through the light of splendour, which is just as much higher than the astral light as the soul is above the body. But the peculiarity of the light of splendour is that it subdues the imagination to the mind and instantly makes the disorder of dreams cease. The Light of Splendour never causes intoxication nor haemorrhage, because it is immaterial like the grace that is its companion [...]. It is, strictly speaking, a connection of the supreme reason with the intelligence of the people. It is a radiation of probity and gentleness.*" (Eliphas Lévi, *Einweihungsbriefe in die Hohe Magie und Zahlenmystik*, Interlaken: Ansata Verlag, 1993, p. 172).

psychologised magical phenomena.[9] As so often with Lévi's works, he exploited and redeployed a sufficient amount of occult ideas of better authors than him, so that today's magical first-time reader will still stumble across many valuable pointers and way-markers for further research. Unfortunately, however, because Lévi lacked any substantial magical experience himself, he held no practical filters to either qualify or understand most of these ancient authors and what they wrote about theurgic magic.

This turned out to be especially problematic with regards to the legacy that he left with his concept of the Astral light. In misreading Jakob Böhme and then penning his own remix in his trademark style of sacral equivocality, Lévi laid the groundwork for generations of magicians to jump off the wrong cliff. Here is an exemplary section as it appears in the first chapter of Lévis's *Dogma*:

> *Imagination is in effect like the soul's eye; therein forms are outlined and preserved; thereby we behold the reflections of the invisible world; it is the glass of visions and the apparatus of magical life. By its intervention we heal diseases, modify the seasons, ward off death from the living and raise the dead to life, because it is the imagination which exalts the will and gives it power over the Universal Agent.*[10]

We will read the original source of Lévi's colportage in a moment. Before that, however, let's pause on the second sentence of the above quote. It is here that Lévi spins the position of human imagination in magic from a receptive organ[11] into the essential formative and active force in magic. Following the same flawed and romanticised

---

9 McIntosh, Christopher; *Eliphas Lévi and the French Occult Revival*, New York: Samuel Weiser, 1974, pp. 149–150.
10 McIntosh, Christopher; *Eliphas Lévi and the French Occult Revival*, New York: Samuel Weiser, 1974, p. 149—It should be pointed out that the German translation reads the second sentence not referring to the agency of human imagination, but to the human soul (Eliphas Lévi, *Transzendentale Magie— Dogma und Ritual*, Basel: Sphinx Verlag, 1995, p. 96).
11 I.e. "the soul's eye," a "glass of visions."

logic on the next page—"Fear attracts the bullet, courage makes it ricochet"[12]—with a single sentence Lévi eradicates the realm of the Other from magic. All that is left in his domesticated, harmless version of the magical art is the world as a vast canvass of astral light, to be painted upon by man's original imagination, guided by the hand of will. Generations of magicians to come continued to reduce magic to the psychologised trinity of human's *will, word* and *imagination* and thus buried deeper and deeper the key that otherwise could have unlocked the door to a classical animistic understanding of magic.

In the magic I am advocating in this book, we are not obsessing over creating things/causes on the *astral realm* according to our own human will, we are instead obsessing over walking out into the *inner realm* where creation has already taken place—not on an eternal, primordial level, but on a level by far exceeding human dimensions of time and duration. That is where we attempt to *see and hear* through a lens that is much more truthful and *real* than our conditioned physical sense of perception. In short, we are attempting to do the exact opposite of what Levi and so many other occult authors after him were rambling about: we are attempting to halt human's addiction with self-generated creation in order to perceive what is there on the inner realm already.

The so-called *creation of astral entities* is one of the most revealing proofs of how little its authors understood about spirit-magic in actual reality. It compares to building a puppet from tooth-picks and chestnuts when right next to you sits an entire ecosystem of real, living spirits ready to engage in purposeful co-creation.

More than two hundred years before Lévi, Jakob Böhme wrote a short treatise under the title "The Inward Looking Eye," as an appendix to his *Psychologia vera or Forty Questions of the Soul* (1620).[13] As with

---

12 Eliphas Lévi, *Transzendentale Magie—Dogma und Ritual*, Basel: Sphinx Verlag, 1995, p. 97.
13 Peuckert, Will-Erich, *Jakob Böhme—Sämtliche Schriften*, Dritter Band, Stuttgart-Bad Cannstatt: Frommann Verlag Günther Holzboog, 1960, pp. 179–184).

all writings of the cobbler-turned-mystic, it is marked by the author's deep first-hand visionary experience, his complex use of the German language, as well as a deep Christian piety. As practicing magicians in the 21st century we have a lot to learn from the humble man of Görlitz. Unlike Lévi's publications, in Böhme's writings words and sentences don't open like trapdoors into cognitive bricolages but into the actual inner realm; the place from which Böhme drew much of his direct and unmediated insights about the nature and dynamics of the Divine.

In the following excerpts of the Inward Looking Eye we want to emphasise what Böhme has to say on the soul's ability to *see*. First, he describes the soul as an *eye* at the threshold of the Abyss.[14] Then he explains that this eye should be imagined as a sphere of glass into which the Holy Spirit descended like a fire. It is this divine fire within the eye of our soul that forms a human's ability to *imagine* i.e. to perceive images *from within*. Thirdly, Böhme now carefully elucidates that what the soul will see depends entirely on what it has attached itself to. In principle, the inward-looking eye could perambulate the entire „wheel of nature, with the four figures," i.e. all of creation as it appears under the dominion of the four mythical beasts of the Throne-Chariot of Divinity.[15]

However, man's inner sight or imagination will only be able to avoid the snares of personal desires, illusions and fears if it is fully grounded in Divinity: Then "its images stand in themselves, in its imagination, in its light, provided they hang on to God." If the soul

---

14 German: *Urgrund*. This term is essential to Böhme's spiritual work and ideally remains untranslated. A more literal translation would give "Ultimate Ground" or "Primeval Ground." I am choosing the term *Abyss* in the sense as it is used in Josephine McCarthy's Quareia course. While it presents a free translation of the original German term, it gives the clearest indication with regards to the magical dynamics referenced: the primordial domain from which life flows and flowers into myriad of forms under the Light of Divinity.

15 See EZ 10, 14 for the description of the animals; also note this implicit reference to the mystical current that is known by using the "divine chariot" to ascend to the heavens, i.e. Jewish Merkavah mysticism.

imagines not from Divinity but if it "imagines from itself" it throws itself into confusion,[16] bitterness and torment. What the inner eye then sees are no longer reflections of the "the Word of God," born from "a fire, which was situated in eternity," but its imaginations will decay into husks and masks of parasites, into images of devils. This, according to Böhme, is an essential secret of the "Divine Magia," to find access to the truthful inner images which are born from Divine imagination, and not from personal fears or cravings.

In other words one could state that the imagination of man and the imagination of Divinity are able to meet halfway in their middle: in the fire of our soul's sphere, where just like in the sphere of an eye, through the fire of the Holy Spirit, we see out into the living forms that have stood in "Nature [...] from eternity."

Let's read the related sections in Böhme's own words.

> The soul is an eye in the eternal Abyss [Urgrund]: A likeness of eternity, a whole figure and image according to the first principle, and [it is formed] like God the Father according to his person, according to the first principle. Its essence and being (where it is pure in itself alone) is first and foremost the wheel of nature with the four figures. [...]
>
> For the Word of God has seized the soul with the eternal Fiat, in the eternal Will of the Father in the center of the eternal Nature, and opened it with the Holy Spirit, or as a fire, which was situated in eternity, blown up, in which then all the figures of the eternal Nature have stood from eternity, and [these figures] have been recognized alone in God's Wisdom in the Divine Magia, as a figure or image without essence from eternity. [...]
>
> The images dwell in the fire of the soul, just as the light dwells in the fire; but they have a different nature, just as the light has a different nature than the fire. Thus the right images of God dwell in the light of the fire of the soul, which light the fiery soul must draw in God's fountain of love, in the Majesty, by its Imagination and Inspiration. And if the soul does not do this, but imagines in itself in its fierce form to the torment of fire, and not in the fountain of love in the light of God, then its nature becomes alike to

---

16 Latin: *turba*.

severity, astringency and bitterness, and so the images of God become Turba [confusion], and devour the likeness of God in the fury.

Thus we give you to understand what soul, spirit, image and Turba are: The soul dwells in itself, and is an essential fire, and its images stand in themselves, in its imagination, in its light, provided they hang on to God; where not, the imagination stands in fearfulness, in the fury of darkness, and is a larva [mask] or image of the devils.[17]

17 Die Seele ist ein Auge im ewigen Urgrund: Ein Gleichnis der Ewigkeit, eine ganze Figur und Bildnis nach dem ersten Prinzip, und gleich Gott dem Vater nach seiner Person, nach dem ersten Prinzip [gestaltet]. Ihre Essenz und Wesenheit (wo sie pur in sich allein ist) ist erstlich das Rad der Natur, mit den vier Gestalten. [...]

Denn das Wort Gottes hat die Seele mit dem ewigen Fiat, im ewigen Willen des Vaters im Zentrum der ewigen Natur gefasst, und mit dem Heiligen Geist eröffnet, oder als ein Feuer, welches in der Ewigkeit gelegen, aufgeblasen, darinnen dann alle Gestalten der ewigen Natur sind von Ewigkeit gestanden, und [diese Gestalten] sind allein in Gottes Weisheit in der Göttlichen Magia, als eine Figur oder Bildnis ohne Wesen von Ewigkeit erkannt worden. [...]

Die Bilder wohnen wohl in dem Seelenfeuer, gleich wie auch das Licht im Feuer wohnt; aber sie haben ein anderes Wesen, gleichwie auch das Licht eine andere Natur hat als das Feuer. Also wohnen die rechten Bilder Gottes im Lichte des Seelenfeuers, welches Licht die feurige Seele muss in Gottes Liebesbrunnen, in der Majestät, schöpfen, durch ihre Imagination und Eingebung. Und so das die Seele nicht tut, sondern imaginieret in sich selber in ihrer grimmigen Gestalt zur Feuersqual, und nicht in dem Brunnen der Liebe im Lichte Gottes, so gehet ihre Wesen in Strenge, Herbheit und Bitterkeit auf, und so werden die Bilder Gottes zur Turba [Verwirrung], und verschlingen das Gleichnis Gottes im Grimm.

Also geben wir euch zu verstehen, was Seele, Geist, Bildnis und Turba seien: Die Seele wohnt in sich selber, und ist ein essentialisches Feuer, und ihre Bilder stehen in sich selber, in ihrer Imagination, in ihrem Licht, sofern sie Gott hängen; wo nicht, da steht die Imagination in der Ängstlichkeit, im Grimm der Finsternis, und ist eine Larve [Maske] oder ein Bildnis der Teufel.

— Judiciously modernised translation of excerpts of: Jakob Böhme, *Das Inngewandte Auge—Das ist eine kurze summarische Erklärung von der Seele und ihrer Bilder, und dann von der Turba, welche die Bilder zerstöret*, in: Peuckert, Will-Erich, *Jakob Böhme—Sämtliche Schriften*, Dritter Band, Stuttgart-Bad Cannstatt: Frommann Verlag Günther Holzboog, 1960, p. 179-184).

Clearing the Glass
OF OUR SOUL

As plainly stated, the trick to apply Böhme's instructions from a perspective of practical magic lies in ensuring our imagination hangs "on to God." Remember, Böhme was a cobbler first who got into mystical philosophy only because of the visions that plagued him. Unlike many other occult authors, for him experience always came first, explanations were only secondary. The term "God" in this context is not the orthodox being sat on a throne beyond creation but signifies the immanent Divinity woven through all of creation which, if only it is seen as such by the practitioner, opens a door from anywhere to everywhere.

So how do we stand back from the *Turba* of our everyday lives and reach for the threshold that is Divinity? Much of our explorations and practical work in *Holy Heretics* are aligned to this goal; specifically the exercise at the end of Chapter II forms an important starting point. What is of eminent interest for us right now is how we can prepare ourselves, the human vessel, for this experience. The *ingenium* to accomplish such mystical work is not (only) inborn but can be drawn towards us like a bird is drawn towards nesting in a particular tree. So how do we make ourselves *attractive* towards mastering the *divine magia* and seeing into the wheel of nature through the lens of our soul's fire?

With the risk of disappointing our desire for exotic rites and arcane arts, one of the most important preparatory steps we can undertake is of a most mundane nature. This, however, does not at all diminish its power and efficacy in regards to the process of inner alchemy we aspire to undertake.

This initial step is to *clear the glass of one's soul*. This implies taking the cloth of our everyday lives and applying it consciously to clean our soul's sphere from the darkness that is our ongoing inner torment and confusion (Turba). The talent (ingenium) we need to draw towards ourselves is knowing how to hold on to a minimal amount of inner peace, even when caught up in the wildest of weathers. *Becoming untroubled* in this sense has little to do with cognitive mindfulness, with deep muscle relaxation or counting our breaths. All of these are helpful levers in the periphery of our work. For we are not aiming to dissociate ourselves from what's going on around us. Instead, we aim to stand in the messy workshop of our lives, fingers burned, hands stained, but souls untroubled. The goal is to live without the darkness of shame or apology, not because you consider yourself superior or because you are cocky or naive about the consequences of your actions but because you are willing to pay the price and settle the bill any honest life will accrue in the end.

What forms the central pillar of in our work to acquire the *ingenium of indifference* is learning how to lead a life that leaves us with a light conscience. Nothing blocks us more from stepping through Divinity in our vision than feelings of guilt, remorse and regret. Quarrelling with decisions we took, not coming to peace with how we showed up in the world is the bigger obstacle to moving forward and crossing the threshold of Divinity.

Clearing the glass of one's soul is a daring and difficult Promethean[18] act of self-empowerment: Prometheus didn't do what he did to please anyone, neither the gods around him nor his mortal ego within him. More importantly, in our case we are not aiming to steal from the gods, we are aiming for a process of purging the glass of our soul from the stains and sediments of a morbid and entirely man-made morality. We are not *taking away* from anyone, but we are finally *taking care* of what is most essentially our own.

---

18 A demigod, one of the Titans who was worshipped by artisans. When Zeus hid fire away from man, Prometheus stole it by trickery and returned it to earth. By way of punishment Zeus chained him to a rock where an eagle fed each day on his liver which grew again each night. He was eventually rescued by Hercules.

Let me slow down here. I cannot overstate how important it is that you and I get onto the same page on this point. For a moment, if that is possible at all, let's ignore all external concepts of ethics, morals or even spiritual codes you have ever encountered in your life. These are not what I am talking about. I am *not* talking about purification as an inner state derived from painstakingly observing religious commandments or philosophical premises. I am speaking of acceptance, of coming to terms with who you have become, partly through circumstances, partly through your own choices.

The result of such a process in practice is precisely not falling in love with who we have become, it is not thinking of ourselves as ultimately flawless or superior to anybody else, not even to our old, yesterday's selves. To gain a minimum level of inner peace is not a competition, not against ourselves nor the heavily redacted biography of any holy woman or man. Instead, it is about the ability to accept the consequences for the decisions we took.

Let's recall the mirrored door from above: Coming to peace with ourselves does not mean seeing ourselves in shiny armour in the mirror of our mind, finally warding off all evil and sins. Instead it means being ready to see ourselves stand tall in this mirror for who we really are. It means inviting ourselves to see our selves with all the flaws, blemishes, shortcomings, and equally all the wondrous talents, skills and gifts that we embody in this very moment. Only then will we be weighed on the scales of Ma'at and that is fine.

To accomplish this process, we have to become equally adept at mastering *indifference* as well as *integrity*. Because of its importance to our path, we have an entire chapter forthcoming that will focus on the virtue that indifference can be. For now it shall suffice to say that our modern world—so obsessed with self-perfection and self-exploitation—has not only forgotten but demonised the wonderful healing qualities that can flow from being indifferent, from being untouched: accepting our fate because we have given it our very best shot, letting go of all the buried guilt, remorse and regret, allowing our failures and shortcomings to step into the light of our sight, and permitting them to sit at the table next to us...

Living with a light conscience is not about tallying achievements but about knowing we have lived life with as much integrity as possible each day—and to accept the consequences for all the rest of it.

You do not get to decide how much pain we will experience on your journey, but it is only you who decides how much drama it will be allowed to unfold. *Indifference*, thought of as a virtue in this context, is the opposite of *drama*; it is what keeps the river's surface flat, even when Charon cuts through it on his ferry.

Once the clearing of the glass has been sufficiently achieved, we will be ready to step into the fire that shines from within it. We will speak more of this process further down in the chapter on *faith*.

For now you might wonder why all this preparation is necessary to achieve something as seemingly simple as using your imagination in magic? Does it really have to take that much? Do you really need to rethink the ethics and code according to which you lead your life? In a world where you might already be lucidly dreaming or have gathered experiences in pathworking—shouldn't this step be more intuitive and organic? Is there not a way in which this will happen *by itself*?

The answer is quite straightforward and unfortunately it is No. For you see, this is the trapdoor and trick with *mastering imagination*: to imagine you had mastered your imagination as a tool for "divine magia" is incredibly easy, it is luring like a sweet poison. All it takes is to enter and then stay within a *fantasy*. Achieving such mastership in actuality, however, is an entirely different challenge. It means going on the expedition to discover and then to enter the ancient arena of magical life-skills. The place where alchemy happens is in the middle of our lives—and we pay the price for it with our entire lives.

Paracelsus still knew about this paradox, and in his usual blunt style he put it down on paper in unmistakable clarity. According to him, mastering your imagination—with all the interdependencies and broad ranging ramifications on your life—is the *only skill* you will ever need to master as a magician: precisely because of how much it demands and how much generative knowledge can flow from it in return.

Here is Paracelsus on how to walk through the door in our mind, out into the SPIRIT world of Otherness.

DE PROBATIONE MAGIAE

The first reason is that a person must be learned from himself and not from other people, because the magia cannot be learned through interpretations but only by coming down from above.

A magician is born like all arts are born, like those who discover new arts, like letters, like mines in the mountains. The magicians have a new spirit that was not created by that human. This spirit is born by asking, by seeking, by knocking, from the heart through the mind.[19]

DE DIVINATIONE

As such, the reason of divination is to be perceived: that the ones who are seeing do not see, the ones who are hearing do not hear, and so on, and yet it is before their eyes. [...] So they were blind, in life they despised the messengers of God. When it was all done, they made them delicious graves. Therefore the spirits of the stars are sent in dreams [and] in other ways, in speculation, in the mind, in the figures to signify a thing; so it is reasonable that such meanings are revealed to the astute.[20]

---

19 *Der erste Grund ist, dass ein Mensch von ihm selbst aus gelernt werden muss und nicht von anderen Menschen, denn die Magia lässt sich nicht lernen durch Interpretationen, sondern alleine dadurch dass sie von oben herab käme.*

   Magus nascitur, sicut omnes artes nascuntur, ut illi qui inveniunt novas artes, ut literas, ut montanica. Magi habent spiritum novum, non creatum ab homine isto. ille spiritus nascitur per petitionem, per quaerite, per pulsate, ex corde per spiritum.
   — Paracelsus, *De probatione magiae*, p. 500, in: Sudhoff, Karl (ed.), *Paracelsus Sämtliche Werke*, Band XII, München und Berlin: Verlag R. Oldenbourg, 1929.

20 *Als solches ist nun der Grund der Divination also wahrzunehmen: dass die Sehenden nicht sehen, die Hörenden nicht hören, uns so weiter, und dass es doch vor ihren Augen liegt. [...] Also blind waren sie, im Leben verachten sie die Gesandten Gottes. Da es alles geschehen war, da machten sie ihnen köstliche Gräber. Darum werden die Geister der Sterne im Traum gesandt, [und] auf anderen Wegen, in der Spekulation, im Gemüt,*

LIBER DE IMAGINIBUS—CAPUT XI

For this we should know, that by our faith and strong imagination alone we may bring the spirit of any man into an image.

Another thing is also possible, namely to receive a voice or an answer from the heavens by our faith and strong imagination alone, without an image or a figure, as often as we want or desire this. For this there is no need of invocation or conjuration such as is recited by the coarse, unintelligent nigromantici and devil-charmers: [These] if they wish to have a spirit or a voice from the air alone, must do mighty conjurationes against all four quarters of the world, with loud calling voice, and to this belong still many ceremonies, making a circle, incense, mortifications, also pure holy clothing, Solomon and his seals—all this is pure monkey play[21] *and seduction from the devil, no doubt originated and taught by a devilish man who is no better than the devil himself, and it is precisely in the devil's school, where the devil himself is overseer and schoolmaster, that such things are learned.*

Therefore, beware, all of you [...] and avoid such people who have gone to the devil's school or have been seduced by the devil's disciples. For this we should know: that all that they are able to do and accomplish with great effort and labour and danger to their lives and souls, we may do also and better than they, by our faith and by our imagination alone. Thereby we can conquer the ascendants according to our desire, and have speech and answer from within, as often as we want, as explained before.[22]

---

in den Figuren ein Ding zu bedeuten; so ist es billig dass solche Bedeutungen den Gescheiten geoffenbart werden.
— Paracelsus, *De divinatione*, p. 502, in: Sudhoff, Karl (ed.), *Paracelsus Sämtliche Werke*, Band XII, München und Berlin: Verlag R. Oldenbourg, 1929.

21 It might be interesting to compare Paracelsus's seemingly crass judgement of Solomonic Magic as "monkey play" to the instruction of Machik Lapdrön, the great female saint and yogini of eleventh to twelfth century Tibet: "*Listen son. Those who have not attained the bodhisattva levels and do not possess clairvoyance cannot understand the minds of others. Those who have not mastered the meditative absorption in visualisation cannot actually invoke gods and demons.*" (Harding, Sarah, *Machik's Complete Explanation*, Boston & London: Snow Lion, 2013, p. 231).

22 *Denn das sollen wir wissen, dass wir allein durch unseren Glauben und unsere kräftige Imagination eines jeglichen Menschen Geist in ein Bild bringen mögen. Es*

LIBER DE IMAGINIBUS—CAPUT XII

Therefore, you should also know that the perfect imagination, which comes from the stars, originates from the mind in which all the stars are hidden. And the mind, the faith and the imagination are to be considered as three different things; for the names are different, but have equal power and strength, for one comes from the other. And I cannot compare them otherwise than with the Divine Trinity; for by mind we come to God, by faith to Christ, by imagination we receive the Holy Spirit. Therefore, like the Divine Trinity, nothing is impossible for these three.

If, then, we come to God on earth with our mind, receive Christ through faith, and the Holy Spirit through imagination, we become like the apostles: We fear neither death, nor prison, nor torture, nor torment, nor poverty, nor labor, nor hunger, nor any other such thing; likewise we can cast out devils, make the sick well, bring the dead to life, move mountains, just as we write of the Divine Trinity. We see an example in the speculation [inner vision], because we see it in the one who speculates and when the thing he

---

ist auch noch wohl ein anderes möglich, nämlich allein durch unseren Glauben und starke Imagination, ohne ein Bild oder eine Figur, eine Stimme oder Antwort aus den Lüften zu erhalten, so oft wir dies wollen oder begehren. Dazu bedarf es keiner Anrufung oder Beschwörung, wie sie die groben, unverständigen Nigromantici und Teufelsbeschwörer aufsagen: [Diese] wenn sie einen Geist oder allein eine Stimme aus den Lüften haben wollen, müssen gewaltige Conjurationes tun gegen alle vier Enden der Welt, mit laut rufender Stimme, und dazu gehören noch viele Zeremonien, einen Kreis machen, Räucherwerk, Kasteiungen, auch reine heilige Kleidung, Salomo und seine Siegel b das alles ist ein reines Affenspiel und Verführung vom Teufel, ohne Zweifel von einem teuflischen Menschen, der nicht besser als der Teufel selbst ist, entstanden und gelehrt worden, und eben in des Teufels Schule, wo der Teufel selbst Vorsteher und Schulmeister ist, dort werden solche Dinge gelernt. Daher hütet euch alle, [...] und meidet solche Leute, die in des Teufels Schule gegangen oder von den Schülern des Teufels verführt wurden. Denn das sollen wir wissen: daß alles das, was sie mit grosser Mühe und Arbeit und Gefahren für ihr Leben und ihre Seele vermögen und zu Wege bringen, das mögen wir auch tun und besser als sie, allein durch unseren Glauben und durch unsere Imagination. Dadurch können wir die Aszendenten bezwingen nach unserem Begehren, und Rede und Antwort von Innen haben, als oft wir wollen, wie vorher erklärt.

—Paracelsus, *Liber de Imaginibus*, pp. 380-381, in: Sudhoff, Karl (ed.), *Paracelsus Sämtliche Werke*, Band XIII, München und Berlin: Verlag R. Oldenbourg, 1931.

*speculates on has a mind. If he now does not desist from it and is seriously interested in it, then he devises the practice from such speculation. For no one can arrive at the practice other than through theory and speculation. To begin with, everything must be speculated. For all crafts and arts also have their origin in speculation and theory. And this is also to be known here, that all times at night, when all bodily things are at rest, secret and silent, it is best and most useful to speculate, to conceive and to imagine. Also in secret, special and suitable places, where one cannot be shouted at, frightened or prevented by people; also with a sober body.*²³

OF THE SOURCE AND ORIGIN OF THE FRENCH DISEASE [I.E. SYPHILIS]

Man is subject to the imagination, and the imagination, although in-

23 *Darum sollt ihr auch wissen, daß die perfekte Imagination, die von den Sternen kommt, die entspringt dem Gemüt in dem alle Sterne verborgen liegen. Und das Gemüt, der Glaube und die Imagination sind als drei verschiedene Dinge anzusehen; denn die Namen sind unterschiedlich, haben aber gleiche Kraft und Stärke, denn es kommt eines aus dem anderen. Und ich kann sie nicht anders vergleichen als mit der Göttlichen Trinität; denn durch das Gemüt kommen wir zu Gott, durch den Glauben zu Christi, durch die Imagination empfangen wir den Heiligen Geist. Darum ist auch diesen dreien, wie der Göttlichen Trinität, nichts unmöglich.*

So wir nun auf Erden mit unserem Gemüt zu Gott kommen, durch den Glauben zu Christi und durch die Imagination den Heiligen Geist empfangen, so werden wir gleich den Aposteln: Wir fürchten weder den Tod, noch Gefängnis, weder Marter noch Pein, Armut, Arbeit, Hunger noch anderes dergleichen, ebenso können wir Teufel austreiben, Kranke gesund machen, Tote lebendig machen, Berge versetzen, gleich wie wir es von der Göttlichen Trinität schreiben. Ein Beispiel sehen wir an der Spekulation [inneren Schau], denn wir sehen, einer der da spekuliert und hat deren Ding ein Verstand, darin er spekuliert. Lässt er nun nicht davon ab und ist ihm ernstlich angelegen, so ersinnt er in solcher Spekulation die Praktik. Denn keiner kann zu der Praktik kommen, anders als durch die Theorie und Spekulation. Es muss erstlich nur alles spekuliert sein. Denn auch alle Handwerke und Künste haben ihren Ursprung aus Spekulation und Theorie. Und das ist hier auch zu wissen, dass alle Mal bei der Nacht, wenn alle leibliche Dinge ruhen, heimlich und still sind, am besten und nützlichsten zu spekulieren, zu mentiren und imaginieren ist. Auch an heimlichen, besonderen und dazu geeigneten Orten, wo man nicht von den Leuten beschrien, erschreckt oder verhindert werden kann; dazu auch mit nüchternem Leib.

— Paracelsus, *Liber de Imaginibus*, pp. 383-384, in: Sudhoff, Karl (ed.), *Paracelsus Sämtliche Werke*, Band XIII, München und Berlin: Verlag R. Oldenbourg, 1931.

visible and untouchable, nevertheless works corporeally into a substance and through this substance, as if it were the substance itself. [...] It follows then that imagination is more than nature and governs it, it takes away the innate quality and terrifies[24] man that heaven no longer knows him, nor the nature of the earth. For he has escaped from them all through the imagination.[25]

SPECULATIO
Fantasy or Inner Vision?

FROM these quotes we realise how closely interwoven the two critical terms *imagination* and *speculation* are in Paracelsus's occult oeuvre. Let's dissect both and resolve the tension, if not seeming contradiction, some of the above sections hold with Paracelsus's better known and explicitly medical works.

The most abbreviated definition of these two Paracelsian terms would be to identify *speculation* as an inborn faculty, a dormant capability of the human mind. This aligns to the the mid 16th century usage of the adjective *specular* as "reflective" (from Latin *speculum* "a mirror"), and later on in the 17th century as "assisting in vision; affording a view."

---

24 The German word "entsetzten" could also be read as an old expression for *deforms* in the sense of changing man to a degree that they are no longer recognised by the natural order of heaven or earth.

25 *Der Mensch ist der Imagination unterworfen, und die Imagination, obgleich unsichtbar und unbegreiflich, wirkt doch körperlich in eine Substanz und durch diese Substanz hindurch, als sei sie die Substanz selbst. [...] Daraus folgt dann, dass die Imagination mehr als die Natur ist und sie regiert, sie nimmt die angeborene Eigenschaft hinweg und entsetzt den Menschen, das ihn der Himmel nicht mehr kennt, noch die Natur der Erden. Denn er ist durch die Imagination denen allen entwichen.*
— Paracelsus, *Vom Ursprung und Herkunft der Franzosen*, pp. 329-330, in: Sudhoff, Karl (ed.), *Paracelsus Sämtliche Werke*, Band VII, München und Berlin: Verlag R. Oldenbourg, 1923.

Imagination on the other hand is the activated state of this faculty; it is speculation in action and driven by *something* into a particular direction. Without differentiating this overtly, Paracelsus now utilises *speculation* in two very different and contradictory senses – depending on what this *something* is. So the essential implicit question becomes: what is activating, driving and guiding this inner perceptive organ of the human mind?

Now *human speculation*, in Paracelsus's works, describes any act where one's cognitive mind is guided from within man itself, that is through human ratio, will, lust, desire etc. In this operative manner Paracelsus is often deriding the function of speculation as highly inferior to making first-hand experiences. He compares it to sophistry[26] and never ceases to stigmatise it as the essential flaw and source of evil of the sciences of his time.

Here is a good example of Paracelsus scolding *human speculation* as a faculty that ceaselessly produces random theoretical fantasies but adds little to understanding the actual nature of man and the cosmos:

> [*To philosophize inwardly*] *creates no teaching except for what man himself speculates.* [...] *The outer philosophy grows from no speculation, but it grows from the human being and shows and learns what the inner one is. Because such is a teacher, it is necessary to leave speculation and to pursue that which is not shown by speculation, but by interpretation and demonstration. Now here lies the tension and the dispute that my opponents speculate and I teach from nature. Now speculating is fantasising and fantasising makes a fantasist. Now the fantasy is not built on any ground, but it is left to everyone to fantasise as much as he wants. In the effect it is not different than one who wishes: He has nothing, only because he wishes it. So it is with those who speculate and fantasise — it is nothing what they speculate and fantasise.*[27]

---

26 Sudhoff, Karl (ed.), *Paracelsus Sämtliche Werke*, Band VII, München und Berlin: Verlag R. Oldenbourg, 1923, p. 267.

27 [*Im Innern zu philosophieren*] *gibt keine Lehre, denn was der Mensch selbst spekuliert.* [...] *Die äussere Philosophie wächst aus keiner Spekulation, sondern sie wächst aus*

This is Paracelsus speaking to an audience of traditional scholars and medics on the "foundations of all medical insights and the duties of the medic" in his hallmark "immediacy and depth of soul."[28] He finished his Paragranum around the year 1530.

It will be most insightful to now compare the above quotation with a small treatise, which dates from the early period of Paracelsus's work, and in which he deals with the human condition, Ein Büchlein (Philosophia) de generatione Hominis.[29]

Here we find the term speculation explicitly differentiated from *fantasy*. The latter is explained to derive from the element of air and the quality of lust, and has to be *placed into the speculation of man* in order for fantasy's dormant seed to become actualised, or in Paracelsus's terms, to turn into a *matter*. It's the capability of human speculation, however, that creates, shapes and finishes all fantasies. Thus speculation as a faculty underlies the human ability to fantasise, but is not identical with it.[30]

The notion that fantasising is a particular state of activating the underlying human ability to speculate, but not the capability as such, is further emphasised in Paracelsus's treatise on raving madness (Taubsucht, as he calls it or, in modern German, Tobsucht). Here Paracelsus diagnoses that these obsessive people overload their minds with too much "extraneous speculationes."

---

dem Menschen und zeigt und lernt was der innere sei. Dieweil nun solcher Lehrmeister sei, so ist es von Nöten, die Spekulation zu verlassen und dem nachzugehen, das nicht aus Spekulieren angezeigt wird, sondern aus Deutung und Darlegung. Hier liegt nun die Spannung und der Streit, dass meine Gegner spekulieren und ich lehre aus der Natur. Nun ist spekulieren fantasieren und fantasieren macht einen Fantasten. Nun ist die Phantasie auf keinen Grund gebaut, sondern es ist einem jeden frei anheim gestellt soviel zu fantasieren wie er will. Im Effekt ist es nicht anderes als einer der wünscht: Er hat doch nichts, nur weil er es wünscht. So ist es mit jenen die spekulieren und fantasieren b es ist doch nichts was sie spekulieren und fantasieren.

—Paracelsus, Paragranum, pp. 141-142, in: Sudhoff, Karl (ed.), *Paracelsus Sämtliche Werke*, Band VIII, München und Berlin: Verlag R. Oldenbourg, 1924.

28 Sudhoff, Karl (ed.), *Paracelsus Sämtliche Werke*, Band VIII, München und Berlin: Verlag R. Oldenbourg, 1924, p. 8.
29 Ibid., Band I, XLIV.
30 Ibid., Band I, pp. 293–294.

As far as the essence of insanity is concerned, namely of those sick people who have overloaded their reason with foreign reason, that is, with more than what corresponds to their office, they take all foreign speculationes and bring everything into their head. And when these speculationes are in their head and are gathered together, then they are called cheap Mirmidones.[31] *So when they are together, they are in conflict, each one warring against the other, and so it becomes a skirmish, as when a band of people beat each other. [...] All these things the brain must fulfil; but when such has happened to the brain, then the brain lies below and the fixed ideas above and continue to rule this fantasist.*[32]

Let's summarise. The human mind (German: *Gemüt*) holds the innate capability to *see* i.e. to *speculate* in the original sense of the Latin word *speculare*.[33] This ability is not produced out of itself but can only come to life if the mind is illuminated. When man is not standing in their own way but truly looking out into the world, their mind can be illuminated by the Light of Nature. Herein lies the secret of knowing how to read the Book of Nature i.e. finding access through experiment, examination and interpretation to the natural wisdom of poisons and antidotes, the essence and efficacy of plants, stones, trees, animals and even humans.

---

31 A Paracelsian neologism for swirling, fixed ideas born from fantasy.

32 *So es das Wesen der Unsinnigkeit anbelangt, nämlich jener Kranker, die ihre Vernunft mit fremder Vernunft überladen haben, das ist, mit mehr als ihrem Amt entspricht, die selbigen nehmen an sich alle fremden speculationes und bringen alles in ihren Kopf. Und so nun diese speculationes in ihrem Kopf sind und versammelt sind, so heissen sie billglich Mirmidones. So sie also beieinander sind, so sind sie zwieträchtig, ein jeglicher will gegen den anderen und so wird ein Scharmützel daraus, gleich als wenn ein Haufen Volk einander schlägt. [...] All diese Dinge muss das Gehirn erfüllen; so es aber um das Gehirn geschehen ist, so liegt das Hirn unten und die fixen Ideen oben und regieren diesen Fantasten weiter.*
— Sudhoff, Karl (ed.); *Paracelsus Sämtliche Werke*, Band VII, München und Berlin: Verlag R. Oldenbourg, 1923, p. 103.

33 Latin: *speculare*: 1570s, "reflective" as in a mirror (from Latin *speculum* "a mirror"), since 1650s also understood as in "assisting in vision" or "affording a view."

Now, if man closes their physical eyes,[34] the Light of Nature gives way to other sources of illumination of the mirror of our mind. Most commonly, as we all experience in dreams, the light of fantasy is taking hold of our our ability to *see from within*. According to Paracelsus, born from a combination of the element of air and man's inborn desires it conjures up fantastical images in front of our inner eyes. It is in this context that Paracelsus affirms "speculating is fantasising." That is, the state of man seeing into the light of fantasy or imagination guided by subjective lust and fear.

Therefore, we have to understand that the light of fantasy is the light of our imagination, explicitly whenever it appears unguided by firm will and clear faith. It is in this state that humans are especially open to uncontrolled exposure and contact with actual *daimones*. To these living spirits a human's unguided imagination is an open gateway, an exposed interface into their minds. Thus, while the light of imagination can breed fantastical illusions born from air and lust, it can also breed images seeded by spirits. Distinguishing these two and becoming adept in filtering and facilitating specific kinds of *contact* establishes much of the canon of magical skill-building.

However, the work of the true magician, according to Paracelsus, is different again from both of the above modes of *seeing*. Neither do they advance their practice through the Light of Nature alone nor through the light of fantasy. Instead, through knowledgeable application of will and faith, they take control of their ability to *see from within* and direct their perception into the Light of Divinity. Thus, their imagination becomes filled and enlivened by the Light of Divinity.[35]

---

34 The *eye* is used here to represent all other physical senses as well. *Inner vision* flows and operates in a synaesthetic manner i.e. it can express itself through all human senses, depending on each magician's individual talents and skills.

35 For the purpose of our current training exploration we will not indulge in the fact that ultimately the *Light of Nature* and the *Light of Divinity* hold one and the same source. While that is true, it reflects a stage of practice that

The above diagram might help to illustrate these essential differences of how man can leverage their mind's ability to *see*: In order to see into the Light of Divinity we have to make a 180 degree turn from our normal vista into the world and learn to gaze into the speculum of our own mind. Here, however, we ensure this speculum no longer acts as a mirror i.e. reflects our gaze back at us. Instead, we begin to polish this speculum of our inner eye and soul. Once sufficient amounts of impurity and stains have been removed, the speculum of our mind turns from a mirror into a *glass*, a window through which we can see into the Light of Divinity.

It is important to emphasise this critical point: the very inner organ that perceives the Light of Nature as the mirror of our eye needs to be thrown into utter darkness and then carefully cleansed from the stains and sediments of our mundane lives and subjective fantasies. Only then will it reveal itself as *glass, through which* we begin to see the Light of Divinity and can learn to stride out into the inner realm.

Try to see this vision clearly in your mind: man standing tall, illuminated by the Light of Nature into which s/he is born. The light of nature's sun shines upon their eye, their heart and hands. Now this human has learned how to loosen and flex their inner form. So they step out of their physical body, turn around and look into the back of their own eyes and heart and hands. If the glass of their inner human has grown clean from the impurities of the world and I, Me, Mine, it suddenly changes its nature, giving way to an entirely different mode of seeing from within: their own human form no longer acts as a mirror to the light from the outside but suddenly becomes a clear glass to the light from the inside. They have become transparent to the Divine. That is the moment the magical journey begins.

---

in many ways transcends the work of the shamanic goês who consciously aims to work with the experience of radical Otherness. In the following diagram, however, we do indicate that both sources of "light" are interconnected in the "speculum" of creation.

INNER MAN   PHYSICAL MAN

In anticipation of the next chapter, we can summarise that above all the magician depends upon three kinds of *inner paraphernalia* in their work as an adept:

The *Speculum*, or the cleared looking glass of their soul's eye through which they will travel out into the inner realm. Under the illumination of the Divinity, they will venture amongst forms and beings of *radical Otherness*, which in themselves are not eternal but of much higher degrees of ontological integrity than the forms and beings in the physical world.

The *Well*, or the spring of the human heart. This is what in traditional ritual magic is often reduced in size to a cup or a chalice. In our work, though, we allow it to extend and grow. Thus, it turns into a deep and broad well at whose rim the magician stands and listens to the voices coming up from deep underground. This the *Urgrund* or *Abyss* that Böhme refers to recurrently: the primordial domain from which life flows and flowers into myriad of forms under the Light of Divinity.

The *Staff*, or wand of will. This is the magician's ability to calm all fantasies, all voices of I, Me and Mine, of their subjective lust and fear. It also represents the magician's ability to become indifferent and immune to outside spirit voices distracting from their present work. Centred in the silence of their mind, they hold onto the staff of their will and point it to the intention of their faith. Holding this staff tightly requires equal measures of knowing how to handle fearless indifferences as well as unconditional faith. This staff, not unlike the broomstick of the witch, is the medium of the magician's journey.

Here now we see the *pentacle* (speculum of our soul), the *chalice* (well of our heart), and the *staff* (spear of faith) residing side by side in their original essence, ready to be joined by the hand of the adept to enable travel, creation and destruction *in vision*.

As complex as this might seem, it will become entirely organic once approached through an appropriate practical framework. To illustrate this, I'd encourage you to perform Josephine McCarthy's *Flame of the Void* exercise as it is given in the appendix of this book with kind permission by its author. —Take a look at it now, read it carefully and come back here afterwards.

As you can see, this is not a complex operation at all. And yet if you look carefully, you'll find all three of the inner paraphernalia of the adept fused into one: the flame *is* the speculum, the void *is* the well, and your intent *is* the staff.

My hope is that through such practice and perspective we can begin to see where magic truly resides. So many outer manifestations of magical practice are nothing but "monkey play" as Paracelsus rightly says. In most cases they are harmless, often useless, and nothing but a distraction from the work that actually matters and ultimately creates magical impact. The latter is not measured by the level of sophistication and variation of our outer paraphernalia but by our ability to handle, to fuse together and to successfully operate the inner tools of our craft: The glass of our soul's eye, the well of spirits that speaks from our hearts, and the staff of our will and faith that determines the direction of our journey like an arrow through the night.

In the following chapters we will explore a framework specifically designed for this book and based upon more than twenty years of magical practice. It is intended to enable us to begin to excavate and apply these inner paraphernalia not only through magical work, but more importantly through the lens of our everyday lives.

Nothing could express the intention of this framework better than Paracelsus words at the end of the following quote from his Book of the Images of Idolatry (Liber de imaginibus idolatriae). Let's see if we can manage to carve what we need from within—even a holy wo/man carved from the rock of our dormant selves—rather than piling up ever more dead bodies of gurus, saints & demons around us.

> But you of the common mind do not want to understand the commandment of Christ and God the Father properly: You throw the wooden images out of the churches. What do they do to you? They do not bite, they do not bark, they do not lie, they do not deceive. Why do you throw them into the furnace? Why do you burn them? Burn the images that condemn your body and soul! These are the images that belong out of the churches. What is there in the wood, what is there in the stone, what is there in the walls of the churches? Why do you purify the temple of the masonry? Not so! Thou shalt cleanse the temple of thy heart, and cast out of it the evil images that thou hast therein, not out of the masonry.
>
> Sweeping out the walls and casting out the idols justifies nothing, for it is only hypocrisy. But go into the temple that is within.
>
> Throw out from you the profanation, the adultery, the manslaughter, your deceit, your blasphemy and the like. Purify it! This is the temple that is to be clean, and do not justify yourself on the masonry. It gives you neither salt nor lard, there is nothing but hypocrisy; your heart remains always defiled. For while thou dwellest on the outward, the devil doth not tarry on the inward. [...]
>
> Throw out the living images that damn your body and soul. [...] Throw out the enemy, not from the outer walls but from your heart. And cast out the unchastity of the thoughts, of the images you imagine. [...]

God wants to have a pure heart and not the outward justification. [...] The house of Christ is a house of prayer; that means it is the heart of the one who prays. The wall is a stone house and not a house of prayer. [...] So you shall recognise the images: if you want to cleanse the temples, let it be the one inside and not the one outside. [...]

But if you make your temple clean and keep it clean, you will not need a carver or a stonemason. You will be yourselves and carve for yourselves what you need, and the consecrated bishop, which does not perish, you will prepare for yourselves inwardly. This is your reward, if you eschew the idolatrous image that God has forbidden.[36]

---

36 *Aber ihr des gemeinen Verstandes wollt das Gebot Christi und Gott des Vaters nicht richtig verstehen: Ihr werft die hölzernen Bilder aus den Kirchen. Was tun sie euch? Sie beissen nicht, sie bellen nicht, sie lügen nicht, sie betrügen nicht. Warum werft ihr sie in den Ofen? Warum verbrennt ihr sie? Verbrennt die Bilder, die euch Leib und Seele verdammen! Das sind die Bilder, welche aus den Kirchen gehören. Was liegt am Holz, was am Stein, was liegt an den Mauern der Kirchen? Warum reinigst du den Tempel des Gemäuers? Nicht also! Du sollst reinigen den Tempel deines Herzens, und aus demselben werfen die bösen Bilder, die du darinnen hast, nicht aus dem Gemäuer. Das Auskehren der Gemäuer und das Hinauswerfen der Götzen rechtfertigen nichts, denn es ist nur ein Heuchelei. Sondern gehe in den Tempel der inwendig ist. Da werfe hinaus von dir die Schändung, den Ehebruch, den Totschlag, deinen Betrug, deine Blasphemie und dergleichen. Den reinige! Das ist der Tempel der rein sein soll, und nicht rechtfertige dich an dem Gemäuer. Es gibt dir weder Salz noch Schmalz, es gibt nichts denn eine Heuchelei; dein Herz bleibt allemal befleckt. Denn dieweil du mit dem auswendigen dich aufhälst, dieweil säumet sich der Teufel mit dem inwendigen nicht. [...] Wirf hinaus die lebendigen Bilder, die dir Leib und Seele verdammen. [...] Den Feind wirf hinaus, nicht aus dem Gemäuer sondern aus deinem Herzen. Und wirf aus die Unkeuschheit der Gedanken, welcher Bilder du imaginierst. [...] Gott will ein reines Herz haben, und nicht die äussere Rechtfertigung. [...] Das Haus Christi ist ein Bethaus; das bedeutet es ist das Herz desjenigen der betet. Das Gemäuer ist ein steinernes Haus und nicht ein Bethaus. [...] Also sollt ihr die Bilder erkennen. So ihr doch wollt die Tempel reinigen, lasset es den inwendigen und nicht den auswendigen sein. [...] So ihr aber euren Tempel sauber macht und sauber haltet, so bedürft ihr keines Bildschnitzers noch Steinmetzes. Ihr werdet es selber sein und euch selbst schnitzen, was ihr bedürft, und den geweihten Bischoff, der nicht vergeht, werdet ihr euch inwendig bereiten. Das ist euer Lohn, wenn ihr das abgöttische Bildnis sein lasst, das Gott verboten hat.*
— Paracelsus, *Liber de imaginibus idolatriae*, in: Goldammer, Kurt (ed.), *Paracelsus—Sämtliche Werke*, 2. Abteilung, *Theologische und Religionsphilosophische Schriften*, Band III, Stuttgart: Franz Steiner Verlag, 1986, pp. 282-283.

CHAPTER IV

Paracelsian Magic

You, Paracelsus

IMAGINE being born at the end of the 15th century, the son of an illegitimate German nobleman and doctor and a monastic Swiss wife. The fact that your parents ended up together, not just for a single night but as man and wife, was unheard of. How come a nobleman would marry not only this far below their own class but what is more, a woman that had vowed to lead a life dedicated to God alone? The circumstances of your birth had only been made possible by the violation of the most essential social norms of the time. From the moment of your birth your life was marked as a violation of spiritual as well as feudal conventions. Thus unsurprisingly, given how unique your parents were as a couple, it came with the territory that all avenues to making a living were blocked for them. There was no road that would lead to a place of their own in a society caught in the chaos of overturning the Middle Ages into a new dawn.

But the oddities of your entrance into this world do not stop there. Recent research into your human remains suggest—yes, we still have a good section of your skeleton, despite the five hundred years passed[1]—even your development in your mother's womb took its own unique path. Today it seems not unlikely that your original foetus chromosomatically had been female. However, due to a rare condition of your adrenal gland your unborn body began to produce a reduced amount of cortisol and aldosterone and yet exaggerated amounts of male hormones. This in turn triggered a series of events, both with regards to the formation of your foetus as well as in your childhood development, that we best leave to describe by experts. What they suggest, though, is that in laymen's term you were a woman on the inside, with the shell of a man grown over it on the outside.[2]

The anthropological examination of the Paracelsus skeleton showed that characteristic female features are present at the pelvis. Furthermore, certain

---

1 Kritscher, Herbert/Hauser, Gertrude/Reiter, Christian/Szilvässy, Johann/Vycudilik, Walter, "Forensisch-anthropologische Untersuchungen der Skelettreste des Paracelsus," in: Heinz Dopsch, Kurt Goldammer, Peter F. Kramml (ed.), *Paracelsus (1493–1541), «Keines andern Knecht...»*, Salzburg: Pustet, 1993, p. 53–61.

2 Let's keep this simple: had somebody taken a chromosome sample of yours, they would have identified you as a woman. Equally, looking at your skeleton alone, researchers would have identified you as a woman as well. However, in contrast to this, your visible sexual characteristics—as developed through hormonal stimulus in the foetus—would have identified you as a male. This condition is often called "congenital adrenal hyperplasia." I am sure you would have hated that term, and maybe preferred the more colloquial expression "Pseudohermaphroditism."

female aspects can be recognized in the area of the skull. This cannot be reconciled with the clinical picture of eunuchism but would be due to the possible presence of a so-called "Congenital Adrenogenital Syndrome," a clinical picture that could be explained not only by the physique and appearance of Paracelsus but also by his nature and life. In this syndrome, there is a recessively inherited defect in the formation of enzymes that are important for individual steps in the biosynthesis of adrenal hormones. The ailment is based on a genetic disorder that occurs in one out of 5,000 births in Central Europe.

Under such hormonal condition, children grow faster than normal i.e. they are taller than their peers, but as a result of a subsequently early closure of the growth plates they also have premature growth arrest. As adults they barely reach a height of 1.6 m. Early, in the third decade of life, a prominent anterior baldness begins. Affected individuals are often of above-average intelligence but psychologically difficult, prone to irascibility, often shy, and usually live secluded lives. There is infertility, and sexually the patients are uninterested.

Whether Theophrast Bombast von Hohenheim was chromosomatically determined as a woman, grew into the body of an apparent man due to a genetic defect, or whether it was merely his restless life, his urge to research, or deliberate self-restraint and mortification that led to this famous physician and scientist remaining without a wife, will hardly ever be entirely determined.[3]

Well, my friend, from the moment of your inception you clearly did not like averageness. Equally, you would not bow to nature's polarities. After all, why choose between male and female when you could be both? And yet, how come such a clean and simple choice led to so much isolation and suffering throughout your lifetime? It seems, embedded in this potential biological condition,

3 Kritscher, Herbert/Hauser, Gertrude/Reiter, Christian/Szilvássy, Johann/Vycudilik, Walter: "Forensisch-anthropologische Untersuchungen der Skelettreste des Paracelsus," in: Heinz Dopsch, Kurt Goldammer, Peter F. Kramml (ed.), *Paracelsus (1493–1541), «Keines andern Knecht»*, Salzburg: Pustet, 1993, p. 61, translation by author.

we already find one of your life's central struggles: the contest to unapologetically express what first-hand experience strikes you as true and yet which within the conditions of your time has neither place nor name.

A child like yourself—incredibly intelligent, equally irascible, and yet entirely without equals, growing up in grave poverty on a destitute Swiss mountain farm: how much would it have needed his mother? Nevertheless, even following her early death when you were merely nine years old (1502), she still didn't belong to herself. As a former servant of the monastry she had become property of the Catholic Church, and in her death so had you, her illegitimate son. Even after your own death in 1541 the Catholic Church was not shy in expressing this "birth-right" over you and claimed a precious silver goblet from your inheritance for the damage the Church had suffered by your mother's absconsion. Under such circumstances, how did you grow up to experience the merit of every human's personal freedom as well as the value of true charity? Well, as we know from all the records you left behind, you grew up fighting for both with the sword of your tongue and the chalice of your healing hands.

Now, dear reader, as you have slipped into the skin of Paracelsus, from this inimitable outlook, raise your gaze and imagine seeing a veritable ocean of a life voyage. Imagine yourself emerging from it as a highly skilled doctor, as a passionate spiritual man, as an alchemist, a magician and a radical folk-healer, striding out on entirely new and unknown paths. In the course of your arduous life you will spend most of your time alone, fall victim to countless political intrigues and become accustomed to changing the garb of the famous and vaunted innovator with the barren saddle of the fugitive and persecuted charlatan. Yes, that's it: through a life of hardships and disappointments, through a life amidst the embers of your faith, the fire of your research and the flames of your wrath, you have become absolutely free from the opinions, the whims and the intrigues but equally of all the affections of your fellow men. You have become a loner who strides on lonely paths.

The most naked, stark depiction of your life has come upon us in a letter from your former *famulus*. While it reads larger than life, we know much of it must be true for we hear the same details of your lifestyle attested from later sources.[4] Here is the letter in a longish excerpt:

> As for Theophrastum Paracelsum, (he is now long dead) – when he was alive, I came to know him so much that I would not easily desire to live with such people as I have lived with him. For apart from his miraculous and fortunate cures in every kind of illness, I did not notice in him any godliness or any erudition, and I used to wonder very much after seeing many things appear that are written by him and claimed to have been left to posterity which I would hardly dream of ascribing to him. So much was he devoted to drinking and boasting day and night, while I stayed with him for almost two years, that he could hardly be found sober for an hour or two, especially after he had left Basel and was celebrated in Alsace amongst the nobles, peasants and farmers like a second Asclepius.
>
> Nevertheless, when he was at his drunkest and, coming home, used to dictate to me some of his philosophy, it seemed to hang together so neatly that it could not have been improved by a sober person. I was anxious to translate it into Latin, and there are also some of these books which have been translated into Latin, partly by me and partly by others. All night long, as long as I stayed with him, he never undressed, which I attributed to his drunkenness. And very often he came home around midnight, always drunk, to sleep. Dressed as he was, his sword with him, which he claimed to have received as a gift from a torturer or executioner, he threw himself on the bed, and now and then, in the middle of the night, when he had hardly slept, he would get up with his sword drawn, like a frenzied man, throwing it to the floor against the wall, so that sometimes I thought he would cut off my head, and was afraid of that. It would take me many days to describe everything I went through with him. He always had his charcoal corner, with constant fire, soon his Alcali, soon his Oleum sublimati, soon

---

4 Peuckert, Will-Erich,, *Theophrastus Paracelsus*, Stuttgart-Berlin: Kohlhammer Verlag, 1941, p. 307 and p. 429.

the king Praecipitati, soon his Arsenic oil or Crocus martis or his whimsical Opodeltoch and I don't know what kind of concoction boiling. For he almost choked my living spirit once with his boiling, when he ordered me to look at the spirit of his alembic; I had held my nose a little too close to it—the glass that lay on top of the alembic was taken away a little, so that I was almost choked and strangled by the virulent smoke and steam that hit my mouth and nostrils so that I fainted and only regained consciousness by him sprinkling cold water on me.

In between he pretended to be able to prophesy many wonderful things and to know strange arcana and mysteries, so that I did not easily get anything from him in secret, nor did I ever dare to touch anything, since I was always afraid of him. He expended a lot of money, so much so that he sometimes kept neither penny nor nickel, as far as I knew, and the next day he again showed me his purse full of money, so that I not infrequently wondered how he had got so much again. Almost every month he had a new coat made, and the other coat he wore he gave away to the first person who met him; but it was so stained that I never wanted one from him again, and even if he had given it to me, I would not have wanted to wear it.

In curing and healing ulcers he performed almost miracles where there seemed little hope, forbidding no kind of food or drink in healing, but carousing with his patients day and night to his heart's content, so that he cured them, as he used to say, with a full belly. The powder of Praecipitate with Theriac or Methridatum or made into pills with cherry juice, he used for purgations in all kinds of diseases. With his Laudanum, as he called pills in the form of mouse droppings which he used in unequal numbers only in the extreme distress of diseases, as if taking refuge in the holy anchor (as they say), he boasted so much that he did not even refrain from claiming that he alone, only by the use of these, could bring the dead back to life, and this he actually proved now and then when I was with him, and they who seemed to be dead suddenly came back to life.

But I never saw or heard him pray, nor did he ask about any spiritual exercise, nor about the evangelical doctrine, which at that time began to be revered and practiced among us and was very carefully and diligently pursued by our preacher, which he not only despised, but also threatened that he would once again set straight Luther and the Pope, as well as Galen and Hippocrates, and that no one who had written about the holy scriptures so far, both the older and the younger, had ever hit the right core of the scriptures, but only the outer shell, so that they only hit the shadows and explained them. And I don't know what other nonsense he brought up, which I am ashamed to tell.

Nothing attracted him to women at all, so that I think he never knew one at all. In the beginning he was very moderate, so that he did not drink wine until his twenty-fifth year; but later he learned to drink in such a manner that he challenged whole tables full of peasants to drink, and also won in drinking and quaffing, now and then sticking his finger down his throat and thus resembling a pig...[5]

---

5 Was Theophrastum Paracelsum betrifft, (er ist jetzt lange tot), als er noch lebte, habe ich ihn so sehr kennen gelernt, daß ich mit derartigen Menschen zu leben, wie ich mit ihm gelebt habe, nicht leicht begehren würde. Denn abgesehen von seinen wunderlichen und glücklichen Heilungen in jeder Art von Krankheiten, habe ich an ihm weder irgendwelche Gottseligkeit noch irgendwelche Gelehrsamkeit bemerkt, und ich pflege mich sehr zu wundern, nachdem ich so manches erscheinen sehe, das von ihm geschrieben und der Nachwelt hinterlassen zu sein behauptet wird, welches ich ihm kaum im Traum, zuschreiben würde. So sehr war er Tag und Nacht, während ich fast zwei Jahre bei ihm verkehrte und wohnte, dem Trunk und der Prasserei ergeben, daß man ihn kaum eine Stunde oder zwei nüchtern fand, besonders nachdem er von Basel fortgereist war und im Elsaß unter den Edeln, Bauern und Bäuerinnen wie ein zweiter Äskulap gefeiert worden war.

Dessen ungeachtet, wenn er am betrunkensten war und, nach Hause gekommen, mir etwas von seiner Philosophie zu diktieren pflegte, so schien sie so ordentlich zusammenzuhängen, daß sie von einem nüchternen Menschen nicht hätte verbessert werden können. Ich war beflissen, sie ins Lateinische zu übersetzen, und es gibt auch einige von diesen Büchern, die, teils von mir und teils von andern ins Lateinische übersetzt worden sind. Die ganze Nacht, solange ich bei ihm wohnte, hat er sich nie ausgezogen, was ich seiner Trunkenheit zuschrieb. Und sehr oft kam er gegen Mitternacht, stets betrunken, nach Hause, um zu schlafen. So wie er angezogen war, sein Schwert bei sich, das er von einem Folterknecht oder Henker geschenkt bekommen zu haben behauptete, warf er sich aufs Bett, und dann und wann, mitten in der Nacht, wenn er kaum geschlafen hatte, stand er auf mit seinem gezogenen Schwert, wie ein Rasender, schmiß es zu Boden gegen die Wand, so daß ich manchmal glaubte, er würde mir den Kopf abhauen, und davor Angst hatte. Viele Tage würde ich brauchen, wollte ich alles schildern, was ich bei ihm durchgemacht habe. Immer hatte er seinen Kohlenwinkel, mit ständigem Feuer, bald sein Alcali, bald sein Oleum sublimati, bald den König praecipitati, bald sein arsenisches Öl oder Crocus martis oder seinen wunderlichen Opodeltoch, und ich weiß nicht, was für Gebräu kochend. Denn er hätte mir einmal mit seiner Kocherei fast den lebendigen Geist erstickt, als er mir befahl, daß ich mir den Spiritus seines Alembiks anschauen sollte; ich hatte meine Nase etwas zu nahe daran gehalten das Glas, das oben auf dem Alembik lag, war ein wenig weggenommen, so daß ich durch den Rauch und Dampf, die in meinen Mund und meine Nasenlöcher schlugen, durch den virulenten Qualm fast erstickt und erwürgt wäre, so daß ich ohnmächtig wurde und erst durch Besprengen mit kaltem Wasser wieder zu mir kam.

Zwischendurch gab er vor, viel Wunderbares prophezeien zu können, und sonderbare Arcana und Mysterien zu kennen, so daß ich im Geheimen nicht leicht bei ihm an et-

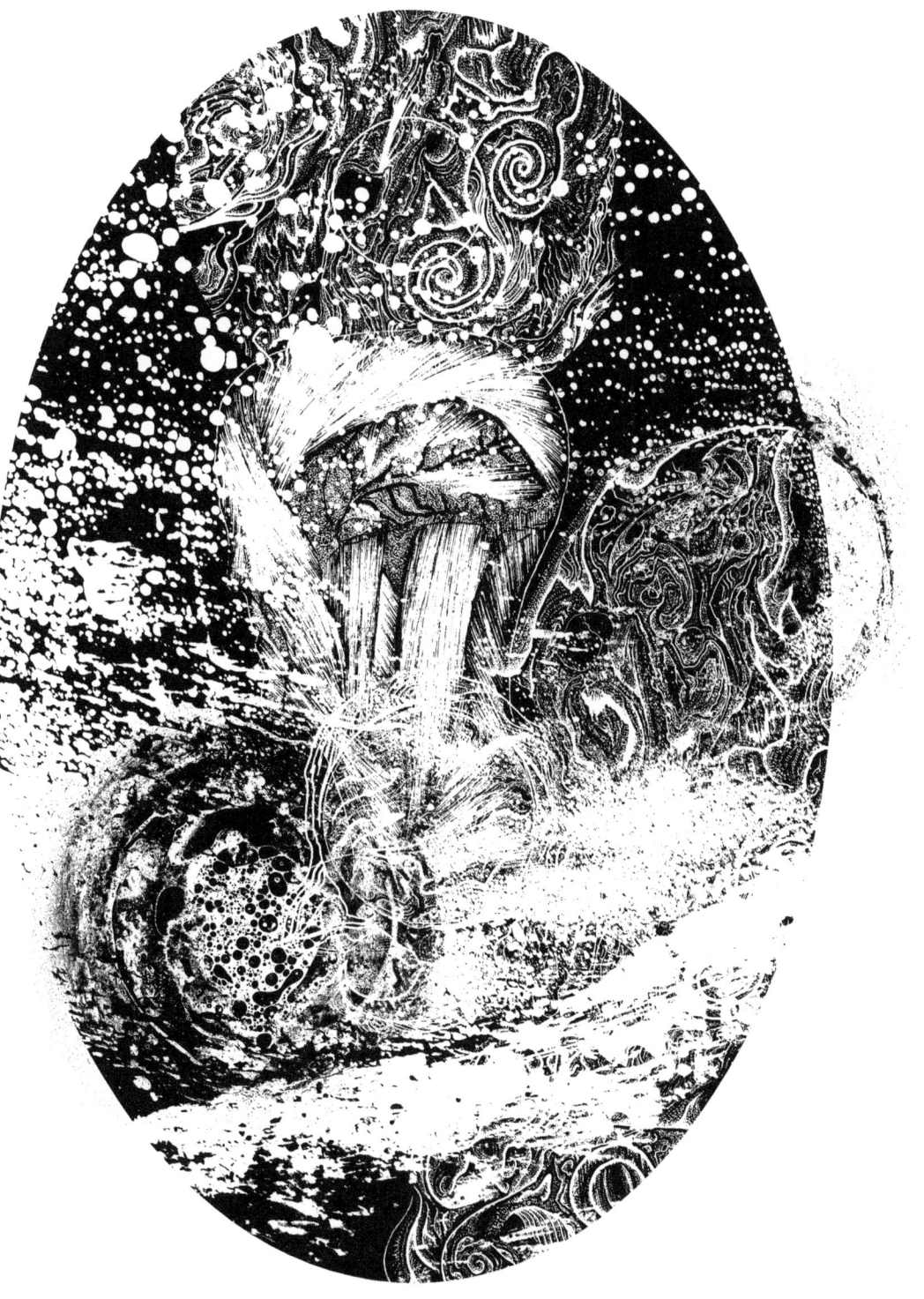

Isn't this ironic: when genius is observed by common people, in their retellings it often takes the form of monstrosity.

So much of what it means to *become ingenium* is quite accurately described in this letter which obviously was meant to deride you, Paracelsus. But here we encounter you in your own flesh, as a man who lives according to his own rules and who doesn't owe a thing to anyone. You are neither a slave to the coin nor to the day time or the night hours; you have begun to live according to nothing but your own rhythm and tides. Now, of course, we witness you off balance, as usual for a man seeking the tempests. You are trying to tame and

---

was heranzukommen, noch jemals etwas anzurühren wagte, da ich mich immer vor ihm fürchtete. Er brachte viel Geld durch, so viel, daß er manchmal weder Heller noch Pfennig behielt, so viel ich wußte, und tags darauf zeigte er mir wiederum seinen Geldbeutel voll Geld, so daß ich mich nicht selten wunderte, wodurch er wieder so viel bekommen hätte. Fast jeden Monat ließ er sich einen neuen Rock machen, und den anderen Rock, den er anhatte, verschenkte er dem Ersten, der ihm begegnete; er war aber so befleckt, daß ich nie mehr einen von ihm begehrte, und wenn er ihn mir auch gleich geschenkt hätte, ich hätte ihn nicht tragen wollen.

Im Kurieren und Heilen von Geschwüren verrichtete er fast Wunder, wo wenig Hoffnung zu sein schien, keine Art von Speisen oder Getränken beim Heilen verbietend, sondern mit seinen Patienten Tag und Nacht nach Herzenslust zechend, so daß er sie, wie er zu sagen pflegte, mit vollem Bauche heilte. Das Pulver von Praecipitat mit Theriak oder Methridatum oder mit Kirschensaft zu Pillen gemacht, gebrauchte er für Purgierungen in allen Arten von Krankheiten. Mit seinem Laudanum, so nannte er Pillen in der Form von Mäusedreck, welche er in ungleicher Anzahl nur in der äußersten Not der Krankheiten, wie zum heiligen Anker (wie man sagt) seine Zuflucht nehmend, eingab, sich so brüstete, daß er sich auch nicht entblödete zu behaupten, daß er allein, nur durch den Gebrauch von diesen, Tote zum Leben zurückbringen könne, und das hat er dann und wann, als ich bei ihm war, tatsächlich bewiesen, und sie, die tot zu sein schienen, plötzlich wieder zu sich kamen.

Aber ich habe ihn nie beten sehen oder hören, noch fragte er nach irgendeiner geistlichen Übung noch nach der evangelischen Lehre, welche zu der Zeit bei uns verehrt und geübt zu werden anfing, und von unserm Prediger sehr sorgfältig und fleißig betrieben wurde, welche er nicht nur verachtete, sondern auch drohte, daß er noch einmal Luther und dem Papst, ebenso wie nun Galen und Hippokrates, den Kopf zu rechtsetzen werde, und daß niemand, der bisher über die heiligen Schriften geschrieben habe, sowohl die Älteren als die Jüngeren, den rechten Kern der Schriften noch nie getroffen hätten, sondern nur die äußere Schale, so daß sie nur die Schatten träfen und erklärten. Und ich weiß nicht, was er noch für andere Nichtigkeiten vorbrachte, die ich mich schäme zu erzählen.

Es zog ihn gar nichts zu Frauen, so daß ich glaube, daß er überhaupt nie eine erkannt hat. Im Anfang war er sehr mäßig, so daß er bis zu seinem fünfundzwanzigsten Jahre keinen Wein trank; aber später hat er so zu trinken gelernt, daß er ganze Tische voll von Bauern zum Trinken herausforderte und auch im Trinken und Saufen gewann, ab und zu seinen Finger in den Hals steckend und so einem Schwein gleichend...

— Johannes Oporinus (1507-1568) in a letter to Johannes Weyer from 1555, in: Peuckert, Will-Erich, *Theophrastus Paracelsus*, Stuttgart-Berlin: Kohlhammer Verlag, 1941, pp. 143-147.

subside the fire of your mind—as well as the loneliness inflicted by genius?—through swigging and carousal. But what would have been your choice: going permanently mad while sober, or rather temporarily while drunk? Truly, you weren't kissed by the muse but fired at by her. And yet the ceasefire stolen from schnaps and beer never lastet long into the night. Here you are in the candlelight again, long past midnight, holding the hilt of Azoth as your only anchor, dictating a new philosophy of medicine, of magic, of alchemy and astrology to a famulus who, while being the closest person to you of all, did not understand a single word you were saying.

Give me a better scenery to depict the loneliness of genius, a better setting to illustrate the price we all might have to pay for genuinely *becoming ingenium*?

In the middle of the Second World War your congenial autobiographer, Will-Erich Peuckert, could hardly keep his own pen down when commenting on Oporius's libellous and yet illuminating letter:

> *A fellow in Sturm und Drang, and next to him a petty bourgeois! A man of genius, flaring up within himself, and this Johannes Oporinus who counts up for the pious at heart how many times he has gone to pray. A Wagner who lacks the courage and all inner desire even to be licentious—what has this pathetic little Hooray Henry ever understood about his lord and master? And yet, the whole roaring striker, young like Spring, can be recognised in these blasphemous lines! It can be seen how one bursts in here without bridle and hold, how he guzzles with peasants, how he makes merry with the students—and how all this is only the outward furiousness of an incomprehensible discerner. He philosophized in drunkenness, one must translate it, because one cannot grasp this rising from the depths into the light.*[6]

---

6 *Ein Kerl in Sturm und Drang, und neben ihm ein kleiner Spießer! Ein genialischer, in sich auflodernder Mann, und dieser Johannes Oporinus, der dem im Herzen Frommen nachzählt, wie viele mal er beten gegangen sei. Ein Wagner, dem auch zum Liederlichsein der Mut und alle innere Lust gebricht b was hat dies schäbige Bürgerlein von seinem Herrn und Meister je begriffen? Und es ist doch der ganze frühlingsjunge brausende Stürmer in den Lästerzeilen zu erkennen! Es ist zu sehen, wie einer hier*

But if you, Paracelsus, cannot be judged from the outside, how then can we understand you from the inside? So much could be offered for an answer and yet we will have to attempt to condense it to a few lines.

You said the human we want to be when we are dead is the human we create when we are alive.[7] You understood life as an alchemical fire—not as a mere metaphor but as a *lived reality*. It is this fire that alters our souls's condition while we are bound in flesh and matter, so our soul becomes a vessel and form that can pass over the threshold of death. This vessel of the Divine spark that we are has to be woven from faith and the stars, from the inner and outer firmaments, from free will and from mastering our ascendant. "As heaven is finished, so man begins," you said.

When on such a journey, civil etiquette simply is no factor of import. If anything, the petty man's guilt, everyday shame, anticipatory obedience and enforced gentleness are the very ropes that require hewing away. You didn't judge yourself by the cleanliness of your coats or the direction you lay in your bed. Your star was of a different kind: you judged yourself over whether you would risk everything, over and over again, when faced with political intrigue and the power games of the academic establishment, to stay true to yourself. You died a poor man—yet you could have easily died like a *monarch*. You chose the path against the grain, not even for us as the beneficiaries of your written works but because you held onto the faith that this is what humans are here for.

Unshakable *faith* in your own ideals and unconditional *indifference* to the world's judgement of you. Relentless *perfection* in mastering your many crafts, and yet always holding onto agile *improvisation* and

---

hereinbricht ohne Zaum und Halt, wie er mit Bauern kneipt, wie er mit den Studenten fröhlich ist b und wie das alles nur die äußere Ungebärde eines unbegreiflichen Erkennenden ist. Er habe im Suff philosophiert, so muß man es sich übersetzen, weil man dies aus den Tiefen in das Lichte Steigende nicht zu fassen weiß.
— Peuckert, Will-Erich, *Theophrastus Paracelsus*, Stuttgart-Berlin: Kohlhammer Verlag, 1941, p. 147.

7 Peuckert, Will-Erich, *Theophrastus Paracelsus*, Stuttgart-Berlin: Kohlhammer Verlag, 1941, p. 294.

not letting any cut or blow of fate strike you in the marrow and leg. Your own life's virtues, Paracelsus, might shine brighter even than your work.[8]

FOUNDATIONS OF ANIMISTIC SPIRIT PRACTICE

¶ The Human Constitution
¶ The Inner Ascendant
¶ An Ecosystem of Spirits

ONE of the essential premises of Paracelsian cosmography is the foundational assumption that each man has an inner firmament which is responsive to but holds the potential to operate independently of the celestial firmament. Thus, there is only one sky in the macrocosms, but another sky and horizon within each human.

As we will see, this simple idea led Paracelsus to develop a unique and highly complex constitution of the *inner man*. While rarely studied, it provides the essential foundation for his many breakthrough insights on the causes and treatments of diseases as well as on the animistic spirit-practice underlying his medical, philosophical and theological writings. The multilayered concept of the inner firmament indeed can be understood as the theoretical bridge via which Paracelsus led Late Medieval thinking into a new era.

Given the broad consequences of this framework and the fact that Paracelsus continued to develop it over the course of more than

---

8 For an explicit exploration of these four aspects of the magical craft, see the last chapter.

twenty years of research, experimentation and writing, the present essay cannot reasonably do it justice. Rather, it is meant as an initial outline for further studies to build upon. In the spirit of Paracelsus's work, such studies should expand both deeper into the man's massive oeuvre and help us bring his wisdom into the 21st century. Equally, they should expand into our own personal practice and help us turn, test and develop the words of this genius on the anvil of our own experience.

The Human Constitution

IN Western Magic we often speak of an inner Divine flame which each man holds in their soul. This spark forms a tie between each soul and Divinity in its unformed state from which all souls once emanated. It is in this sense that man holds the potential to become divine, not in their embodied form, but in excavating and consciously reconnecting with this divine spark that is embedded in their heart-space.

Paracelsus's inner firmament is conceived in the exact same manner: in addition to a divine spark man also holds sparks of the seven planets comprising our solar system or macrocosm. These sparks are not hidden or hibernating within us but take a most active role. It is the weave of these seven sparks—or planetary intelligences and cosmic forces—which continuously interact with the four elements. The latter, according to Paracelsus, are not at all the tangible representations of fire, air, water and earth, but rather their inner alchemical principles. The four elements provide the essential building blocks of all subtle and material creation.[9]

---

[9] The building blocks of the elements themselves are constituted by the three

Together, these seven generative and destructive celestial forces in combination with the four elementary forces define, create, adjust and evolve the state of man's physical and psychological constitution at any given moment in time.[10]

As it was critical to any successful act of healing or magic, Paracelsus then very explicitly describes the way in which this process comes to life: He distinguishes the corporeal substances—among these first flesh, bones and blood—from all the incorporeal forces within a human body. The latter he identifies as the various facets of the inner firmament, for anything that "is not corporeal, that same is a star, an astrum."[11] The collective of all these inner stars, or inner *senses* as he calls them as well, is what establishes the human soul.

The properties of one's soul thus are defined by the condition of one's inner firmament. And yet again, this firmament fans out into a sevenfold realm: In descending order of creation these are (1) the realm of the apocalyptical stars,[12] (2) the stars of the ascendants, (3–6) the stars of the four realms of the elements, and finally (7) the stars ruling over the realm of imagination.[13]

---

dynamic principles of Sulphur, Sal and Mercury. These latter principles, however, operate below the threshold of material matter as we observe it. A modern comparison of atoms (equivalent to the realm of the elements) and quarks (equivalent to the operating level of sal, sulphur, mercury) might help to illustrate how these two levels of creation are mutually dependent and interlaced in Paracelsus's worldview.

10 See: Sudhoff, Karl (ed.), *Theophrastus von Hohenheim, gen. Paracelsus, Sämtliche Werke*, Band XII, München: Otto Wilhelm Barth, 1932, p. 495.
11 Ibid.
12 The term "apocalyptical" should be read in its original Greek meaning in this context i.e. as *uncovering,* or *revealing.* In the spirit of John's Book of Revelation, for which he held great respect, Paracelsus uses the term often to relate to prophetic divination. In this context, the "apocalyptical stars," thus are the fixed stars of the outer firmament. (For Paracelsus's specific use word the word see e.g. Sudhoff, Karl (ed.), *Theophrastus von Hohenheim, gen. Paracelsus, Sämtliche Werke*, Band XIV, München: Otto Wilhelm Barth, 1933, p. 188.
13 See: Sudhoff, Karl (ed.), *Theophrastus von Hohenheim, gen. Paracelsus, Sämtliche Werke*, Band XII, München: Otto Wilhelm Barth, 1932, p. 495.

With that, we begin to see the complexity and yet the expressed clarity of the constitution of the inner firmament or human soul within Paracelsus's work. Specifically, he posits that in order to become a "whole astronomer" one has to consider all of these seven realms and the diverse manifestations of the celestial forces within them. To illustrate the importance of this insight, Paracelsus gives the following example:

> *I present this only because it is not enough, nor is it sufficiently spoken about in astrology, to recognise Mars in the sky alone where it looks like a glowing coal. But above it there is another Mars and four in the four elements and one more in the imagination. What is this blacksmith who can only make a horseshoe and not the nail? What is the carpenter who can make only chips and not joints? In an art everything should be perfect and united, and there nothing should be excluded, but what belongs together, that should be learned together.*[14]

As microcosm and macrocosm, of course, mirror each other, we find the same realms on both sides — and the human experience caught up in the middle of it.

Each human is constantly exposed to, touched and affected by a complex fabric of dynamic external forces. Just as within man, so on the outside these forces are made up by the four elements as well as the seven major celestial influences. Collectively, these forces have no interest in man's health or sickness, in the human species' prosperous evolution or degenerative destruction. Because they op-

---

14 *Solches lege ich allein deshalb dar, da es nicht ausreicht noch genügend darüber gesprochen wird in der Astrologie den Mars nur im Himmel zu erkennen, der doch nur einem glühenden Kohlen gleich aussieht. Sondern über demselbigen ist ein anderer Mars und vier in den vier Elementen und noch einer in der Imagination. Was ist das für ein Schmied, der nur ein Hufeisen machen kann und den Nagel nicht? Was ist der Zimmermann, der nur Späne machen kann und nicht Fugen? Es soll in einer Kunst alles vollkommen sein und liegen, und da soll nichts ausgenommen werden, sondern was zusammen gehört, das soll zusammen gelernt werden.*

— Sudhoff, Karl (ed.), *Theophrastus von Hohenheim, gen. Paracelsus, Sämtliche Werke*, Band XII, München: Otto Wilhelm Barth, 1932, p. 496.

erate against a wider and broader canvas of purpose than merely the human domain. The way these macrocosmic forces affect the human sphere is hence a side-effect of each of these forces pursuing their own inherent nature as embedded into the vast woof of the macrocosm.

Thus, according to Paracelsus, if nothing else interfered with man's constitution our species would be a plaything of the matrix of chthonic and celestial cosmic forces. Compare it to a game of chess: the four elements construct the corporeal figures, the celestial movers define the rules of manoeuvre. For anybody entangled in the game the way a chess figure looks and the way it *manoeuvres* on the board would not appear as two separate things but as being woven into one entity. A pawn is a pawn, both because of how it appears and the way it is able to move on the board. In the same way, elementary and celestial influences come together to set into motion and continuously keep spinning the wheel we call evolution.

Your liver, your lungs, your body, you yourself—we are all constructed according to the same principles of combining celestial influences (ability to manoeuvre or act) and elementary forces (substance generating powers). Now we begin to see the essential ecology inherent in Paracelsus's cosmos: any element of creation, be it a single blood particle or the entire human species, is but a figure on the eternal chess-board of creation. The players of this game are *all of us*, each single object of creation following the inner choir of its inherent firmament. The aim of this game is not at all for "man to win," but for creation to recognise itself.

The Inner Ascendant

> *The imprint, that is, according to Paracelsus's usage of the term, the inner compulsion. Not out of the outside, not out of the "boundaries" that take place in any material order, only out of the inner compulsion, the essence, being happens,—only the imprint, the astrum, the "life-force" lets that develop which is laid out in a body. Therefore, it is not the disease, its material appearance, but what created it, its incorporeal cause, which must be recognised and assailed in its nature, and one must act against the ascendants, that is against what gives birth to them, what drives them, and not against a body.*[15]

Now that we have understood the general design of the human constitution according to Paracelsus, let's unravel the particular function of the Paracelsian Ascendant.

Despite the complexity of the term it is with this function that Paracelsus gave us a most precise idea of a what guides and rules over a human's ability to manoeuvre on the chessboard called creation.

In Early Modern astrology, the ascendant signifies the celestial sign[16] rising during the hour of one's birth, which holds particular relevance and power over determining one's fate.[17] Equally, each moment or hour holds their own ascendant, colouring it in its particular and dominant quality. It is in this sense that in Paracelsian language the term *ascendant* can either be read in the sense of a dis-

---

15 *Die Imprimierung, das ist nach Paracelsi Wortgebrauch der innere Zwang. Nicht aus dem Äußeren, nicht aus den in irgendwelchen materiellen Ordnungen sich vollziehenden 'Grenzen,' nur aus dem inneren Zwang, dem Wesen heraus geschieht das Sein, b nur die Impressio, das astrum, die 'Lebenskraft' läßt das in einem Körper Angelegte sich entwickeln. Deshalb auch muß nicht so die Krankheit, ihre materielle Erscheinung, sondern was sie gemacht hat, ihre unkörperliche Ursache, in seiner Natur erkannt und angegriffen werden, und wider die Aszendenten muß man handeln, also wider dieses sie Gebärende, Treibende, und nicht wider einen Leib.*
— Peuckert, Will-Erich, *Theophrastus Paracelsus*, Stuttgart-Berlin: Kohlhammer Verlag, 1941, p. 201.

16 As well as in correlation to it the corresponding planet.

17 Peuckert, Will-Erich, *Theophrastus Paracelsus*, Stuttgart-Berlin: Kohlhammer Verlag, 1941, p. 281.

position (if referring to one's ascendant of birth) or as a dominant, *driving force* (if referring to a moment in time).

Finally, there is a third meaning of the word *ascendant*, and unfortunately it is here that things turn slightly more complex. In addition to the quality of one's constitution or the quality of time, the term ascendant is also used to determine a *spirit* that holds an elevated or dominant position over us. In the Late Medieval techniques of deriving the name of one's *holy daimon* from the native's birth chart, we often see two of these meanings collapse, the daimon's namebeing derived from the planet rising on one's birth chart. With Paracelsus, however, these are two discrete meanings of the term ascendant.

So in summary we can read the term ascendant in three differing yet interrelated senses: to describe one's constitution, to describe the dominant quality of a moment in time, or to describe the dominant spirit guiding one's life. The latter, though, does not need to remain one and the same over the course of one's life but may be altered. Finally, not only man as a whole is assigned an ascendant, but each component part of the "microcosm" receives their own dynamic ascendant. Thus inner organs, diseases, qualities of time or locations, all hold their own ascendants.

With this in mind, let's take the time to read several extensive direct quotes from Paracelsus's writings on the ascendant.

The following passages have been taken from Paracelsus's vast oeuvre to illustrate the depth of his thinking on the nature of the ascendant. At the same time, each quote presumes the reader is familiar not only with common medical and astrological knowledge of the Late Middle Ages but also with Paracelsus's particular language and terminology. Despite these natural limitations when quoting Paracelsus out of context, I still believe collectively these sections will provide not only rich food for reflections but an accurate initial outline of the composition of the Paracelsian ascendant.

> *Since now in man lies heaven, and [as it] cannot be otherwise, know this, all you physicians, that in man lie all ascendants. Now who will claim*

that man is subject to one [single] ascendant but only the outer parched astronomer? The physician must make this clear and discover it; for as many ascendants as heaven is capable of, so many is man capable of. Thus man is put into many hundred beings. [...] For heaven is man, and man is heaven, and all men are one heaven, and heaven only one man.[18]

If the ascendant can find the sick [to strangle them], the ascendant can also find the sick [to sustain them]. Everything is twofold; where disease is, is medicine, where medicine is, is disease.[19]

Let us suppose that one had come from Granada and was arriving in Cologne and wanted to go to Gdansk; now another would have come from London and also wanted to go to Gdansk and would also arrive in Cologne, and in Cologne they would come together to an inn. And in the same inn one would already be there; and the three would sit together and come to the conviction that the third also wanted to go to Gdansk. Now the three would go together, so the first two would lead the third who would now come from Cologne and would not have wanted to go out there, but since he had come into the company, it would take him with it. Now it follows that this one, who has been in Cologne, receives his nature in this manner: where the two come, there he also comes. They come to Gdansk etc., there he also comes, and thus together with the two beings that of the third is

---

[18] *Dieweil nun im Menschen der Himmel liegt und [es] nicht anders sein mag, so wisset hierin, ihr Ärzte alle, dass im Menschen liegen alle Ascendenten. Nun wer will behaupten, dass der Menschen einem [einzigen] Ascendenten unterworfen sei, als allein der äussere ausgedorrte Astronom? Der Arzt muss das klar machen und entdecken; denn so viele Ascendenten der Himmel vermag, so viele vermag der Mensch. Also wird der Mensch in viele hundert Wesen gesetzt. [...] Denn der Himmel ist der Mensch und der Mensch ist der Himmel und alle Menschen ein Himmel und der Himmel nur ein Mensch.*
— Sudhoff, Karl (ed.), *Theophrastus von Hohenheim, gen. Paracelsus, Sämtliche Werke*, Band VIII, München: Otto Wilhelm Barth, 1924, pp. 99-100.

[19] *Kann der Aszendent den Kranken finden [um ihn] zu würgen, so kann auch der Aszendent den Kranken finden [um ihn] zu erhalten. Es ist ein jegliches doppelt; wo Krankheit da Arznei, wo Arznei da Krankheit.*
— Sudhoff, Karl (ed.), *Theophrastus von Hohenheim, gen. Paracelsus, Sämtliche Werke*, Band III, München: Otto Wilhelm Barth, 1930, p. 108.

also found. So it is there too. If a child is born, be it what it may, pilgrims pass through there and also come to the city, that is the firmament. Now the child follows the same pilgrims, goes with them as it has found them on the road and does not know itself, where from and where to, because it has never been on earth, can do nor know anything on it. So the messengers take it along and lead it.[20]

"But now it may happen that the child obtains a different messenger, a father, a praeceptor[21] who shows the child other things than the pilgrims... Now such are also spirits in heaven. And the same spirit is also there and also pleads that he be a pilgrim and lead the child a different way, not as the stars have to lead him, but according to his will. Now I suppose that such a spirit would also be mixed in there and would also be an ascendant together with the others; now it is necessary that this ascendant is also recognised because it will do more than the stars; because in the ascendants, which are spirits, there is gambling, drinking, whoring, courting, warring, cursing, breaking of oaths, blasphemy, stealing, murdering, robbing..."[22]

20 *Ich setze, es käme einer gegangen von Granaten und käme gen Köln und wollte gen Danzken (Danzig); nun käme einer von Lunden (London) und wollte auch gen Danzken und käme auch gen Köln, und zu Köln kämen sie zusammen in ein Wirtshaus. Und in demselbigen Wirtshaus wäre einer vergebens da; und die drei säßen zusammen und würden eins, daß der auch gen Danzken wollt. Nun die drei zögen miteinander, so führen die ersten zweien den dritten, der nun aus Köln käme und nicht da hinaus gewollt hätte, sondern da ist er in die Gesellschaft gekommen, die zeucht ihn mit sich. Nun folgt auf das, daß dieser, der zu Köln ist gesein, seine Natur empfängt also: wo die zween hinkommen, da kommt er auch hin. Sie kommen gen Danzken usw., da kommt der auch hin, und also bei der zweien Wesen wird das des dritten auch gefunden. Also ist es da auch. So ein Kind geboren wird, es sei, wie es wolle, so ziehen Pilger da durch und kommen auch in die Statt, das ist das Firmament. Nun folgt das Kind denselbigen Pilgern nach, geht mit ihnen, so es sie doch auf der Straße gefunden hat, und weiß selbst nicht, wo aus und wohin, denn es ist nie auf Erden gesein, kann noch weiß nichts auf ihr. Also nehmens die Boten an und führen es.*
— Paracelsus, in: Peuckert, Will-Erich, *Theophrastus Paracelsus*, Stuttgart-Berlin: Kohlhammer Verlag, 1941, p. 281.
21 Latin for *teacher, instructor, tutor, preceptor*.
22 *Nun aber mag sichs begeben, daß das Kind einen andern Boten erlangt, einen Vater, einen Praeceptoren, der das Kind auf andere Sachen zeucht denn die Pilger Nun über das so sind auch Geist im Himmel. Und derselbige Geist ist auch da und fleißt sich auch, daß er ein Pilger sei und das Kind führe einen andern Weg, nicht wie die Stern*

Know that we do not bring an ascendant with us from birth, we take it ourselves. Thus, if a man wants to lie, he finds his ascendant in heaven; if he wants to be truthful, he finds his ascendant; if he wants to court, he finds his ascendant; if he wants to steal, he finds his ascendant, and so with all things.[23]

Because the inexperienced astronomers speak wrongly about the nativities and ascendants. As I am born under Scorpio and as I come under Aries, I am an Arietist and Scorpio has nothing more to do with me, therefore it no longer remains my Ascendant, for as long as I submit myself [to the revolving influences of the stars], as I have written in de nativitatibus. Therefore here the manner is to be changed after the way of the firmament, and [the goal is to] never make oneself submissive to another ascendant and conjunction. As even if I were born to be hanged and if the spiritus firmamenti were thus in me, as we then have of the spiritibus humanis, if I want it to be broken I move under another planet and leave the former, thus it is broken. And even if the inclination remains with me, the effect is not there. So often a pious man becomes a thief and an evil influence in the outer perception of men, as is written in de spiritibus.[24]

---

an ihm zu führen haben, sondern seinem Willen nach. Nun setze ich, ein solcher Geist wäre da auch eingemischt und wäre auch ein ascendens mitsamt den andern; jetzt ist not, daß dieser ascendens auch erkannt werde, denn er wird mehr ausrichten, denn die Sterne; denn in den Ascendenten, die Geister sind, da ist Spielen, Saufen, Huren, Buhlen, Kriegen, Fluchen, Ehbrechen, Gotteslästerung, Stehlen, Morden, Rauben.
— Paracelsus, in: Peuckert, Will-Erich, *Theophrastus Paracelsus*, Stuttgart-Berlin: Kohlhammer Verlag, 1941, p. 282.

23 *Wisset, daß wir von Geburt keinen Ascendenten mit uns bringen, wir nehmen ihn uns selbst. Also findet einer im Himmel, will er lügen, seinen Ascendenten, will er wahrhaftig sein, seinen Ascendenten, will er buhlen, seinen Acsendenten, will er stehlen, dergleichen, also mit allen Dingen.*
— Paracelsus, in: Peuckert, Will-Erich, *Theophrastus Paracelsus*, Stuttgart-Berlin: Kohlhammer Verlag, 1941, p. 282.

24 *Denn falsch reden die unerfahrenen Astronomen von den Nativitäten und Aszendenten. Als ich bin geboren unter dem Skorpion und so ich komme unter den Aries, so bin ich ein Arietist und Skorpion hat nichts da mit mir mehr zu schaffen, darum bleibt er nicht länger mein Aszendent, denn so lange ich mich unterwerfe als ich de nativitatibus geschrieben habe. Darum hier die Art nach des Firmaments Art zu verändern ist und sich nimmer unterwerflich machen einem anderen Aszendenten und Konjunktion. Als auch so ich geboren wäre erhängt zu werden und wär der spiritus firmamenti*

Every thing that is in the human body has its own ascendant in itself. That is the same ascendant, his own heaven, which serves him alone and nothing for the other limbs. The origin of this woe thus takes itself from the ascendant which you may also call constellationem particularem. If a limb has a displaced sky and ascendant, the pain is here now. [...] Because heaven in its potency is equal to [human] reason that does one thing today and another tomorrow. And since we and heaven are one creature, we are also the same. For our reason is no more than heaven's and heaven's no more than reason's. As man makes his order as he wants, so heaven does it too. Man is considered according to his reason, but heaven is not considered, but the unified potential in both is the same, considered and unconsidered. So we form heaven and heaven forms us, that we go wrong ways on both sides as long as we build on ourselves. Because as it is possible for heaven to err and to go astray, so it is also possible for our reason. And if it is possible for us, it is also possible for heaven. We understand that there is a being above all of this which we must pursue, which is alone without error, and not after our kind. Because if we go after ourselves, we go into diseases, just as heaven leads to them, if it is not as it should be. [...] Now the sky has its course and as long as the course, so long is the woe. If this is to be turned around, the subjectum must strongly resist it. So then when it [the sky] sees it, its course is over, and in that manner the limb will be closed [to the displaced celestial influence], just like someone who flees the winter in a room or the heat in a cellar.²⁵

---

also in mir, wie wir dann den spiritibus humanis haben, will ich das gebrochen werden zeuch ich unter einem anderen Planeten und lasse den stehen, so ist er gebrochen. Und ob mir schon die Art bleibt so ist doch der Effekt nicht da. Also wird oft ein frommer Mann ein Dieb und einer bösen Influenz, als de spiritibus geschrieben steht, de externis sensibus hominum.
— Sudhoff, Karl (ed.), *Theophrastus von Hohenheim, gen. Paracelsus, Sämtliche Werke*, Band III, München: Otto Wilhelm Barth, 1930, p. 18.

25 *Ein jegliches Ding, so im Leib des Menschen ist, hat in ihm selbst sein eigen Aszendenten. Das ist der selbe Aszendent, sein eigener Himmel, der ihm allein dient und den anderen Gliedern nichts. Aus dem Aszendenten, den ihr auch constellationem particularem heissen mögen, nimmt sich der Ursprung dieses Wehes also. So ein Glied einen verrückten Himmel und Aszendenten hat, so ist jetzt das Weh da. [...] Denn der Himmel in seiner Potenz ist gleich der Vernunft, die heute das macht und morgen ein anderes. Und dieweil wir und der Himmel ein Geschöpf sind, so sind wir auch gleich.*

> Now understand also that in man lie the children of the ascendants, that is, of the heavenly body, in the same way as Adam is to be understood against his father, that is, against heaven and earth. [...] So also know that man has in himself the attracting power from heaven. From this it follows that the inner ascendants, signa, planets etc., if they rule in the course of the microcosm and come into the desire [i.e. astrological activation] of the outer firmament, they attract these [influences] to themselves like the earth attracts the rain. If that celestial attraction is healthy, it is good; if not, it is poison.[26]

In essence, we see Paracelsus's ascendant connected to time and dynamic movement: Just as the horizon line of heaven is in constant motion, constantly revealing another sign, another planet, so too

---

> *Denn unsere Vernunft ist nicht mehr als der Himmel und der Himmel nicht mehr als sie. Also macht der Mensch seine Ordnung, wie er will, also machts auch der Himmel. Der Mensch ist besinnt nach seiner Vernunft, der Himmel aber ist nicht besinnt, aber die einig potentia in beiden gleich, besinnt und unbesinnt. Also praefigurieren wir den Himmel und der Himmel uns, das zu beiden Seiten Irrwege gehen, so wir auf uns selbst bauen. Denn dem Himmel möglich ist zu fehlen und Irrwege zu gehen, so ist es auch unserer Vernunft möglich. Und ob es uns möglich ist, so ist es auch dem Himmel möglich. Dabei verstehen wir, dass ein Wesen ist über dies alles, dem selbigen müssen wir nachgehen, das ist allein ohne Irrung, und nicht nach uns. Denn so wir uns nachgehen, so gehen wir in die Krankheiten, wie auch der Himmel darein geht, so er nicht ist, wie er sein soll. [...] Nun hat der Himmel seinen Lauf und so lange der Lauf, so lange ist das Weh. So nun das soll gewendet werden, so muss das subjectum ihm stark widerstehen. Also dann so er [der Himmel] das sieht, so ist sein Lauf aus, und das also, das das selbige Glied verschlossen wird, wie einer, der den Winter in einer Stuben flieht, oder die Hitze in einem Keller.*
> — Sudhoff, Karl (ed.), *Theophrastus von Hohenheim, gen. Paracelsus, Sämtliche Werke*, Band I, München: Otto Wilhelm Barth, 1929, pp. 154-158.

26 *Nun also verstehe auch das, dass im Menschen die Kinder der Aszendenten liegen, das ist, des Gestirns, in der gleichen Weise wie Adam gegen seinen Vater zu verstehen ist, das ist gegen Himmel und Erden. [...] Also wisset auch auch dass der Mensch die anziehende Kraft hat in sich vom Himmel. Aus dem folgt nun, dass die inneren Aszendenten, Signa, Planeten, etc. so sie herrschen im Lauf des Mikrokosmos und kommen in die Begierlichkeit [d.h. die astrologische Auslösung] des äusseren Firmaments, so ziehen sie diese an sich wie die Erde den Regen. Ist jene himmlische Anziehung gesund, so ist sie gut, wo nicht, da ist sie Gift.*
— Sudhoff, Karl (ed.), *Theophrastus von Hohenheim, gen. Paracelsus, Sämtliche Werke*, Band VIII, München: Otto Wilhelm Barth, 1924, p. 166.

the human constitution is constantly changing in tune with these tides.[27] Thus, Paracelsus confronts us with a human constitution that is far less fixed and determined than what traditional astrology had established: man's ascendant does not remain stable and fixed but moves with (or at least is influenced and superimposed by) the tides of time. Moreover, man stands between the firmament of the macrocosm and their own inner microcosm, and holds the Herculean responsibility of correcting deviations, aberrations or overexposures in the constellations that arise between these two firmaments.

An Ecosystem of Spirits

No human can accomplish this task by themselves, but we all depend on divine assistance. For the human mind with all its reason and ratio is just as fallible as the celestial macrocosm in achieving perfect balance—or at least a somewhat graceful motion through the storms of cosmic tides. Each one of us, therefore, depends on a "being that is above all of this" and the ability to establish communion and to receive guidance from this source that resides beyond the sublunar realm.

A monotheistical mystical reading would identify this being as capital-G God; a magical reading, however, could insert any kind of spirit into this equation, whose influence and guidance aligns to our present purpose. Paracelsus explicitly states that once we were able to consciously assign our ascendant-spirit then these "will do more than the stars." Regretfully, in real life for most humans this

---

27 See: Sudhoff, Karl (ed.), *Theophrastus von Hohenheim, gen. Paracelsus, Sämtliche Werke*, Band VII, München: Otto Wilhelm Barth, 1932, pp. 284–286, or Sudhoff, Karl (ed.), *Theophrastus von Hohenheim, gen. Paracelsus, Sämtliche Werke*, Band VIII, München: Otto Wilhelm Barth, 1932, p. 110.

process happens entirely unconsciously and automatically. Thus, their ascendant-spirits are not only of volatile and temporary nature but also more attuned to enable egotistical desires, hedonistic pleasures and morbid habits than fulfilment of their human "potentia."

To summarise, the Paracelsian ascendant does not only portray humankind as a spirit-interfacing species. Instead, and on a much more ambitious scale, it recognises each living cell, each minuscule aspect of the vast hive of creation as infused with spirit consciousness. Thus, it dissolves the artificial boundaries between man and the world. Instead, it outlines an Early Modern animistic worldview: Paracelsus recognises the human spirit as essentially enlaced in a spirit ecosystem that begins with our blood cells and extends out as far as the Empyrean Heaven.

> The life of every thing is a spiritual being, an invisible and incomprehensible thing and a spirit and a spiritual thing.[28]

> The spirit in the body is incomprehensible, invisible [...] The same spirit is essential, sensitive, visible and tangible to other spirits [...] I have a spirit, the other one has one as well; the spirits know each other [...] they practice their language with each other.[29]

> For the cause of diseases is not physical; therefore spirit is to be used against spirit.[30]

---

28 Das Leben eines jeden Dinges ist ein spiritualisch Wesen, ein unsichtbares und unbegreifliches Ding und ein Geist und ein geistlich Ding.
— Sudhoff, Karl (ed.), *Theophrastus von Hohenheim, gen. Paracelsus, Sämtliche Werke*, Band XI, München: Otto Wilhelm Barth, 1928, p. 329.

29 Der Spiritus im Leib ist unbegreiflich, unsichtig [...] Der selbige Geist ist wesentlich, empfindlich, sichtlich und greiflich anderen Geistern [...] Ich habe einen Geist, der andere hat einen; die Geister kennen einander [...] sie üben ihre Sprache miteinander.
— Sudhoff, Karl (ed.), *Theophrastus von Hohenheim, gen. Paracelsus, Sämtliche Werke*, Band I, München: Otto Wilhelm Barth, 1929, p. 217.

30 Denn die Ursache der Krankheiten sind nicht körperlich; darum Geist gegen Geist gebraucht werden soll.
— Sudhoff, Karl (ed.), *Theophrastus von Hohenheim, gen. Paracelsus, Sämtliche Werke*, Band VIII, München: Otto Wilhelm Barth, 1924, p. 178.

This now is the consequence that Paracelsus wants each of us to recognise and adapt to: his anthroposophical cosmology is an open revolt against a worldview of fixed beliefs and orthodox truths. Instead, each diagnosis, each day is meant to be a new expedition. Each hour calls upon us to take a fresh glance at what is happening in this present moment. Because not only time flows in a merciless, never-ending stream, but all of reality does and with it does the definition of *what is true right now*.

Finding truth, forming identity, gaining solid ground of where we stand in this world is not a once-in-a-lifetime event. Identifying one's ascendant and all the character-forming forces rippling out into our lives from them, is an ever evolving stream of interwoven forces, moments, and opportunities. So while there is no solid ground for man to retreat to in order to pin down their personal identity, character or essence, Paracelsus offers a different kind of security. It is not to be found in any axiomatic insights over *who were are* but in the presence of the community of spirits with whom *we are together with*. Stopping the stream of reality, only to land with fixed, permanent truths, is a most foolish adventure to waste a life on. Finding the swarm of beings that flow with us in this stream, beginning to see and account for one's own importance to this hive of living spirits, however, is a most propitious endeavour. Paracelsus might have called it a *good life*.

Let's conclude this chapter with a few forward-looking, pragmatic reflections. What then, you might ask, can I take away for my own practice from the concept of the Paracelsian ascendant? As you would expect, neither Paracelsus nor I would offer a fixed answer to this question. Instead, let's open the vista towards a few essential questions for your own practical explorations.

> ¶ Paracelsus acknowledges that "the spirits know each other [...] they practice their speech with each other." This then seems to be the gateway skill of the magician, to switch their human, outer senses for their inner ones and to learn to speak

and listen in the *language of spirits*.³¹ When you look at your own practice today, what is your learning laboratory, what are your practical experiments to build this capability within yourself?

¶ If we break down the above reality into the reality of our own bodies, we understand that each organ within us holds its own spirit, its own fluctuating ascendant, and its unique vibrating chord of *sympathy* into the macrocosm around us. Josephine McCarthy's book *Magical Healing* (TaDehent Books, 2019) offers plenty of practical exercise to begin working as a medical mage in a Paracelsian sense. Especially relevant, in our present context, are the two chapters on *Visionary Healing*, as well as the final one on *Self-Healing and Maintenance*.

¶ Return to the quote above where Paracelsus speaks of the travelling spirits (from Granada and London via Cologne to Gdansk) who found your soul in a pub and took you along on their ride.—How does this reality translate to your present biography? How much are you journeying on your own path versus following your stars' journeys as a passenger? Recall what Paracelsus stated in no ambiguous terms about our ascendants: the one who wants to become a liar will find a star that allows him to do so; and yet the one who was determined by their ascendant to end as a hanged man can still revert and change their inherent patterns.—Once you have thought about how these realities apply to your own present life, bring in another thought for meditation: How do Paracelsus's reflections apply to the magic you practice? Elementary, daimonic, chthonic or celestial magic, whatever your practice or path—in which manner are you attempting to redraw the image of yourself through this work? As

---

31 For further reading on this topic as a cornerstone of Paracelsus's teachings see: Pagel, Walter, *Das Medizinische Weltbild des Paracelsus, seine Zusammenhänge mit Neuplatonismus und Gnosis, Kosmosophie*, Band I, Wiesbaden: Franz Steiner Verlag, 1962, pp. 73–75.

magicians, we are all golems of mysterious clay and our own co-creation. Who will you be?

¶ Finally, under whose tutelage or guardianship do you intend to undertake this work? As Paracelsus mentioned, it is possible for heaven to err just as much as it is for human reason to do so. As long as we blindly follow either the stars or our own feeble human will, we are likely to *walk into disease*. But to break the *c(o)urses of ego and astrum* and to liberate ourselves so we can truly choose our own path, we have to "strongly resist" as well as to unite ourselves with "a being above all of this."—Depending on the magical work at hand, I have united forces with a broad array of spirits—from chthonic land beings to underground mountain spirits, from Olympic intelligences to Ancient Egyptian deities. Our choice of magical and spiritual allegiances is endless. And yet, what I can confirm from lived experience is that each choice I made had irreversible consequences. It shaped the golem I am becoming to be in ways that I could not traverse backwards on. Call it an oath, a pact, an initiation, whatever man-made term fits your practice and paradigm. Deciding and acting upon whom we choose to share a swarm, a hive, a skin with, counts among the most essential choices we will make in our lives. Choose wisely, magician.

In our modern Western world today, we still find ourselves surrounded by echos of Paracelsus's innovations such as in chemotherapy or homeopathy.[32] What has been largely overlooked, however, is that Paracelsus also established the foundation for a modern animistic worldview and spirit practice. This practice was intended to be applied to and explored in various disciplines such as medicine, chemistry, theology, astrology, and practical magic. It is upon us, to restore this knowledge and practice today.

---

32 For a balanced summary of Paracelsus's medical legacy and innovations see: Pagel, 1962, pp. 27–32.

THE PLOW
WE PULL

So then, if our rule is such, and this is our order, we must refrain from saying: If God wills it, He will make me well; if He wants me to eat, He will give me bread. No, not so, for He is not a baker, He shall not eat by sweat, He is not our thresher; it shall be us, and our labour shall bring it to pass, that it may be respectable and beneficial to us. The yoke has been tied to us and placed on our backs. And what belongs to the work procure, nothing omit, the iron to the plow, and the art to bring the iron from the rock, to make the plow from the iron, frugally learned.[33]

THE anvil of life is a place we escape with death, not a moment before. We go up in one last fiery blaze, or fall from the iron in a final spark.

And yet, our position is not at all a passive one. Life throws many blows at us, it heats the embers around us and quenches us in black waters. And yet, we are not only a nakedly exposed lump of iron, slowly growing towards a blade with each additional day on the anvil and at the grinding stone. We hold agency ourselves. Our spirit extends into all elements of this workshop: Indeed, we are under the hammer. But we are also part of the fire, we are part of the water, and we are part of the hand that guides this work.

---

33 *So nun unsere Regel also ist und das ist unser Orden, so müssen wir absehen von dem, das wir sagen: Wenn es Gott will, so wird er mich gesund machen; will er dass ich esse, er wird mir wohl Brot geben. Nein, eben so nicht, denn er ist kein Bäcker, er soll nicht im Schweisse essen, er ist nicht unser Drescher; wir sollen es sein und unsere Arbeit soll es zu Stande bringen, das uns ansehnlich sei und vorteilhaft. Uns ist das Joch aufgebunden, und auf den Rücken gelegt. Und was zur Arbeit gehört dazu beschaffen, nichts unterlassen, das Eisen zum Pflug, und die Kunst, das Eisen aus dem Stein zu bringen, aus dem Eisen den Pflug zu machen, genügsam gelernt.*
— Sudhoff, Karl (ed.), *Paracelsus Sämtliche Werke*, Band XII, München und Berlin: Verlag R. Oldenbourg, 1929, pp. 240-241.

Paracelsus often used the term of the *plow* to refer to the grind and strain of everyday work.[34] To him, the raw experience of walking while having tied a yoke on our back is an unavoidable fact of reality. Paracelsus, however, adamantly emphasised that each one of us can decide for themselves whose plow they pull. That is, into whose hand and meaning we place our work.

Here is a little exercise I'd like to invite you to. You can do this quite casually; it does not require any grand preparations. You can do it next time you go for a walk, next time you take out your dog or set out for a run. You can do it briefly, truly in a moment, a few minutes will be perfectly fine.

So next time you have a moment to walk or run undisturbed, in your mind's eye evoke the following vision. Around your shoulders is tied a yoke of light. The strings tying it to you are made from light and so is the yoke itself. Attached to the yoke are the strong ropes of a plow which rests on the ground some seven or eight feet behind you. As you walk, the plow of light opens the ground. Steadily, with each step, you carve the ground and leave it opened behind yourself. Following your steps, like a long trace of light, runs a deep furrow through the land, carved by your plow of light. Do not worry right now what will be sown into it. Just concentrate on the vision of the plow of light, bound to the yoke on your shoulders, hooked deep into the ground, following each of your steps, preparing the earth. Walk for a while, run for a while with this vision in mind. Not asking for purpose or origin of this image, just be present with the plow of light that you are pulling through the land.

Then, after you have sufficiently connected with the vision, ask yourself: Do you feel like an ox in this vision, or like a worker of Divinity? Have you been placed under this yoke or picked it up in free will? And what is it your plow is preparing the ground for? See if you can connect with the land and witness how it is changed by your plow... Now the question emerges: If you cannot walk away

---

34 E.g. Sudhoff, Karl (ed.), *Paracelsus Sämtliche Werke*, Band XIV, München und Berlin: Verlag R. Oldenbourg, 1933, p. 266.

from this yoke, if you are destined to pull this plow, what decisions are truly yours? Who are you in this work? What *are you good for?*

One illusion we have to cut through with the scalpel of truth is this: *magic* is not going to be the rescue vehicle that will lift anybody out of the hard and bruising work that is life. For as long as we live, none of us will ever walk without yoke and plow. But it is ours to choose when and where we apply our work.

Unfortunately, as it turns out, it's all too easy to pull our plow in circles, turning its fertilising powers void and yet our muscles increasingly strained and our shoulders raw. For many of us, self-laceration and self-destruction are not unfortunate peak moments, marked by abnormality and transience. Instead they are experiences of a status quo which creation can maintain calmly and effortlessly over many lives and cycles. If we bet on outside help arriving anytime soon, we have locked ourselves into losing.

The experience I am referring to here has nothing to do with access to wealth or financial resources. Yes, simply securing one's (family) income in a time of decaying social and healthcare systems can be a brutal and often mind-numbing experience. What I am relating to here, though, is the experience people are having *with themselves when not even involved in mundane work.* I.e. I am pointing to the psychosocial drama and habitual dysfunctional games many of us choose to play with themselves and each other in the very moments when we are free from paid labour.

For a moment, let's put ourselves into the position of an angelic observer. Here they are, mankind. This species of marvellous earth-bound workers, gifted with the spark of divinity, bound into flesh, drops of celestial dew on their hearts, chthonic grime on their hands, the plow of telluric work evenly following each of their steps. What power and potential encapsulated in these tiny, fragile creatures!

And then it all goes to waste, plows pulled in circles, seeds put to waste, bones broken in the work. We seem to be filled with so much paradox, so many antagonistic forces, pulling a plow in a straight line over a field of our own choice already might have to be acknowledged as an heroic act in itself.

More commonly, though, we follow well trodden circles laid out by our past: Repeating the traumas of our childhood, projecting the shadows we cannot accept, fearing what we cannot comprehend, insisting to receive before we allow ourselves to give, and dreaming of validation rather than otherness.

The divine grace and beauty embedded into each human sleeps underneath a cocoon of celestial influences. Mundane work will be mundane work. We are bound to fall into bed battered and exhausted one way or the other. But it is upon us to choose whether this work, whether this being exposed to the inevitable grindstone, slowly over time polishes away this cocoon, like rust and impurity, until it grows so thin and transparent we can finally, and for the first time, begin to see our Self shine through it.

Whose plow will you pull, and over which ground, Paracelsus asks us. And with this question, Paracelsus addresses the one force humanity holds as an ally to pull themselves out of the downward spiral of self-destruction and insignificance: *free will*.

For you see, our holy daimon, the Olympic Spirits, Henoch or Lilith, Scirlin or the witch's familiar, none of them will ever be able to stop an experience that we are choosing to be in. We shoulder the plow. Stretched in the yoke, we are offered freedom: for there is no farmer but us, we choose both field and furrow. We also choose the seed that we bring into the embrasure. Only the pulling we do not choose, only the perspiration we do not choose. At once we are oxen and angels.

So before we can awaken to our angelic selves, we have to stop behaving like oxen. Acknowledging and embracing that we are born and lead much of our lives as the latter is a step many people never get to take.

In the following we will explore why incarnated man is entirely built as a beast. A beast that is pushed, primed and guided by unconscious celestial influences which express themselves as urges and fears.

The good news is that these celestial chains can be broken. The planetary ties that run through ourselves can be welded anew and changed. Through this, even blood ties running back rivers of generations can be redirected or cut off. It blows one's mind entirely to see the vast possibilities of change and self-empowerment creation holds in store for us. And yet none of these, ever, will happen *against our will*. Even wanting this change might not be enough. What it takes is to embrace life with all its blows and chaos, its pitfalls and temptations, and to use all this joy *and* adversity in order to break the planetary-metal cocoon and draw out what is hidden inside each one of us.

Ironically, when we observe human history and even modern people's lives, endurance of suffering and pain doesn't seem to be the problem here. The amounts of suffering we inflict upon ourselves even outside of our day-jobs, in the moments when we are free from paid labour, would be a marvel to any angelic observer. Rather than the fear of suffering, what truly might be holding us back is something much more mundane and boring: the fear of leaving familiar territory.

Try to get someone to break away from the scaffold of deeply engrained, reassuring and orientation providing daily habits, and you'll quickly despair. The ascent of the unknown at the horizon of our lives is what makes so many of us turn their back to dawn. The approach of radical Otherness is what drives people deeper into the cave of illusions. For even when in pain, when afraid and scared, we can still believe we know *what we are, who we are* and *what our story is*. — This might be it then: we will rather accept being part of a tragedy than stepping out onto the tightrope of Otherness, not knowing what our story will be... and who we might become within it.

On your own journey into radical Otherness I am offering up the figure of *Paracelsus* as a role model, as a personal encouragement and ultimately as a travel companion. Even if you never read his inspired works, there is so much genius left in his biography and the hazardous life decisions he took. Seeing the amounts of audacity and determination, how much heat and how many hammer blows on the anvil he was willing to take time again should have an impact upon us. It should impact how we lead our own lives. To me, Paracelsus biography and his lifestyle is an open hand, a palm into which I can place my own. And invisibly yet firmly it pulls me forward towards a version of myself which just a minute ago I didn't even had the faith to discern.

THE PLANETARY COCOON

> *Know therefore, dear sirs and good friends, that the books which have come to you and to me from the ancients have not been able to please me. For they are not perfect, but an uncertain writing which serves more for seduction than for the proper, simple way. Which also caused me to forsake them. Now it is true that a disciple cannot be without a master. The disciple must learn from the master. And this has always been in me, where the master is who teaches, whereas the writers may not be respected as masters. I have thought of this: If there were no books on earth, if there were no doctors, how would we learn? So it turns out that Medicine can be learned without a human master. But how and in which way I have discussed here, and the very "books" which lie at the foundation of the invention of all arts. What these are, then, follows in this book in which we understand and may well remember that man should not seek his salvation in man as in a single master; but let man go and seek the foundational books, to become perfect in them.*[35]

35 *So wisset nun, lieben Herren und gute Freunde, daß die Bücher, so an euch und an mich von den Alten her gelanget sind, mich gnügsam zu sein nit gedeucht hat. Denn sie sind nicht vollkommen, sonder ein ungewisse Schrift, die mehr zu Verführung dienet denn zum rechten schlichten Weg. Welches mich auch veranlasst hat, sie zu verlassen. Nun ist es wahr, ein Jünger mag ohne einen Meister nicht sein. Der Jünger muß vom Meister lernen. Und das ist je und je in mir gelegen, wo der Meister sei, der da lehre, dieweil die Schreiber für Meister nicht mögen geachtet werden. Auf solches hab ich gedacht: wie wann kein Buch auf Erden wäre, gar kein Arzt, wie müßt gelernt werden? So befindet sich, daß die Arznei one Menschenmeister wohl mag gelernt werden. Wie aber und in welchem Weg, hab ich hier erörtert; dieselbigen Bücher, die dann in Erfindung*

And further: Paracelsus has no greater enemy than the Galenic Medicos who persuade themselves when they come across a book that they read, they already know what it says. But the highly learned dolts do not consider that Paracelsus wrote his books Stylo Magico. So also their brain is full of wit that Intellectus Magicus cannot enter. Therefore they cry, magia is sorcery, beware it is the devil's work. Since magia is not sorcery, but the greatest wisdom of divine works, and a cogniser of hidden nature.[36]

—ALEXANDER VON SUCHTEN

PARACELSUS differentiates two different ways in which the celestial forces can take effect in man: direct and indirect. The former Paracelsus summarises under the term *dona* (Latin: gifts or talents) which can unfold their potential without man's direct assistance in a natural manner; the latter he terms *scientia*, and they have to be carried out by man. Thus, the *dona* are celestial gifts in the form of naturally evolving forces embedded in man, the *scientia* are "human action ignited by heaven."[37]

The *donae* are then split into the following forces:

Membrum aegrorum: the reflection of actions and dynamics in the macrocosm into the microcosm.

---

aller Künsten die rechten Hauptbücher sind. Welche nun dieselbigen sind, folgt in diesem Buch hernach, darinnen wir verstehen und wohl mag gedenken, daß der Mensch sein Heil im Menschen nicht suchen soll, als in einem einigen Meister; sonder den Menschen fahren lassen und suchen die Hauptbücher, in denselbigen vollkommen zu werden.

— Paracelsus; *Labyrinthus Medicorum Errantium*, in: Goldammer (ed.), 1955, p. 69

36 *Und weiter: Paracelsus hat keinen grössern Feind/dann die Galenische Medicos, die überreden sich/wann sie über ein Buch kommen/dasselbige lesen/wisen sie schon/was es sagt. Aber die hochgelehrten Dölpel betrachten nicht/daß Paracelsus seine Bücher Stylo Magico beschrieben, So ist auch ihr Hirn voller Witz/daß Intellectus Magicus nicht hinein kan. Darumb schreyen sie/Magia ist Zauberey/hütet euch/es ist Teuffelswerck/da doch Magia keine Zauberey/sondern die allergröste Weißheit Gottlicher Werck ist/und eine Erkennerin verborgener Natur.*

— Alexander von Suchten (1520-1575), quoted after: Will-Erich Peuckert, *Pansophie—Ein Versuch zur Geschichte der weissen und schwarzen Magie*, Berlin: Erich Schmidt Verlag, 1956, pp. 312-313.

37 Peuckert, Will-Erich, *Theophrastus Paracelsus*, Stuttgart-Berlin: Kohlhammer Verlag, 1941, pp. 375–376.

Augurium: the foreshadowing of future events as found in the animal realm.
Divinatio: the inspiration of the stars into man.
Inclinatio: the occult influence of the celestial realm on man.
Impressio: the urge and desires that rule large parts of human behaviour.

Paracelsus saw the effect of these natural forces upon man to take effect both on the inside and outside of the microcosm i.e. they express themselves in both physiological as well as psychological conditions and dynamics.

It is essential that we, as modern readers of the 21st century, take sufficient time to truly comprehend the mode of operation that Paracelsus saw embedded within both *donae* and the *scientiae*.

However, in attempting to do so we need to keep in mind that Paracelsus's terminology often is ambivalent and ambiguous. Terms assume different meanings depending on the realm of creation they are put into context with. This also holds true for the word pair of *scientia* and *magia* in Paracelsus's writings. Thus, our attempt cannot be to provide a comprehensive reading of these terms but rather a specific one as they relate to the mode of functioning of the *Musa Sagax* within man.

The best bridge we might be able to walk over, leading our understanding back from the 21st to the 16th century, may lie in comparing this mode of functioning to the way psychoactive substances take effect in humans. If we swallow a plant containing psychoactive substances, such as *Atropa belladonna L.*, *Datura stramonium L.*, or *Hyoscyamus niger*, we expect the physical component of the plant, once chewed and absorbed by our mucous membranes, to take direct effect on our mind. We expect the plant to alter and induce a particular kind of thinking and sensing the world around us. No longer can we differentiate in such a scenario between our own mind and the plant-mind. For a limited period, our respective minds are shared and blur into one.

We know the same to be true for some traditional plants whose leaves hold such strong toxins that skin contact alone is sufficient to trigger their poisonous effect. In such cases we do not need to eat components of the plant, but simply make physical contact with it, especially if it touches our outer mucosal membranes e.g. in our eyes. Again, without any surprise to our modern Western scientific world, we would expect under such circumstances that the plant affects both the way *in which* we think as well as *what* we think while we are intoxicated or *in contact* with it.

Now according to Paracelsus this way of being affected by the natural world is not at all confined to psychoactive plants. Quite the contrary in fact: each object of creation, from the tiniest particle to giant mountains and the sky itself, holds the potential to unfold its embedded *contact poison* within our body and mind. While an abyss of silence and otherness separates the average human from experiencing such contact consciously, it is precisely the mage who is mastering the skill of how to create and comprehend such contact experiences.

Let's take this idea in for a moment. Paracelsus lived in a world where each object, if approached in the right manner, holds the potency to form a link with our mind and to *rub off* on the *way* we think as well as *what* we think. This is why Paracelsus pays such paramount attention to the faculty of human *imagination*, as it forms the foundational capability to step into (inner) contact with the language of the natural world. Or in his own words: to read in the *light* and *book of nature*.

Here is another metaphor that may prove helpful in illustrating how this process works. Think of your imagination as a field of metal shavings, scattered throughout your body. The movement of these metal splinters is what is constantly generating human thoughts, ideas and mental images. At any given moment this *field of imagination* is affected by a wide array of influences; and yet some particular forces will take predominant effect. The human mind thus forms a sounding board or echo membrane to the influences of the natural world.

This now is the planetary cocoon we referred to in the previous chapter: a field of splinters of (sub)consciousness, constantly shifting under the influence of the celestial dynamics, which is loosely held together by the fence of our skin. In modern terms we like to call this planetary cocoon our personality.

But let's return to our exploration of *magica* and *scientia*. To create conscious contact with one particular plant, stone, animal etc., first of all the mage would need to know how to temporarily tone down all other contacts. In the emerging silence they could stretch out their consciousness towards the *Other*, like a spirit over water. Then they would listen, look at, inhale, taste and pay attention- with all their senses to begin to perceive the world through the induced images, words, scents and sounds of the object in front of them. Effectively, the mage would gradually learn how to temporarily share their mind with the mind of the plant, stone, herb etc. in front of them. Today we still know and expect this process to take place when ingesting psychoactive cocktails such as ayahuasca; for Paracelsus, however, such experience lay dormant in all objects of nature.

The term *scientia*, according to Paracelsus, was thus essentially interconnected with *magia*. Together they form the outside and the inside of Paracelsus's *cosmosophia* which only becomes accessible to humans through the integrated simultaneous application of both practices.

While the desired sharpness of distinction and clarity of definition are somewhat construed, we could expound the terms as follows. *Scientia* in this context indicated the process of drawing out the occult knowledge embedded in the natural objects around us by creating proximity, observing and experimenting. *Scientia* was the essential foundation for any kind of first-hand *experience*;[38] it was about identifying and tuning into the knowledge-signal of the

---

38 Paracelsus, *Labyrinthus Medicorum Errantium*, in: *Theophrast von Hohenheim, gennant Paracelsus. Die Kärntner Schriften*, Klagenfurt: Amt der Kärntner Landesregierung, 1955, p. 97; also: Brandl, Simon, *Mystik und Magie im Frühparacelsismus*, Berlin: De Gruyter, 2021, p. 6.

Other. For Paracelsus, therefore, genuine alchemy was a prime example of the method of *scientia*.[39]

> *"Scientia" is not an asset, not an "Art," not a trained professional competence and ability, but the realisation emanating from the object of interest, the peculiar „knowledge" of the object which in the act of experience turns into a realisation of the unique way of being of the object as an other. So in essence [scientia is] a highly philosophical process of cognition!*[40]

Magia, on the other hand, was the mirror process within the human mind. In order to create genuine contact, just exposing ourselves to a foreign signal was not enough. What was of equal importance was knowing how to decipher and interpret the incoming information, mental images, or other sensory imprints. Paracelsus therefore emphasised repeatedly "that the things are all revealed through magia."[41]

Thus, *magia* in this particular context refers to the art of preparing the receiving field of our consciousness to take in and decode the incoming signal. It was the inspired process of interpreting, meaning-making, and contextualisation otherness into the world of the microcosm.[42]

---

39 Paracelsus, *Labyrinthus Medicorum Errantium*, in: *Theophrast von Hohenheim, gennant Paracelsus. Die Kärntner Schriften*, Klagenfurt: Amt der Kärntner Landesregierung, 1955, p. 93.

40 *"Scientia" ist kein Besitzstand, keine 'Kunst,' keine antrainierte fachliche Kompetenz und Befähigung, sondern in von seinem Gegenstand ausgehendes Innewerden des ihm eigentümlichen "Wissens," das im Erfahrungsakt zu einem Innehaben der Existenz-Eigenart des Gegenübers wird. Also im Grunde ein höchst philosophischer Erkenntnisvorgang!*
— Kurt Goldammer, *Der Göttliche Magier und die Magierin Natur*, Kosmosophie Band V, Stuttgart: Franz Steiner Verlag, 1991, p. 46.

41 Paracelsus; *Labyrinthus Medicorum Errantium*, in: *Theophrast von Hohenheim, gennant Paracelsus. Die Kärntner Schriften*, Klagenfurt: Amt der Kärntner Landesregierung, 1955, p. 112.

42 Goldammer, Kurt, *Der Göttliche Magier und die Magierin Natur*, Kosmosophie Band V, Stuttgart: Franz Steiner Verlag, 1991, p. 47.

Such process was not performed by the cognitive mind as the primary actor. Rather, the planetary cocoon of celestial influences had to come to rest and open the stage of our perception to something different altogether. A critical catalyst had to be added in order to unlock the effect of magia: the *Holy Spirit*, or in other terms the *Light of Nature*. It was the latter that enabled man to personally experience the mysteries of the Scripture and to gain a divinely inspired position of insights and revelation outside of a religious context.[43] According to such a worldview, science and magic, research and revelation do not at all contradict or exclude one another. Instead, they are essentially interwoven aspects of man's Faustian attempt of turning the key in the lock of the world in order to assume their position as a "sapiens" or mage within the ecosystem of creation.[44]

As has become obvious, we are faced with a paradox here. From the vast corpus of Paracelsus's unpublished manuscripts we have to recover the practice of a sophisticated learning process taking place between man and the natural world. At the same time Paracelsus himself advises us that this learning process cannot be taken from books but is only taught by nature herself.[45] At the heart of this paradox sits Paracelsus's deeply *sensual experience* of both *scientia* and *magia*. For both terms illustrate manners of applying ourselves to the world in a way that releases the experience of a sensual encounter, of an intimate relationship.

It would be wise to suggest that the best way to create first hand experience of such a *sensual understanding of scientia and magia* is to consider them as erotic experiences. Just for a moment imagine the world as your lover. Your hands, your entire own body then becomes a tool of *scientia*. The way you touch the world has to become a lover's touch: a careful, caressing approximation, a deeply respectful, mutual exploration of intimacy. If I place my hand here, how does the world's body respond? If I breathe over this stone, how does the

---

43 Goldammer, 1991, p. 53.
44 Goldammer, 1991, p. 52.
45 Goldammer, 1991, p. 53.

stone react? If I lend my ear to this river, how does the perception of the river open up and unfold? Each movement in this erotic experience is made up of two components, touch and response, call and answer, of placing awareness onto something which responds with its own kind of magic. *Scientia* and *magia*. Searching, knocking and listening for the answer. Or in Paracelsus's own words, the more the hidden knowledge embedded in all things created reveals itself to us, the more we will fall in love with the world: "The more knowledge there is in a thing, the more love."[46]

Finally, we also should acknowledge that this experience is *erotic* only in the understanding of *speaking through our senses*, in the subtle alternation between touching and being touched in return. However, it is not at all a *romantic* experience: while the magician is in the embrace of the world, carefully moving from one tactile contact to the next, they also should be measuring, recording, and respecting the blows on the anvil. Adhering to scientific standards while performing atavistic forms of ancient magic easily pays off in a slightly enhanced life expectancy.

In this manner, a modern scientist can stand in a laboratory in full body suit, surrounded by sterile glass and high-tech gear, and still practice *scientia* and *magia* in a Paracelsian sense. Similarly, a shaman crouching in a cave, reaching for the underworld, will still need to guard themselves not to get lost in the (erotic) act as such. Instead, we always keep our guards up and act with unmoved objectivity and full accountability. These are basic characteristics of what Paracelsus would have expected of any *sapiens*.

> *For whatsoever any man seeketh, that shall be given him. And where your treasure is, there also is your heart. In which you will also be granted [access].*[47]

---

46 Paracelsus; *Labyrinthus Medicorum Errantium*, in: Theophrast von Hohenheim, gennant Paracelsus. Die Kärntner Schriften, Klagenfurt: Amt der Kärntner Landesregierung, 1955, p. 115.
47 Ibid., p. 80.

[...] man [has] a knowledge of such secrets that he does not let himself be seduced by the book but hangs on to the treasure. But if man does not know this, he clings to that which he [then still] knows: drinking, whoring, gambling, warring, sloth etc. Then this is true once: he who does not know God does not love him; he does not know anything about him. He who does not know the Trinity does not believe in it, therefore he does not love it. He who does not know Mary does not love her. He who does not know the saints does not love them. He who does not know nature does not love it. The one who does not know anything does not see anything in the same one, despises her. His belly is his God. But the more knowledge there is in a thing, the more love. He who does not understand or know the poor does not love them. All things lie in knowledge. From the same then flow the fruits against the same. Knowledge accords faith. For he who knows God believes in him. He who does not know him does not believe in him. Each one believes as he knows. So also in medicine; each one does as much as he knows in nature. He who knows nothing does nothing. What he does, he copies as a painter copies a picture. Now there is no life in him, so also in that same physician.[48]

---

48 [...] der Mensch [hat] ein Wissen von solchen Heimlichkeiten, daß er sich vom Buch nicht verführen lässt, sondern an dem Schatz hängt. So aber der Mensch das nicht wüßte, so hängt er an dem, das er [dann noch] weiß: dem Saufen, dem Huren, dem Spielen, dem Kriegen, der Faulheit etc. Dann das ist einmal wahr: der Gott nicht erkennt, der liebt ihn nicht; er weißt nichts von ihm. Der die Trinität nicht weißt, der glaubt sie nicht, darum liebet er sie nicht. Der Maria nicht kennt, der liebt sie nicht. Der die Heiligen nicht kennt, der liebt sie nicht. Der die Natur nicht kennt, der liebt sie nicht. Derselbige, der also nichts erkennt, der sieht nichts bei demselbigen, [der] verachtet sie. Sein Bauch ist sein Gott. Je mehr aber die Erkenntnis ist in einem Ding, je mehr die Lieb. Der den Armen nicht verstehet, noch erkennt, der liebt ihn nicht. Alle Ding liegen in Erkenntnis. Aus derselbigen fließen alsdann die Früchte gegen demselbigen. Die Erkenntnis gibt den Glauben. Denn der Gott erkennt, der glaubt in ihn. Der ihn nicht erkennt, glaubt in ihn nicht. Ein jeglicher glaubt, als er kennt. Also in der Arznei auch; ein jeglicher tut, soviel er kennt in der Natur. Der nichts erkennt, tut nichts. Was er tut, das malet er ab, wie ein Maler ein Bild abmalt. In dem ist nun kein Leben, also in demselbigen Arzt auch.
— Paracelsus; *Labyrinthus Medicorum Errantium*, in: *Theophrast von Hohenheim, gennant Paracelsus. Die Kärntner Schriften*, Klagenfurt: Amt der Kärntner Landesregierung, 1955, p. 115.

In an earlier chapter we suggested the definition of *magic as a relationship*, and even more precisely as one's ability to *cultivate relationships of radical Otherness*.

In Paracelsus's magico-medical works we now encounter a most explicit and specific application of this insight: together, *scientia* and *magia* enable the mage to stand in a living relationship and dialogue with the natural world. It liberates the *philosophus adeptus* from the Enlightenment's solitary confinement of their rational mind and throws them back into an ecosystem of voices, images and perceptive worlds which are constantly rocking against the shore of their dreams and skins.

The Practice of Scientia & Magia[49]

IF we inquire further how precisely *scientia* and *magia* are meant to be brought into practice, we find surprisingly clear instructions.

Paracelsus, first of all, repeats the assertion that not everyone will be able to perfect this art. Each one of us holds their gifts (*dona*). And while it is possible to partly liberate ourselves from the influences of the outer heavens, it would be foolish to reject the particular treasure of talent each one of us was given by birth.

Thus, if we hold a talent for *magia* we have to learn to put our elemental body to rest (the cocoon) and awaken the senses of our inner body, or as Paracelsus puts it, of our *sidereum corpus*. It is by applying, seeing and working through our inner senses that we begin to recognise the underlying patterns and dynamics of not only diseases and illnesses but the entire world of creation.

---

[49] Paracelsus often uses the Latin terms *magia* as well as *magica* interchangeably to refer to *magic*. For easier reading we have adopted the correct term *magia* here and in the following.

While engaged in this manner of working from the inside, the lines between ourselves and the spirits begin to blur: Paracelsus emphasises that the remedy *is a spirit*. Equally, the (sidereal) spirits speak to us to reveal their insights like "a letter sent to one over a hundred miles."

> *And so notice that everyone has their particular way, that is donum, into which they are born. In the same donum they should foster themselves so that they come to its end, not learn their innate scientiam from other creatures. For it is given to them alone, not to the other from whom they want to learn. Why then would the pear tree learn from the sloe? Why the fig tree from brier? Why would the sweet want to eat the sour?*[50]

> *Now if the remedy is to have a certain foundation which does not hail from the head's invention (but should follow a true indication and teaching), then you should know at first that the diseases are hidden, as also is the remedy. And there is nothing amongst these two that must be done, nor invented, by the earthly one; but it must be done by the sidereum corpus for that it sees into nature as the sun sees through a glass. Now it is to be known in which way the hidden things are found which are not visible to the earthly body. So it follows that the things are all revealed by magicam and by their kinds, as by gaballiam and gaballisticam etc. They are the same that reveal all secrets in hidden nature. And it is necessary and proper that a physician be instructed and familiar with them. If he is not, he is a madman and a good-for-nothing in medicine who is more inclined towards deception than towards truth. This is proved by himself. For magia is anatomia medicina. In the same way as a butcher cuts up an ox and one sees everything that is in it and how it is which cannot be seen through the skin,*

---

50 *Und also merkent, daß ein jeglicher sein besondere Art hat, das ist donum, in das er geboren wird. In demselbigen dono soll er sich fürdern, daß er zu demselbigen End komme, und nit lerne von andern Creaturen sein angeborne scientiam. Dann ihm ist sie allein geben, dem andern nit, von dem du lernen willt. Warumb wollt dann der Birnbaum von der Schlehen lernen? Warumb der Feigenbaum von Dörnen? Warumb wollt das Süß das Sauer fressen?*
— Paracelsus; *Labyrinthus Medicorum Errantium*, in: Goldammer (ed.), 1955, p. 101.

so magia cuts up all the corpora of the medicine in which are the remedia that are in the same corpus.[51]

Since the help of the sick is a spiritus, and lies hidden from the elemental body, and is only visible to the sidereal body, it follows that magia has to teach, and not Avicenna, nor Galen. And only magia is the praeceptor, schoolmaster and paedagogus to find and teach the remedy, the help of the sick, and [to make] that same visible.[52]

Just as a letter sent to one over a hundred miles, which is understood in the mind, in such a form, also in the manner of a letter, the firmament reaches out to us. Now look for the messenger, you doctors, where you will find him who went to and fro to you.[53]

---

[51] *Soll nun die Arznei einen gewissen Grund haben, der nicht aus dem Kopf gehet in Erdichtung (sonder er soll gehen durch ein wahrhaftigs Anzeigen und Lehren), so sollent ihr anfänglich wisen, daß die Krankheiten verborgen seind, auch die Arznei. Und nichts ist unter denen zweien, das durch den irdischen muß getan, noch erfunden werden; sonder es muß durch den sidereum corpus geschehen, daß derselbig sicht in die Natur, wie die Son durch ein Glas. Nun ist jetzt weiter zu wisen, in was Weg die verborgen Ding gefunden werden, die dem irdischen Leib nit sichtbar sind. So folgt nun auf das, daß die Ding alle durch magicam offenbar werden und durch ihr species, als durch gaballiam und gaballisticam etc. Dieselben sind, die da offenbaren alle Heimlichkeit in verborgner Natur. Und ist von nöten und billig, daß ein Arzt in derselbigen unterricht und bekannt sei. Wo nit, so ist er ein Irrer und ein Gutwöller in der Arznei, der mehr zum Betrug gericht ist dann zur Wahrheit. Das beweist sich an ihm selbst. Dann magica [i.e. magia] ist anatomia medicine. Zu gleicher Weis wie ein Metzger ein Ochsen zerlegt, und man sicht alles, das in ihm ist und wie er ist, das durch die Haut nit mag gesehen werden, — also zerlegt die magica alle corpora der Arznei, in denen die remedia sind, was in demselbigen corpus ist.*
  — Paracelsus; *Labyrinthus Medicorum Errantium*, in: Goldammer (ed.), 1955, p. 112.

[52] *Derweil nun die Hilf der Kranken dermaßen ein spiritus ist, und liegt verborgen vor dem elementischen Leib, und allein dem siderischen offenbar, — jetzt folgt nun, daß magica zu lehren hat, und nit der Avicenna, noch Galenos. Und allein die magica ist praeceptor, Schulmeister und paedagogus, zu finden und lehren die Arznei, die Hilf der Kranken, und dasselbig sichtbar.* —Ibid., p. 113.

[53] *Gleich als ein Brief, der einem über hundert Meilen geschickt wird, desselbigen Gemüt verstanden wird, in solcher Gestalt, auch in Briefsweis, das Firmament an uns langet. Nun schauet jetzt umb den Boten, ihr Arzt, wo ihr ihn findet, der euch da hin und herging.* —Ibid., p. 82.

[...] *such man is blind with seeing eyes, deaf with hearing ears, with his nose he smells nothing, with his hands he feels nothing, his body feels nothing. The seer sees inwardly, but outwardly he sees no more, he hearkens speech but understands no more the outward word, he has sound of every thing, but understands it no more. For he is engrossed and sunken and drowned in the inward vision like a child in a beautiful trinket or like a fool in a painting. Such a man seems to be without his five outer senses and is considered by the world to be the greatest of fools, but by God he is the wisest of all men, whom he lets know his own wisdom and see into what is hidden, more than all philosophers and worldly wise men.*[54]

As we saw in the second chapter of this book, Paracelsus is aiming to teach us "clean practice." His language is only abstract for so long—until we have actually experienced the effects of *magia* in our own bodies, minds and lives.

Once this experience has taken place, we realise that Paracelsus's ambiguity of language, his repeated use of Latin terminologies, and his masterful application of metaphors from the natural world are not at all shortcomings or diversions. Rather they are the only proper way to describe in writing the kind of reality we are dealing with: applied *magia* in itself is *not* an altered state of consciousness nor a hidden feature of the human psyche. Thus it evades psychological language, just as much as religious terminologies tend to do. Instead, magic *pushes through* altered states of consciousness, it knows how to open up the human psyche in order to venture out

---

54 [...] *dieser Mensch ist blind mit sehenden Augen, taub mit hörenden Ohren, mit seiner Nase riecht er nichts, mit seinen Händen tastet er nichts, sein Leib empfindet nichts. Der Seher sieht wohl innerlich, aber äußerlich sieht er nicht mehr, er hört wohl reden, versteht das äußere Wort nit mehr, er hat wohl Hall und Ton von jeglichem Ding, versteht es nit mehr. Denn er ist vergafft und versunken und ertrunken in die Innenschau wie ein Kind in einen schönen Kram oder wie ein Narr in ein Gemälde. Ein solcher Mensch scheint ohne seine fünf äußern Sinne zu sein und wird von der Welt für den größten Stocknarren gehalten, ist aber bey Gott der aller Weiset Mensch, den er sein Heymlichkeit wissen laßt und in das Verborgen hineinsehen laßt, mehr denn alle Philosophi und Weltweisen.*
— Sudhoff, Karl (ed.), *Paracelsus Sämtliche Werke*, Band XIII, München und Berlin: Verlag R. Oldenbourg, 1931, p. 383.

through that hidden door, through the cracked cocoon, and into the spirit realm.

Upon arrival in this realm we quickly realise that radical Otherness is abundant, that it has to be endured, navigated and learned to be appreciated. As we explored above, true spirit relationships are marked by evading all man-made traditions, by repelling our sense of normality, and oftentimes by overwhelming us with a sense of paradox and contrariness.

All of this was obvious to Paracelsus. And yet, with the splendid exception of Will-Erich Peuckert, it was an enigma to most of his modern day researchers and commentators such as Karl Sudhoff (1853–1938) or Kurt Goldammer (1916–1997). Confronted with Paracelsus's medical brilliance and yet the almost daemonic ubiquity of magical ambiguity in his works, they read the latter as a shortcoming and as a failure to shake off the shackles of a narrow-minded, superstitious Medieval mindset.

From the perspective I gained by researching Paracelsus for several years I'd venture to presume he might not have cared much about the exegetical approaches to his written works. It might be fair to presume that it would have been entirely trivial to him whether one managed to unlock all aspects of the linguistic puzzles laid out in his many books. What would have been of primary concern to him, however, would have been the applied practice, the *experientia* his writings led us to explore for ourselves.

Fritz Perls once famously stated that all kinds of cognitive reflections on true practice only distinguish themselves by the amount of *shit* they heap into our minds. Similarly, Paracelsus might have quickly retreated to the nearest pub when confronted with overly academic attempts to dissect his manuscripts.[55] What mattered to

---

55 *I distinguish three classes of verbiage production: Chickenshit—this is "good morning," "how are you," and so on; bullshit—this is "because," rationalization, excuses; and elephant shit—this is when you talk about philosophy, existential Gestalt therapy, etc.—what I am doing now.*
— Perls, Fritz, *Gestalt Therapy Verbatim*, Gouldsboro: The Gestalt Journal Press, 1992, kindle edition, p. 63.

him above all was the practice we derive from contact with him. May this practice be medieval or modern, medical or magical, or all of that at once. Both Perls and Paracelsus would have agreed that the two legs upon which our practice walks are Now and How.[56]

CELESTIAL INCLINATIONS

THERE IS A CRACK, A CRACK IN EVERYTHING. THAT'S HOW THE LIGHT GETS IN.

—LEONARD COHEN

Let's take a closer look then at how we ready ourselves for the experience of magia in a Paracelsian sense. The good news is that, unlike Leonard Cohen's quote, we do not need to crack the cocoon of celestial influences that anchor directly in our human beingness. Nothing needs to be broken away or cut off in order for us to experience what Paracelsus sometimes termed Musa Sagax and more frequently referred to as the Light of Nature.

However, some of the crooked and thick-skinned aspects of our planetary cocoon might need to be ground off and polished so that the light of nature can shine through from within.

Let's listen to Paracelsus directly and the emphasis he placed on learning from this occult light and magical muse.

> Much have I thought and reported of the magia, yet [more] often of the invention of the secrecy of nature in these books, and also in others. Therefore you should know this in all brevity, that the book magica inventrix should be well learned by every physician. Even if all the books perish and die, and

---

56 Ibid., p. 64.

all the medicines with them, still nothing is lost, for the book inventrix finds it all again and even more. This is an anatomy of art.⁵⁷

Tell me, what does it mean to enter through the proper door into medicine? Through Avicenna, Galen, Mesue, Rhasim etc.? Or through the light of nature? For there are two entrances: one is in the books discussed, another is in nature. Whether now it is not fair, reader, that there is an oversight, which door is the entrance and which is not? Namely, this is the proper door, which is the light of nature, and the other [mode of entrance] is [like] entering from above through the roof; for they do not agree. Different are the codices scribentium, different the lumen naturae; different the lumen apotecariorum, different the lumen naturae. If then they are not of one way, and yet the right way must be one only, I consider that book to be the right one which God himself has given, written, dictated and set. And the other books, according to their reasoning, may advise, [and] opinionate, may give as much as they would; [but] nothing is taken from nature.⁵⁸

57 *Viel habe ich gedacht und gemeldet der magica, [und] noch oftmals der Erfindung der Heimlichkeit der Natur in diesen Büchern, auch in anderen. Darum sollt ihr das Wissen nach der Kürze, das dis Buch magica inventrix bei einem jeglichen Arzt sol wohl gelernt werden. Ob als dann alle Bücher verdürben und stürben und alle Arznei mit ihnen, so ist doch noch nichts verloren; denn das buch inventrix findet es alles wieder und noch mehr dazu. Das ist eine Anatomie der Kunst.*
— Sudhoff, Karl (ed.), *Paracelsus Sämtliche Werke*, Band XI, München und Berlin: Verlag R. Oldenbourg, 1928, pp. 205-206.

58 *Sagen sie mir, welches ist zur rechten Tür hinein gegangen in die Arznei? Durch den Avicenna, Galen, Mesue, Rhasim, etc. Oder durch das Licht der Natur? Denn da sind zwei Eingänge: einer ist in den besprochenen Büchern, ein anderer ist in der Natur. Ob nun nicht billig sei, Leser, dass da ein Übersehen gehalten werde, welche Tür der Eingang sei, und welche nicht? Nämlich die ist die rechte Tür, die das Licht der Natur ist, und die andere ist oben zum Dach hinein gestiegen; denn sie stimmen nit zusammen. Anders sind die codices scribentium, anders das lumen naturae; anders das lumen apotecariorum, anders das lumen naturae. So sie nun nicht eines Weges sind und doch der rechte Weg in dem einen liegen muss, achte ich, das Buch sei das rechte, das Gott selbst gegeben, geschrieben, diktiert und gesetzt hat. Und die anderen Buecher nach ihrem Bedenken, concilia, opiniones geben so vil als sie mügen; der Natur ist nichts genommen.*
— Ibid., p. 169.

What the Musa Sagax and Alstoos gave me in medical insights allows me to make clear statements, as I am also known as the author of similar expert opinions.[59]

The last quote is of particular importance as it is taken from the only extant letter of Paracelsus to the great humanist Erasmus of Rotterdam (1466–1536). As such, it was an official document of significant importance even to Paracelsus, and he chose his words carefully. It is the only known instant of the term *musa sagax* in his entire written work. Thus, it was a term he coined for this particular situation and with the intent to express himself in a manner that would be authentic and genuine, and yet accessible and acceptable to one of the greatest minds of the northern Renaissance.

The Latin word *sagax* stems from the Indo-European root *sag-*, *to seek, track, trail*. It is also found in the Latin word *sagire, to perceive, to seek to know*. As an adjective *sāgax, sāgacis* thus refers to someone or something *of keen perception* and is also found in the English term *sagacious*.[60] In Paracelsian language, however, *sagax* is synonymous with *adept* as we can see derive from his posthumously published magnum opus, the Philosophia Sagax.[61]

Therefore, in the letter to one of the most influential scholars of his time, Paracelsus openly declares that his wisdom does not stem from books or other formally established sources but from an occult type of *muse* which is accessible only to the adepts. It is this muse of the adepts, as in the direct inspiration of a spirit in the classical

---

59 *Quae mihi musa et alstoos tribuit medica, candide apud me clamant: similium iudiciorum manifestus sum auctor.*
— Paracelsus in a letter to Erasmus of Rotterdam (1526), in: Sudhoff, Karl (ed.), Paracelsus Sämtliche Werke, Band III, München und Berlin: Verlag R. Oldenbourg, 1930, p. 379.

60 According to Julius Pokorny's book, *Indogermanisches etymologisches Wörterbuch* (Bern: Francke, 1959, 1989) the root-word *sāg-* is best translated as *to seek, track, trail*. The other term mentioned by Paracelsus in this context, *Alstoos*, unfortunately has remained enigmatic to this day.

61 *Astronomia Magna: oder die gantze Philosophia sagax der grossen und kleinen Welt*, Michael Toxites (ed.), Frankfurt am Main: Martin Lechler for Hieronymous Feyerabend, 1571.

sense, which "the young doctor invokes, and under which aegis he places himself."⁶²

It might have come as little surprise that Erasmus's response was friendly but noncommittal. While he admitted his surprise about the precise remote diagnosis Paracelsus had given in the letter, he did not offer an invitation in return. Even for someone of such unquestionable standing like Erasmus, dealings with Paracelsus might have seemed risky at best.

Over the course of his life, Paracelsus paid dearly for his overt and direct commitment to the *musa sagax* and the *magica inventrix* as his main teachers. Despite, or maybe because of, the countless examples of his almost miraculous medical achievements, the hostility and attempts of character assassination from scholars all over continental Europe remained unnumbered and highly effective.

> *They say he can write of nothing but of luxu and venere; they mock his bald head, they call him the forest donkey of Einsiedeln, they write that he is a plagiarist and think that I purloin my work, although my current library, as everyone knows, does not contain six sheets, and about all this my secretaries testify that such (what I write) comes from the mouth and I have not read a book in ten years. One of them thought I was dumb (foolish), the other one thought I was a nigromantist and what they liked to invent more from the magical. They were prompted to do so by the thief and rogue who sat behind their ears. And the great cures, which I have proven throughout many kingdoms, languages and countries, over other physicians, over their patrons and all books [...] they have attributed the same to the devil as if I had accomplished such through the Belzenbuck."⁶³*

62 Peuckert, Will-Erich, *Theophrastus Paracelsus*, Stuttgart-Berlin: Kohlhammer Verlag, 1941, p. 137.
63 *Sie sagen, er könne nichts als nur von luxu und venere schreiben; sie spotten seiner Glatze, sie heißen ihn den Waldesel von Einsiedeln, sie schreiben, er sei ein Plagiator und meinen, ich stehle meine Arbeit, obwohl doch meine gegenwärtige Bücherei, wie einem jeden zu wissen ist, sechs Blätter nicht umfasst, und über das alles meine Sekretäre bezeugen, daß solches, (was ich schreibe), vom Mund geht und ich in zehn Jahren kein Buch gelesen habe. Einer hielt mich für taub (närrisch), dem ändern war ich ein Nigromantist und was sie mehr mochten aus dem Magischen erdenken. Dazu ursachte*

We quote the above to emphasise how daunting and risky it remained throughout his life for Paracelsus to admit to the occult sources of his learning. And yet it also illuminates how important these must have been to himself as he never attempted to conceal, socially sanitise or academically gentrify the source of his knowledge and experience. Musa sagax: she was the only bride he ever wooed.

In order to understand what enabled Paracelsus to unlock this source of natural wisdom we shall have to return to the *donas* mentioned above. In particular, we will need to take a closer look at the *inclinations*. As we will see, Paracelsus maintained a precise theory and a related practice as regards this process.

Like any good theory, it not only explains how Paracelsus gained access to the musa sagax but how any one of us could achieve the same. For it is a theory of what constitutes and enables human ingenuity or, in other words, what allows us *to become ingenium*. As Will-Erich Peuckert remarked, even today, five hundred years later, we still do not have a better explanation or more precise language when acknowledging the unique effects of a particular celestial inclination as human "genius."[64]

We have already examined the human constitution according to Paracelsus's cosmosophia and in particular the role of the celestial *ascendant*. According to the five categories of *donas*, the ascendant would have been understood as an *imprint*. The ascendant expresses itself as deep-rooted urges and desires which are closely related to our fate patterns and yet, according to Paracelsus, are shifting and changing with the tides of time.

---

sie der Dieb und Schalk, der ihnen hinter den Ohren saß. Und die großen Kuren, so ich durch viel Königreiche, Sprachen und Länder trefflich bewiesen hab, über andere Ärzte, über ihre Patrone und alle Bücher, [...] haben sie dieselbigen eher dem Teufel zugelegt, als ob ich durch den Belzenbock solches vollbrächte.
— Will-Erich Peuckert and Paracelsus, in: Peuckert, Will-Erich, *Theophrastus Paracelsus*, Stuttgart-Berlin: Kohlhammer Verlag, 1941, p. 208.

64 Ibid., p. 376; also see: Sudhoff, Karl (ed.), *Paracelsus Sämtliche Werke*, Band XII, München und Berlin: Verlag R. Oldenbourg, 1929, pp. 103–122.

As so often with Paracelsus, there is no hard line between what separates imprints from inclinations. However, the latter category is both broader as well as even more temporal and fluid in its impact upon man. In particular, it is the celestial inclinations that define the individual structure and qualities of the human mind. One's ability to think creatively across traditional categories of learning and knowledge, to see possibilities where others don't even register a path, in short, one's ability to innovate was a direct effect of the particular donas or gifts the celestial inclinations had bestowed upon an individual. In this manner, such genius was not simply inborn or embedded in one's blood (in contemporary diction: in one's DNA). Rather, it was a dynamic expression of the specific spirit relationships one had embedded oneself into.

Of course, even during Paracelsus's time very few people would have been considered capable of altering and changing their creative capabilities consciously. And yet that is precisely what Paracelsus expected from the human he sometimes tagged as an alchemist, more frequently as *philosophus adeptus* and in particular with regards to himself as a student of the musa sagax.

A man's inclinations could be changed. They could be rearranged. They were expressions of choices made by celestial spirits as well as by the recipients of their influences, humans. Such choices, similar to a contract, could be dissolved and new ones could be drafted and signed. Yes, one was born into a particular weave of celestial influences; and yet even long thereafter one could become an *adoptive son or daughter* of a particular spirit. Again we realise how essential Paracelsus's strong emphasis of the volatile, fluid and constantly (r)evolving relationship between inner and outer firmaments is. To him, the inner man was never completed, finished or perfected.

As long as our souls were clothed in this garment of heavenly fabric, we could engage in the difficult yet highly rewarding process of unravelling the webbing, pulling in new threads, and thus changing both our perception of the world and our means of expression in it.

Paracelsus's teachings of the celestial inclinations and of each man's ability to reforge them was an open revolt against the Catholic doctrine of spiritual dependency as well as against the general Medieval mindset of predetermination. What Paracelsus offered was not only a doctrine of hope and empowerment, but he rekindled the fire of genuinely Pelagian self-responsibility and Promethean accountability. Divinity had not hidden the key to all of creation in some occult and remote crypt. On the contrary, it had woven it into the most openly accessible and obvious place of all: into the inner firmament of each human.

As such, standing in a living relationship with the *musa sagax* was not the privilege of the elected few but it was a road open for travel to anyone. It's precisely this aspect of Paracelsus's deeply democratic worldview that explains his bitterness and bile against the traditional scholars of his time. He was neither a nigromantist nor a genius, he was a man who had made the choice to learn directly from the light of nature, who had walked the narrow path to arrive at this source of wisdom unbound. The same path was open to all other men, certainly to all privileged scholars and noblemen, had they only mustered the same courage, commitment and care to actually explore it.

To Paracelsus, life was a constant negotiation process between the stars' agendas and ours. It meant realising the human mind as our central instrument: a vessel, a hive, a choir of consciousnesses. *Magia* now was the art of deliberately filling this vessel with a certain substance, of bringing to the foreground certain members of the hive, of amplifying particular voices of the choir—and locking into our relationship with them, and electing them as our teachers.

As we shall see from the following quotes, this process of a chosen student-teacher relationship between a particular planet and man could be initiated from either side. The celestial bodies could choose an adopted son or daughter amongst the human beings. Conversely, humans could reforge the ties that bound them to certain celestial inclinations by alchemical processes applied to themselves.

Therefore a medicus should be an astronomus, so that they may know the celestial inclinations that work through the whole skin.[65]

The wise man should shake off the Inclinationes, Impressiones, Influentia like the donkey shakes off the horse flies.[66]

So that you may understand: in the same manner as a pupil learns from his schoolmaster, so may a man learn in Adepta Philosophia through the heavenly Praeceptores. [...] For in all ways, what a man may learn from other men, that may he also learn from the stars, and that with more foundation and understanding. [...] If man can learn wisdom from others, it is all the more possible to learn it from the stars. [...] This is the right way to make man perfect in the light of nature.[67]

Know then that there are two heavenly bodies, one celestial and one terrestrial, one of folly and one of wisdom. And in like manner as there are two worlds, a small world and a great world, and as the smaller governs the greater, so also the heavenly body microcosmi governs and overcomes the heavenly body coelesti. For this here you ought to know, that God created the planets and all the other planets of heaven, not for the purpose that they should govern man and be lords unto the same, but for the service of man, that they should serve him as do other creatures. Although it is true that the upper stars give their inclination and sign man and all other earthly bodies with natural signs after their kind. Yet this is not a dominion or governing

---

65 Darum soll ein Medicus sein ein Astronomus, auf dass er wisse die himmlischen Inclinationes, die da wirken durch die ganze Haut hinein.
— Sudhoff, Karl (ed.), *Paracelsus Sämtliche Werke*, Band XI, München und Berlin: Verlag R. Oldenbourg, 1928, p. 87.

66 Der Weise soll die Inclinationes, Impressiones, Influentia abschütteln wie der Esel die Bremsen. —Ibid., p. 228.

67 Daß ihr also verstehen sollt: Zu gleicher Weise wie ein Schüler von seinem Schulmeister, also mag auch der Mensch lernen in Adepta Philosophia durch die himmlischen Praeceptores. [...] Denn in allen Wegen, was der Mensch mag lernen von anderen Menschen, das mag er auch von den Sternen erfahren, und zwar mit mehr Grund und Verstand. [...] Kann der Mensch Weisheit lernen von anderen, so ist umso möglicher sie zu lernen von den Sternen. [...] Derart ist die rechte Weise den Menschen vollkommen zu machen im Lichte der Natur. —Ibid., Band XII, p. 99.

power, but a predestinated command and office, only so that nothing may remain hidden, but through external signs the internal power and virtue may be recognised.[68]

Now know further [...] that the heavenly body itself governs man and produces him according to its purpose. This is to be understood in such a manner that the heavenly body prepares a work and wishes to make it manifest through the human being. And if there is no man who stands in conjunction with the same heavenly body, it takes one for itself, who is like a filius adoptivus. The father owes him nothing, but he is assigned to him, which is not due to friendship, blood or justice. Thus the astrum chooses for itself an adopted son through whom it then acts as if he were its only-begotten son. Now notice of this inclination that it performs its inclination in six-fold form. Namely, once in the person, that is, in flesh and blood, so that it makes a particularly pleasant person, who is also more praiseworthy or more hostile to other people. Further, it often uses the mind of man, that is, that the mind of the same man surpasses the minds of all other men. Thus Solomon was an adopted son in the sense of his person, Julius Caesar in the sense of his mind. Likewise, there are inclinationes who control the spirit, that is, that the same spirit is for all others with happiness, with assaults, with all the things that are due to the spirit. One such adopted son was the Emperor Barbarossa of Swabia. So you should also know about the inclinations of the fourth manner, that the heavenly body prepares a doctrine which it wants to make manifest through man, so it chooses one through

---

68 Auf das so wisset, das zweierlei Gestirne sind, nämlich ein himmlisch und ein irdisch, eines der Torheit und eines der Weisheit. Und zu gleicher Weise wie zwei Welten sind, eine kleine und eine grosse Welt, und wie die kleinere die groessere regiert, also auch das Gestirn microcosmi das Gestirn coelesti regiert und überwindet. Denn das sollt ihr hier wissen, dass Gott die Planeten und alle anderen Planeten des Himmels nicht darum erschaffen hat, in der Meinung dass sie den Menschen regieren und demselbigen Herrn sein sollen, sondern zum Dienst der Menschen, dass sie ihm als andere Kreaturen dienen. Obgleich es stimmt, dass die oberen Gestirne ihre Inclination geben und den Menschen und alle anderen irdischen Körper signieren mit natürlichen Zeichen nach ihrer Art. So ist dies doch keine Herrschaft oder regierende Gewalt, sondern ein prädestinierter Befehl und Amt, damit nur nichts verborgen bleibe, sondern durch auswendige Zeichen, die inwendige Kraft und Tugend erkannt werden.
— Ibid., Band XI, p. 380.

whom it accomplishes it. Thus an adopted son of this kind was Albert Magnus, Lactantius, Wicleff and others. So the star also prepares a special art or a special skill in merchandising. And if she has no born son by whom to accomplish it, she chooses one. Thus an adopted son of art was Albrecht Dürer of Nuremberg, and an adopted son of the Fuggers of Augsburg was the son of commerce. Notice, then, in the sixth specie, that the astrum gives birth to some skill, that is, that the same surpasses all others. For such adopted sons are those who can walk on a rope. So understand the fourth limb and its kinds, how the heavenly courses perform miracles in their adopted sons, that is the Inclinatio.[69]

69 Nun wisset weiter [...] dass das Gestirn den Menschen selbst regiert und denselbigen erzeugt nach seinem Sinn. Das ist also so zu verstehen, dass das Gestirn etwa ein Werk zurichtet, und will das selbige durch den Menschen offenbar machen. Und aber ist kein Mensch vorhanden, der mit demselbigen Gestirn in der Konjunktion steht, so nimmt es sich einen für, derselbige ist gleich als ein filius adoptivus. Demselbigen ist der Vater nichts schuldig gewesen, sondern was er ihm beweiset, das geht aus keiner Freundschaft, Blut noch Gerechtigkeit zu. Also erwählt sich das Astrum einen Adoptivsohn, durch den es dann wirkt, als wäre er sein eingeborener Sohn. Nun merkt von dieser Inclination, dass sie in sechsfacher Gestalt ihre Inclination vollbringt. Nämlich einmal in der Person, das ist in Fleisch und Blut, also dass sie da eine sonderlich angenehme Person macht, die für andere Menschen auch löblicher oder feindseliger ist. Weiter, so verwendet sie oft das Gemüt des Menschen, also dass des selbigen Menschen Gemüt aller anderen Menschen Gemüt übertrifft. Demnach ist Salomon ein Adoptivsohn der Person halber gewesen, Julius Caesar des Gemüts halber. Ebenso gibt es Inclinationes die den Spiritus kontrollieren, also das derselbige Spiritus für alle anderen ist mit Glück, mit Anschlägen, mit all den Dingen, die dem Geist zustehen. Ein solcher Adoptivsohn ist gewesen der Kaiser Barbarossa von Schwaben. Also sollt ihr auch wissen von der Inclinations der vierten Weise, dass das Gestirn etwa eine Doktrin zurichtet, die sie durch den Menschen offenbar machen will, so wählt sie einen, durch welchen sie es vollendet. Also ist ein Adoptivsohn dieser Art gewesen Albertus Magnus, Lactantius, Wicleff und andere mehr. Also bereitet das Gestirn auch eine besondere Kunst oder eine besondere Geschicklichkeit in der Kaufmannschaft. Und so sie keinen geborenen Sohn hat, durch den sie es vollendet, so wählt sie einen aus. Also ist ein Adoptivsohn der Kunst gewesen Albrecht Dürer von Nürnberg, der Kaufmannschaft ist ein Adoptivsohn der Fugger von Augsburg. Also merkt in der sechsten Specie, dass das Astrum etwa eine Geschicklichkeit gebiert, also dass die selbige alle anderen übertrifft. Zur solchen sind Adoptivsöhne solche die auf dem Seil gehen können. Also verstehet das vierte Glied und seine Arten wie die himmlischen Läufe in ihren Adoptivsöhnen Wunderbarkeiten handeln, das ist die Inclinatio.
— Sudhoff, Karl (ed.), *Paracelsus Sämtliche Werke*, Band XII, München und Berlin: Verlag R. Oldenbourg, 1929, pp. 109-110.

*And this is also necessary to know: What the alchemist breaks, that same loses the firmamentary power. If the firmamentary force is to be effective, it must not be broken. Know further that the Philosophia Adepta possesses a special art of composition. Thus in the same way as one naturally mixes many bodies together, so may the sidereal Arcana be composed. From this the names follow, as tyriaca coelestis, methridatum Olympi, suffuff aethereum etc. This is how they are made earthly, such they are also composed firmamentally.*⁷⁰

*When we read the Scriptures, we understand them by the spirit which is given to us by God out of heaven, without which we understand all things earthlywise. Therefore the understanding of man is divided into the natural spirit and the other spirits, one of which is from God and the other from the devil. Therefore it is up to man according to which spirit he wants to understand. The natural body does not accept the divine and thus also the heavenly knowledge; only he who is born again, as Christ demands in his conversation with Nicodemus, only he is able to accept the heavenly and to recognise it. [...] If therefore a man would wish to attain well, he must be experienced in this composition and direct himself into the heavenly effect, that he may be a magus coelestis, a medius coelesti, etc. For all that pertains to the heavenly must run and go forth entirely from the new birth and not at all from the earthly.*⁷¹

70 Und das ist auch zu wissen von Nöten: Was der Alchimist bricht, dasselbige verliert die firmamentische Kraft. Soll nun die firmamentische Kraft wirken, so muss keine Zerbrechen geschehen. Darauf wisset auch weiter, dass die Philosophia Adepta inne hat eine besondere Kunst der Komposition. Also zu gleicher Weise wie man man natürlicher Weise vielerlei Körper zusammen vermengt, also mögen auch die siderischen Arcana komponiert werden. Aus dem folgen die Namen, als tyriaca coelestis, methridatum Olympi, suffuff aethereum, etc. Das ist wie sie irdisch gemacht werden, also werden sie auch firmamentisch komponiert. —Ibid., p. 98.
71 So wir die heilige Schrift lesen, so verstehen wir sie durch den Geist, der uns von Gott aus dem Himmel gegeben ist, ohne denselben verstehen wir alle Ding irdisch. Darum teilt sich hie der Verstand des Menschen nach dem natürlichen Geist und in die andern Geist, so von Gott der eine und der andere vom Teufel sind. Darum liegts nun am Menschen, nach welchem Geist ers verstehen will. Das Göttliche und damit auch die himmlische Erkenntnis nimmt der natürliche Leib nicht an; nur der, der wiedergeboren wird, wie Christs es im Gespräch mit Nikodemus fordert, nur der vermag das Him-

*So through man the heavenly power may be brought into man [...]. So the same man into whom the magia has brought such forces becomes like the same star, as it is in himself, with the same secrets and arcanis. [...] For if it is possible to bring poison into man, medicine with its effect, through man into man, it is also possible to drive the firmamental forces into man through the astronomico magico.*⁷²

SEEING THE LIGHT OF NATURE

THIS process now—man changing the nature of their celestial inclinations through magico-alchemical operations—holds the key to the purpose of all celestial theurgy in a Paracelsian sense.

Rather than extracting this theoretically, allow me to illustrate it by use of a personal digression. In doing so, I am not writing from

---

mlische anzunehmen und es zu erkennen. [...] So nun der Mensch ein gut Erlangen tun will, so muß er in dieser Komposition erfahren sein, und sich in die himmlische Wirkung richten, auf da er ein magus coelestis sei, ein medius coelestis usw. Denn alles, was das Himmlische anbetrifft, das muß ganz und gar aus der neuen Geburt laufen und gehen und gar nicht aus der irdischen.
— Peuckert, Will-Erich, *Theophrastus Paracelsus*, Stuttgart-Berlin: Kohlhammer Verlag, 1941, p. 379; also see: Sudhoff, Karl (ed.), *Paracelsus Sämtliche Werke*, Band XII, München und Berlin: Verlag R. Oldenbourg, 1929, pp. 301-315.

72 *Also mag durch den Menschen die himmlische Macht in den Menschen gebracht werden [...]. Also wird aus dem selbigen Menschen, in den die magica gebracht hat solche vires, gleich der selbige stern, wie er an ihm selbst ist, mit den selben secrets[?] und arcanis. [...] Denn ist es möglich, in den Menschen Gift zu bringen, Arznei mitsamt ihrer Wirkung, durch den Menschen in einen Menschen, so ists auch möglich, dem astronomico magico die firmamentischen vires in den Menschen einzutreiben.*
— Sudhoff, Karl (ed.), *Paracelsus Sämtliche Werke*, Band XII, München und Berlin: Verlag R. Oldenbourg, 1929, p. 122.

the hubris that I have actually accomplished this process but with the knowledge, drawn from the accomplished facts, that I have humbly merely commenced it.

When I started studying first elementary and then planetary magic almost twenty years ago, I came across a strange paradox familiar to many students of this art. The technicalities of the operations seemed to be incredibly clear. What was *occult* in this experience was not at all the path towards making planetary contact and to effect change. Whether I worked with the books of the Golden Dawn tradition or reverted back to earlier sources such as Agrippa's *De Occulta Philosophia*, the *Picatrix*, the astral lore of the *Sabians of Harran* or elements of the *Greek Magical Papyri*, in rough outlines the approach of making contact was sound and clear. From preparatory periods of fasting and purification to invoking the assistance of a supreme Deity, to calling to the guardians of the specific operation, to drawing the spirit of the planet into a vessel of one's choice etc.: the reconstruction of the ritual process proper was not at all a challenge. What remained an enigma, however, irrespective how deep I delved into first and secondary sources, was the answer to the question of why I should undertake this work at all? I.e. once you stand face to face, or more precisely, spirit to spirit with a planetary ruler, what will be your ultimate motive, your purpose, your heart's intent for reaching out through so many lightyears of time and space? Once the magical texts were cleared from the debris of naive juvenile euphoria of proving to oneself that such contact was possible at all, indeed that magic itself was actually possible, only two classical motives seemed to remain: crisis prevention and personal gain.

I remember sitting at my desk in the dark morning hours, after years of assembling and preparing my magical paraphernalia. Finally I was ready, I had arrived at the threshold of the experience I had been waiting for so long. Before me on the table rested my ritual book and showed me the exact sequence of ritual steps to be taken in the rite. I knew the ins and outs of every one of them, felt the routine and automation in my bodily and mental muscles to unlock each phase of the operation. And then, in my mind's eye, I saw myself arriving at the centre of the maze, standing eye to eye with the divinity I had summoned — but now what? There was no way I could ask for personal gain in a life that already felt okay. Intuitively I also knew that anything to be gained would come at a price. A price I most likely would be unconsciously agreeing to, to realise only later, after the event, what exactly I had bartered away. Striking such deals in my mundane life with employers and collaborators, paying with sweat, study and hard labour seemed a much smarter and smoother way of finding my place in the world of humans. Similarly, crisis prevention wasn't the dominant topic in my direct environment. Of course I could have aimed to heal global warming, the pollution of oceans etc. But even in my juvenile narcissistic mind I realised that might be a step too far. So why exactly was I taking the liberty to bother this spirit?

It took me several years, full of experimentation, a lot of failure, wasted efforts as well as some solid successes, to discover my own answer to this question. The resolution was that I was missing life experience to make such a call. I was too young to call for the celestial rulers — and to have any meaningful inquiry. I did not know myself enough at the time, and neither did I know enough of the world. Even without magic, my chest was wide and the world seemed an oyster. I hadn't rocked up hard enough against my own natural limits, dysfunctions and demons yet. Crisis prevention and personal gain were topics of relevance which I had yet to explore and experience through a mundane lens first before I had anything meaningful to ask of a planetary god. Without knowing it at the time, what I had realised was an essentially Paracelsian insight: before I could attempt to change the inclinations of my life, I had to experience them first-hand in all their colourful facets. Before I could attempt to become an agent of celestial change, I had to subject myself and experience mundane change at a much deeper level yet.

So I began to throw myself into the world, even more so than I had done before: I took on low paid internships in America and India, travelled through Rajasthan, and ventured by railway and boat all the way from Berlin to Tokyo. I went from job to job, seeking life experience much more than a career or a professional home. And while doing all of this, I continued to study at IMBOLC, every day, where the curriculum required me to spend nights out in the woods, to work hard and to slowly but steadily walk into the shadows of my own demons and fears. It was a joyful time! Every night I went to bed as a different version of myself. While still bound by my own celestial weave of inclinations, I expanded my horizon as far as I could at the time. I experienced the fluidity of identity, reality and truth; and the essential choice life and I had to make each day, how we wanted to encounter each other.

After about ten years of such joyful and radical involution, I was finally ready to answer the question above: why bother a planetary spirit with my presence? I found my answer in the Arbatel Operation which I later on documented online. Each rite held no other purpose than *the encounter itself*. No crisis prevention, no personal gain. All that I intended was to create a conscious relationship with the spirits whose weavings I had been travelling now for quite some time, inside and out, and in a diverse array of settings. Finally, it was time to meet the directors of the stage play I had been participating in. At the age of almost thirty I felt I held sufficient bruises, scars and general life experience to spot the planets' echo and vibration in the mundane world once I had stood spirit to spirit with them. And, having encountered vulnerability and death, I was respectfully willing to pay the price they would demand. Accepting that I still held little control over what that would be, but much greater ability of regulating myself when confronted with sudden change or loss.

What I learned from these operations was what many magicians before me had learned through theirs: the inner man is a composition of celestial inclinations, each one bound into their elementary resonance organ. Deep within this inner man hovers a flame in their heart-space which can be kindled and used as a gate from both ends. However, for this flame's light to unite with the cognitive mind of the practitioner, the celestial inclinations clouding this contact have to be polished, purified and their weave turned transparent.

This process is much less about *changing* one's celestial inclinations than about self-initiating the inner *rebirth* Paracelsus mentions above.[73] Such rebirth, at least according to my own practice and understanding derived from it, can be initiated by standing eye to eye, spirit to spirit with the forces that create the compound being that we are, as well as all of creation around us. Standing in front of them without any human agenda of our own other than to *see them*, results in an irreversible experience. For seeing first-hand their active weave within ourselves changes everything. It breaks the foolish identification with the celestial cocoon our flame has been placed in. Once we see how Mars, how Venus, how Saturn are woven through our flesh and our blood, our past and our presence, our character and our mind, we can no longer can call these things I, Me or Mine.

If we have used our magical journey so far to become adept in experiencing Radical Otherness, this is the moment when we apply it to ourselves. Seeing our own body, mind and life being made up of the consciousness stream of planetary beings repels our identity away from what is genuinely theirs.

This is the process, if followed through with unconditional commitment, that opens a path for the voice of the *musa sagax* to reach our conscious mind. Once the mist of false identification is cleared from the inner man's eyes and ears, from their tongues and lips, the light of nature can shine through the cocoon of celestial inclinations and make conscious contact with us. Such contact can manifest itself in dreams, in mundane experiences, in intuitions or full books being downloaded into our minds, if only we know how to create the unclouded space and the inner resonance of receiving them.

> *What is the doctrine of God? Answer: To have God and to be absorbed in His will. To get there, you have to labour your entire life to draw out your*

---

[73] In *Holy Heretics* (Scarlet Imprint, 2022) I have given a fully restored version of how this process can be initiated in a ritual setting.

own good, your "springtime," your "good gift" and to bring it to light. A moral life is labour.[74]

Listening to the *musa sagax* is not a pure scientific process, it is the epiphany of applying both *scientia* and *magica* at once. Paracelsus might have never known what specifically the *musa sagax* truly is. Just like after more than ten years of daily work I still do not know what this holy daimon is that I am communing with. Faith, as Paracelsus so elaborately put it, is a critical component of magic. Not as in the blind belief in absolute truths without proof. But as in the state of complete commitment and absolute presence with an experience. Listening, seeing, experiencing with the senses of the inner man, are absolute categories. Doubt (Mercury) clouds them. Fierceness (Mars) obscures them. Desire (Venus) derails them. Fantasy (Moon) blocks them. Grandiosity (Jupiter) silences them. And Fear (Saturn) undermines them.

Opening a space for the *musa sagax* within us means accepting to lead a live as a living dovecot. All our inclinations send their birds into our minds, into our blood and into the cocoons over our hearts. Let's welcome these birds, and let's see them for what they are. They are not us. Not I, Me or Mine. But visitors, the weaves of creation in constant, eternal action. Listening to the *musa sagax* now means carefully electing a teacher in the spirit world—be it merely for a moment or for a lifetime—and then unraveling the notes its birds are sending us. In the dovecots of our minds.

As we have mentioned, there is no shortage but rather an abundance of technical books that provide us with the operative means to achieve such a state: Books on elementary and planetary magic, on celestial theurgy and chthonic goêteia. The missing element to turn these recipes into a meaningful journey, isn't just one more secret ingredient. It is the practitioner's ability and commitment to

---

74 *Was ist die Lehre von Gott? Antwort: Gott haben und aufgehen in seinem Willen. Um dahin zu gelangen, muß man sich ein ganzes Leben lang mühen, um das eigene Gute, den "Frühling," die "gute Gab" herauszuarbeiten und ans Licht zu bringen. Sittliches Leben ist Arbeit.* —Strunz, 1937, p. 44.

create spirit-encounters with the sole, genuine intent of becoming able *to see in the light of nature*.

Aside from technical rituals, operative instructions and occult recipes, what is hardest to achieve is our own attitude in how we encounter all of these. To use our free will, discipline, and the work of a lifetime to turn ourselves into an unobstructed resonance body of creation, into the tight skin of a drum. And then to be one with the hand that plays us...

Here is a little prayer I like to use for myself. Maybe it will prove worthy on your own journey?

Doubt has ceased.	THE DOOR HAS OPENED.
Fierceness has expired.	THE DOOR HAS OPENED.
Desire has vanished.	THE DOOR HAS OPENED.
Fantasy has faded.	THE DOOR HAS OPENED.
Grandiosity has gone.	THE DOOR HAS OPENED.
Fear has fallen.	THE DOOR HAS OPENED.

CHAPTER V

Becoming Ingenium

⸓

THE BOOK OF M
and the
ENS ASTRALE

SEVENTY-THREE years after Paracelsus's death the original manifest of the Rosicrucian brotherhood was published in print. Johannes Valentinus Andreae (1586–1654) had penned it several years before and various manuscript versions had been shared in a small circle for some time. It is widely known that the manifest calls out Paracelsus as a pioneer of their brotherhood, in spirit and in action, despite the fact that he obviously never joined them.[1]

1 Johann Valentin Andreae, *Fama Fraternitas—Das Urmanifest der Rosenkreuzer*

As so often, however, the actual section in the Fama Fraternitatis (Kassel, 1614) is rarely studied in its original wording as taken from the handwritten manuscripts which circulated before the first print edition.

Many Late Medieval or Early Modern magical texts used the technique of hiding their occult secrets in plain sight. They pushed a shiny, dramatic story into the centre of their narrative that would work well enough to capture the average reader's attention. Then they went on to hide the actual messages and occult signposts in the meandering periphery of the same text, where the same superficial readers would easily dismiss them as mere decoration and embellishment.

As we have shown in Holy Heretics, this worked wonderfully in the Arbatel and in regards to the correct way of working with the Olympic Spirit(s). Unsurprisingly, for many centuries now the same technique has worked wonders for the Fama Fraternitas.

One has to read the section that mentions Paracelsus carefully and possibly a few times over to realise how much it truly reveals:

> Certainly we must confess that even then the world was pregnant with great excitement and, having passed through the pains of childbirth, produced undaunted, glorious heroes who violently broke through the darkness and barbarism, leaving it only for us, as the weaker ones, to follow them. Certainly, they were the tip of the fiery triangle whose flames now shine the longer, the brighter and will certainly ignite the final fire of the world.
>
> Such was also, according to his vocation, Theophrastus. Although he did not join our brotherhood, he read the Book of M diligently and enlightened his keen ingenium with it.[2]

Bruderschaft zum ersten Mal nach dem Manuskript bearbeitet, die vor dem Erstdruck von 1614 entstanden sind durch Pleun van der Kooij, Haarlem: Rozekruis Per, 1998, pp. 78–79.

2 *Gewißlich wir müssen bekennen, daß die Welt schon damahls mit so grosser Commotion schwanger gangen und in der Geburt gearbeitet, auch sie so unverdrossene rühmliche Helden herfür gebracht, die mit aller Gewalt durch die Finsternuß und Barbareien hindurchgebrochen und uns schwächern schier nur nachzudrucken gelassen, und*

The mysterious Book of M has inspired many researchers to come up with their own interpretations. Does it stand for Mundi or Matrix as in "the book of the created world?" Does it relate to Magica, revealing Paracelsus as a theurgical doctor? Does it simply stand for Mysterium, thus emphasising the mystical side of his teachings? Or does it indeed refer to the Musa (sagax) of which we have learned above?

None of these arrows hit their target with adequate precision. For Paracelsus himself reveals to us what is meant by the Book of M that holds the agency to ignite and enlighten the human ingenium.

It is in his Volumen Paramirum that he establishes the doctrine of the five entia i.e. the five intertwined realms of being which together lend life to the created cosmos.

> You should understand the ens astrale in this manner. It is a thing which we do not see, but which keeps us and everything that lives and has sensibility alive, and it comes from the stars. And so we say: a fire that burns must have wood; otherwise there is no fire. Note: the fire is a life, but it cannot live without the wood. Therefore note: although this is a rough example, it is still useful enough; the body is a wood, the life in it the fire. Now the life lives from the body. The body must have something so that it is not consumed by life, but remains in its essence. The same is the thing of which we tell you the ens; this comes from the firmament. You say, and it is so, that if the air were not there, all things would fall to the ground, and everything that has life there would suffocate and die. Now note again that there is still one thing that holds the body (which holds life), which is no less to be lost than the air. The air is preserved in the thing and from the same, and if this were not the case, the air would disintegrate. The firmament lives

---

> freylich der Spitz an dem Trigono igneo gewesen, dessen Flammen nun mehr je heller leuchtet und gewißlich der Welt den letzten Brand entzünden wird.
> Ein solcher ist auch in seiner Vocation gewesen Theophrastus, so gleichwohl in unsere Fraternitet nicht getretten, aber doch den Librum M. fleissig gelesen und sein scharffes Ingenium dardurch angezündet.
> —Johann Valentin Andreae, *Fama Fraternitas—Das Urmanifest der Rosenkreuzer Bruderschaft zum ersten Mal nach dem Manuskript bearbeitet, die vor dem Erstdruck von 1614 entstanden sind durch Pleun van der Kooij*, Haarlem: Rozekruis Per, 1998, pp. 78-79.

from the same, and if it were not in the firmament, the firmament would disintegrate. And we call this the M, because nothing higher is created in everything, nothing more; nothing is more useful to the physician to consider. Notice and take note of it well: that we indicate to you the M, not that it springs from the firmament or that it is born in him, or that it was born in him, or that the firmament sent it to us, nothing at all. But this you note: that this M sustains all creatures in heaven and on earth, and all elements live from it and in it.[3]

The *ens astrale* leads us one level deeper into the mystery. It remains an enigmatic term itself and yet it is clearly what Paracelsus describes as the specific M referred to in the Fama Fraternitatis.

Ēns is a Latin word derived from *esse* (being) and translates simply as a thing or a being. In alchemy, *ēns* presents the root word of the *essence* i.e. a fluid extraction condensing within itself all the virtues and qualities of a substance from which it is extracted. The *ens astrale*, therefore, should be translated without overlaying artificial specifi-

---

3   Das ens astrale sollt ihr so verstehen. Es ist ein Ding, das wir nicht sehen, das ferner uns und alles das, was lebt und die Empfindsamkeit hat, beim Leben erhält, und das kommt aus dem Gestirn. Und wir sagen so: ein Feuer, das da brennt, muß Holz haben; sonst ist kein Feuer. Merke: das Feuer ist ein Leben, doch kanns nicht leben ohne das Holz. Drum merke: obwohl das ein grobes Exempel ist, ist es doch brauchbar genug: der Leib ist ein Holz, das Leben in ihm das Feuer. Nun lebt das Leben aus dem Leibe. Da muß der Leib etwas haben, daß er vom Leben nicht verzehrt werde, sondern im Wesen bleibe. Das selbe ist das Ding, von dem wir euch das ens erzählen; dieses kommt aus dem Firmament. Ihr sagt, und es ist so: wenn die Luft nicht wäre, so fielen alle Ding zu Boden, und alles, was da Leben hat, das erstickte und stürbe. Nun merkt hinwiederum, daß noch eins ist, das den Leib hält, (welcher Leib das Leben hält), das ist nicht minder zu verlieren als die Luft. Die Luft wird in dem Dinge erhalten und aus demselben, und wenn das nicht wäre, so zerginge die Luft. Das Firmament lebt aus demselben, und so es nicht im Firmament wäre, so zerginge das Firmament. Und wir heißen das das M, denn nichts Höheres ist in allem geschaffen, nichts mehreres; nichts ist dem Arzte nützer zu betrachten. Auf das merkt und merkt es wohl: daß wir euch das M anzeigen, nicht daß es aus dem Firmament entspringe oder daß es in ihm geboren sei, oder daß das Firmament uns das zuschickte, alles nichts. Aber das merkt euch: daß dies M alle Geschöpfe im Himmel und auf Erden erhalte, und alle Elemente leben aus ihm und in ihm.

— *Volumen Paramirum*, in: Paracelsus, *Werke, Band I, Medizinische Schriften*, Basel: Schwab reflexe, 2010, pp.188-189.

cation or subjective interpretation: it is the *Astral Being*. Now in the above quote Paracelsus explicitly points out that this *Being* (German: *Sein*) is not sent to us by the stars or generated by them.

Thus, we are encouraged to consider the *ens astrale* as an aether-like atmosphere, an all-penetrating substance or vibration which fills and surrounds the world up to the sphere where the earth's atmosphere dissolves into open interstellar space. M, in this sense, is both the very condition of all earthly life as well as the medium through which the celestial spirits take effect within our realm of creation.

> But so understand the ens astrorum: the astra have their nature and their different quality—like humans do on earth. The same astra also have their changes and become the better, the more evil, the sweeter, the more sour, the finer, the more bitter. When they are in their goodness, nothing evil comes from them, but in the evil their wickedness arises. Now note that they surround the whole world like a shell surrounds an egg. Through the shell comes the air and, beginning in it, goes through it toward the centre of the world. Now note: such astra as are poisoned stain the air with their poison. And where the poison then comes, in the same place the same diseases arise according to the quality of the same star, which cannot poison the whole air of the world, but only a part, dependent on its strength. So it is also with the benevolence of the stars.
>
> That is called ens astrale; that is the smell, haze, sweat of the stars, mixed with the air, as the course of the stars renders it. From this comes cold, heat, dryness and dampness and the like, just as their properties are and indicate it. Thus you should note that the stars do not incline anything but only poison the M by their vapour, by which we are then poisoned and weakened. This is the ens astrale, which changes our body in this way for good or evil. The man who is so natured that he is repugnant to the vapour from his natural blood, becomes ill; but he who is not natured against it is not harmed. Nor does it harm him who is so noble and fortified against it that he overcomes the poison from the noble nature of his blood or the

medicine that resists the adulterated vapours of the upper ones.[4]

The *ens astrale* is the medium through which the influences of the celestial spirits affect change and conditioning in all things created. The *ingenium*, on the other hand, is the receiving interface of the *ens astrale* in a human which in return constitutes the qualities of the human mind.

If we wanted to utilise another "rough example," as Paracelsus called it above, we can compare the *ens astrale* to the nervous system of the cosmos, the spirits to its neuronal messengers, and the *ingenium* to the specific receptor within the human brain.[5]

[4] *Aber so versteht das ens astrorum: Die astra haben ihre Natur und ihre verschiedene Eigenschaft—wie auf Erden die Menschen. Die selbigen astra haben auch ihre Veränderungen und werden je besser, je böser, je süßer, je saurer, je feiner, je bitterer. Wenn sie in ihrer Güte sind, kommt nichts Böses von ihnen, aber in der Böse entsteht ire Bosheit. Nun merkt, daß sie die ganze Welt umgeben, wie eine Schale ein Ei. Durch die Schale kommt die Luft und geht, in ihr anfangend, durch sie auf die Mitte der Welt zu. Nun merkt: welche astra vergiftet sind, die beflecken die Luft mit ihrem Gift. Und wo dann das Gift hinkommt, am selben Ort werden die selbigen Krankheiten, nach Eigenschaft des selbigen Sterns, den er kann nicht die ganze Luft der Welt vergiften, sondern allein ein Teil, je nachdem seine Stärke ist. So ist es auch mit der Güte der Sterne.*

Das heißt also ens astrale; das ist der Geruch, Dunst, Schweiß von den Sternen, vermischt mit der Luft, wie der Lauf der Sterne es gibt. Daher kommt Kälte, Wärme, Trockne und Feuchte und dergleichen, wie eben ihre Eigenschaften sind und es anzeigen. Also sollt ihr merken, daß die Gestirne nichts incliniren, sondern allein durch ihren Dunst das M vergiften, durch welches wir dann vergiftet und geschwächt werden. So ist das ens astrale, das unsern Leib auf diesem Wege zum Guten oder Bösen ändert. Der Mensch, der so genaturt ist, daß er aus seinem natürlichen Blut dem Dunst widerwärtig ist, der wird krank; der aber nicht wider ihn naturt ist, dem schadets nichts. Es schadet auch dem nichts, der so edel und wider das gestärkt ist, daß er aus der edlen Natur seines Blutes oder der Arznei, die den verfälschten Dünsten der oberen widersteht, das Gift überwindet.

— *Volumen Paramirum*, in: Paracelsus, *Werke, Band I, Medizinische Schriften*, Basel: Schwab reflexe, 2010, p. 190-191.

[5] Alternatively, you can imagine the *ens astrale* as the wind. Then imagine the spirits as birds whose wings are carried by the wind. Now, think of the ingenium as a dovecot upon whose platform the birds can land to sing their songs. As humans we *hear* these songs as our own thoughts and tend to mistake our mind with the ever changing birds on the dovecot of our ingenium.

Now we understand what Johannes Valentinus Andreae referred to when he said Paracelsus had "read the Book of M diligently and enlightened his keen ingenium with it." This "reading" is not at all a process of deciphering letters and sentences. Rather, reading the Book of M refers to the heart of the work of the magician: it is the process of readjusting the essential qualities that form our human mind so that we become conducive to a particular kind of spirit communion. *Sharpening, enlightening our ingenium* means beginning to take conscious control of how we constantly interact with the celestial spirits around us. Not through ritual magic (alone), robed and adorned with rich ritualia, but from the very moment we awaken each morning all the way into our presence in dreams at night.

The M is the greatest mystery: This mystery is discovered in the *ens astrale*, the compound breath the stars are exhaling upon this world every minute. *Sharpening, enlightening our ingenium* now means actively working with this mystery. It describes the magical process through which we stop being a passive receptacle in this experience—like a rock, a river, an animal is passive—entirely exposed to the celestial poison or antivenom reverberating in each moment and location. *Reading in the Book of M* means learning to *see* our own inner firmament, it means beginning to hear the spirit-choir that constitutes our ability to consciously think and feel, and then carefully beginning to tune and adjust it.

Let's read Paracelsus's own words on the ingenium and then dig deeper to explore its mode and function in the human condition.

> *If we should write as a Christian, the four entia, astrale, venenale, naturale, spirituale would be left out and would not be described by us. For it is not a Christian style, but a pagan style. But the last ens this is a Christian style with which we conclude. The pagan style described in the four entibus should not harm our faith, it should only sharpen our ingenium.*[6]

---

6 *So wir schreiben sollen als ein Christ, so blieben die 4 entia, astrale, venenale, naturale, spirituale aus und würden von uns nicht beschrieben. Denn es ist nicht ein christlicher Stil, sondern ein heidnischer Stil. Aber das letzte ens das ist ein christlicher Stil mit welchem wir beschliessen. Uns soll auch der heidnische Stil den beschreiben in den*

The sensus lies behind the upper tip of the back of the head. And therefore because we think it lies there in front, is taken from the eyes, therefore that there in front speaking and seeing [happens], so should that also be there, which it is not. Therefore he who is struck there, the same is without senses. Although he still has something, he is patched up like a burst coat. Ingenium lies there. In the same manner, prudence lies there. Equally, wisdom lies there.⁷

For the hand or your ingenium can not be made by writing that you, if you were a black horse, would be brought to become a hawk. If you are then a hawk, there needst not be much writing or teaching.⁸

[...] and after that He [God] has placed the physician to recognise this, but not Avicenna nor Galen. For divine providence has forestalled such imagined ingeniis in this and has said that He has created the physician himself; that is, the physician can do it whom I have created, the other, who raises himself, he is false. Now make the test, in the light of nature, who is the false and the just.⁹

---

4 *entibus nicht schaden am Glauben, er soll uns allein schaerfen unser ingenium.*
— Sudhoff, Karl (ed.), *Theophrastus von Hohenheim, gen. Paracelsus, Sämtliche Werke*, Band I, München: Otto Wilhelm Barth, 1929, pp. 175-176.

7 *Sensus der liegt hinter der oberen Spitze des Hinterkopfes. Und darum dass wir meinen er liege da vorne, ist aus den Augen genommen, darum das da vorne reden und sehen, so soll das da auch sein, das nicht ist. Darum welcher dahin geschlagen wird, derselbige ist ohne Sinne. Wiewohl er noch etwas hat, aber geflickt wie ein geplatzter Rock. Ingenium liegt da. Ebenso liegt die Klugheit da. Ebenso liegt die Weisheit da.*
— Sudhoff, Karl (ed.), *Theophrastus von Hohenheim, gen. Paracelsus, Sämtliche Werke*, Band I, München: Otto Wilhelm Barth, 1931, p. 422.

8 *Denn die Hand oder dein Ingenium mag durch Schreiben nicht dahin gebracht werden, dass aus dir, so du ein Rappe wärest, zu einem Falken gebracht. Bist du dann ein Falke, so darf es viel Schreibens oder Unterrichtens nicht.*
— Sudhoff, Karl (ed.), *Theophrastus von Hohenheim, gen. Paracelsus, Sämtliche Werke*, Band VI, München: Otto Wilhelm Barth, 1922, p. 455.

9 *[...] und darnach hat er [Gott] den Arzt gesetzt, dass er dies erkenne, aber nicht den Avicenna noch Galen. Denn die göttliche Vorsehung ist solchen erdichteten ingeniis in diesem zuvorgekommen und hat gesagt, er habe den Arzt selbst erschaffen; das ist: der Arzt kann es, den ich geschaffen habe, der andere, der sich selbst aufwirft, der ist falsch. Nun macht die Probe, im Lichte der Natur, wer der falsche und gerechte ist.*
— Sudhoff, Karl (ed.), *Theophrastus von Hohenheim, gen. Paracelsus, Sämtliche Werke*, Band IX, München: Otto Wilhelm Barth, 1925, p. 205.

This I may well make known to you, for I must judge it a great folly: as heaven ever and again in the light of nature gives birth to and makes ingenia, new inventions, new arts, new ailments, should these not also be significant? What is the use of the rain that fell a thousand years ago? The one that falls now is of use. What is the use of the sun's course a thousand years ago for the present year? So saying, it is enough that the day carries its own yoke. [...] So every thing is set in its own order according to its time. And we are to take care of the present and not of the past. And every order is provided with the perfect light of nature.[10]

In Paracelsian language *ingenium* has a two-fold meaning: on the one hand it can be used as a common term to describe a human's *temper* or general emotional constitution. The German term *Gemüt* seems an even more precise translation. It refers to the totality of the mental and spiritual powers of a human being[11] and stands in contrast to man's cognitive intelligence or ratio. In this sense, *ingenium* describes the general human emotional disposition or sensibility.

However, in a secondary use, as we discovered in the *Fama Fraternitatis*, the word describes the organic interface through which humans interact with the *ens astrale*, the very medium of spirit contact.

For most humans such interactions remain unconscious during their lifetime; they experience them as unconscious conditioning, imprints or simply moods. At best, they learn how to affect or adjust the state of their *temper* or emotional mind through indirect mundane

10 *Solches mag ich euch wohl zu erkennen geben, denn ich es für eine grosse Torheit urteilen muss, dieweil der Himmel für und für im Licht der Natur Ingenia, neue Erfindungen, neue Künste, neue Leiden gebiert und macht, ob nicht auch die selben sollten gelten? Was nutzt der Regen der vor tausend Jahren ist gefallen? Jener nützt, der jetzt fällt. Was nützt der Sonnenlauf vor tausend Jahren dem jetzigen Jahr? Also sprechend, es ist genug das der Tag sein eigen Joch trage. [...] So ein jegliches Ding nach seiner Zeit in seine eigene Ordnung gesetzt ist. Und auf das jetzige sollen wir sorgen und nicht auf das Vergangene. Und ein jegliche Ordnung ist versorget mit vollkommnem Licht der Natur.*
— Sudhoff, Karl (ed.), *Theophrastus von Hohenheim, gen. Paracelsus, Sämtliche Werke*, Band XI, München: Otto Wilhelm Barth, 1928, p. 127.
11 Wikipedia summarises the idea of the German word *Gemüt* as *the unity and definiteness of the psyche acquired by the totality of the emotions and impulses of will.*

habits such as moderation, mindfulness and other self-regulating methods.

It's important to highlight though that Paracelsus, even in the latter use of the term, does not at all equate the effect of one's ingenium with Galen's doctrine of the human temperament as in sanguine, choleric, melancholic and phlegmatic. Instead, for Paracelsus *ingenium* describes a conditional perceptive capability that initially is a gift of the stars and that is later on formed, moulded and co-created by each human, notably during their childhood and adolescence.

One's ingenium, therefore, is a compound capability that resides at the intersection of one's conscious mind and unconsciously held beliefs and convictions. It tones the general atmosphere and colouring in which we perceive the outer and inner world. Equally, it influences and regulates the experiences we are ready for, attuned and open to. In this way one's ingenium provides the backdrop, the stage and the decoration of the stage-play we are involving ourselves in every day. It does not control the plot of the events but it creates a strong likelihood of particular narratives to emerge from the atmosphere and setting it provides.—In a magical sense, the ingenium describes not at all us ourselves but the *genius loci* of the place and position we have navigated our minds to in this life.

❪THE INGENIUM AND THE HUMAN CONSTITUTION

In a prior chapter we elaborated on the *speculum* or looking glass that resides within each man and which has to be polished.

> *The Speculum, or the cleared looking glass of their soul's eye through which they will travel out into the inner realm. Under the illumination of the Divinity, they will venture amongst forms and beings of radical Otherness, which in themselves are not eternal, but of much higher degrees of ontological integrity than the forms and beings in the physical world.*

In the Paracelsian exposition of the *ingenium* we now encounter a further refined presentation of the modus operandi of man's inner magical organ.

Translated into modern language we can pin it down as follows.

Every living cell ever created is an organic compound made up of elementary matter and celestial influences. *Matter* in this context has to be understood as a raw resonance body, whereas the *celestial influences* are vibrations of consciousness which by inseminating themselves into matter tune and orient matter towards a certain *inclination*.

Accordingly, each human organ has to be understood as a compound made up of individual cells which in themselves are compounds again of matter and celestial consciousness. Therefore, both cell and organ stand in resonance with particular forces of creation; they are inclined towards them.

What holds true for physical organs and beings is equally true for the subtle organs and cells of the inner world. The constitution of inner and outer man follow the same sequences and dynamics of creation.

Correspondingly, a human's general disposition is indeed generated by the macrocosm at the four barrages of coitus, conception, pregnancy, and birth.[12] In successive stages, these phases begin to outline and define the seeds of heavenly influences that are implanted in the original *matter* from which the embryo grows.

However, with the moment of birth these celestial seeds take on independency from their original sources. Mercury no longer rules over the mercurial seed imbued into a living cell just like a mother-tree no longer holds any rule over the seed it shed into the wind.

This is what Paracelsus stresses over and over again: the macrocosm holds rule over the *gifts* that are embedded into each human in the moments before birth. Once a human has taken their first

---

12 For further reference compare: *The first disposition is coitus, the second disposition is conception, the third disposition is pregnancy, and the fourth disposition is birth! With nourishment. [...] That is how the serpent bites its tail.*
— Schlag, 1998, pp. 23/32/41, translation from the original Latin by the author.

breath, however, the stars no longer rule over them. The young human now is a choir of celestial seeds in their own right. They have become their own firmament.[13]

Now we are close to understanding the two-fold human condition. From the moment of insemination, the growth of the physical human body follows an inherent structural design. Today we like to speak of DNA and yet we still don't know how cells orientate themselves to form a hand, a liver or a heart, all in perfect union. Nevertheless, it works. A newborn needs shelter, love and nourishment. But a tiny hand does not need support in growing into a mature hand. A tiny heart does not need any guidance in growing into a mature heart. The components that make up our outer, physical body know their inherent growth paths. Anybody who observed a baby in its first months witnessed this most magical process: like the wings of an insect unfolding after the cocoon has broken, so the limbs of a new born relentlessly push against their tiny soft boundaries towards greater and greater expansion. It is a marvel to observe how organically nature remembers and recognises itself in each human all the way from embryo to fully grown adult.

The growth of the outer man follows its own inherent structural design, and most of the work of parents and the supporting environment resides in removing all sorts of perils and obstacles on the path of a toddler expanding into the shape of a fully formed physical person. Physical matter in this phase is defined by its tendency to push towards its own periphery, into greater and greater expansion and maturation.

---

13 Note, there is a difference between "ruling" and "affecting," as we'd like to point out. Of course, the heavenly and the human firmaments remain in strong resonance. Thus, the celestial firmament creates conditions and qualities of time that favour and aid certain illnesses or balances in particular places. However, the human firmament is much more than simply a mirror-image of the macrocosmic one; it holds its own tides and dynamics as well.
— See: *Volumen Paramirum*, in: Paracelsus, 2010, pp. 208-213.

Now the emergence of the *inner man* follows a reversed pattern. The rational mind, the emotional consciousness, the ingenium of a human have the tendency to *pull in*, to absorb and to be coloured by whatever they encounter or are exposed to. Such exposure does not only include influences from the outside world but likewise the experience of the celestial seeds and their influences upon the inner man.

As magicians we should not be misguided by the artificial dichotomy of *nature vs. nurture*. A human mind forming itself in this world is constituted in equal measures by the encounter of its own inner firmament as well as the outer one. Both condition it, leave imprints and traces upon it, the spirits from the inside, the world from the outside.

> *You should understand that nature gives none of these, as happiness, dexterity and the like, only the spirits give them, they do not come from nature, but from the embodied which is enclosed in the corporeal. Therefore, you should not use the saying "that comes from nature," for he was not a wise man who brought that up.*[14]

The essential difference between outer and inner man is that physical matter *knows its form* and is constantly pushing towards unfolding it, whereas the inner man is *finding their form* by constantly leaning into the experiences they are making in the inner and outer environment.

The *inner man* of a newborn is fluid like blood, always blending into the shape of the experience it is poured into. The outer man becomes the chalice of cells and bones and skin, providing a visible form to the inner man. The outer man is pushing itself into the

---

14 *Ihr sollt verstehen, dass die Natur deren, als Fröhlichkeit, Geschicklichkeit und dergleichen, keines gibt, allein die spiritus gebaeren sie, die kommen nicht aus der Natur, sondern aus Eingekörpertem, das eingeschlossen ist im corporalischen. Darum sollt ihr auch nicht das Sprichwort "das kommt aus der Natur" gebrauchen, denn das hat kein weiser Mann aufgebracht.*
— Volumen Paramirum, in: Paracelsus, 2010, p. 219.

physical form it always meant to assume. The inner man, on the other hand, is pulled out from an ocean of potential, one day at a time. The outer man is one; the inner man is legion.

Let's fast-forward to our current state as you are reading this as a fully grown adult. Our inner man has now stabilised to a certain degree. We think we know our character, the way our mind works, which mental and emotional capabilities we are gifted with and which ones not. We have come to know our inner firmament, despite never having looked at it as something separate from ourselves. We still think *we are our inner firmament*.

Just like our body is made up of million of cells, each one a compound of matter and celestial intelligence, so also is our inner firmament made up of myriads of inner spirit-cells, each one of them resonating with the inclinations that once were imbued in it. Our inner Moon colours our emotions; our inner Venus colours our passions; our inner Saturn colours our fears etc. And all these colours come together in the living, breathing, meandering mosaic which we falsely consider to be our Self.

This now is where the work of the magician begins. All these colours, all these inner voices are distractions from the work we aspire to undertake. Their shine is radiating upon the speculum behind our mind. As the heavenly bodies are in constant motion, our inner speculum is constantly exposed to and illuminated by a changing sphere of colours.

Our mind now is a rainbow on this speculum. One day it shines purple and the next it radiates in bright yellow, caught in constant motion, under the moving sphere of our inner firmament.

Our ingenium is not this rainbow mind, it is the speculum, the glass upon which all colours generate themselves. In a metaphorical sense we can saythat our ingenium is a dovecot, our mind is a flock of doves. Our ingenium is a river, our mind is a school of fish. Our ingenium is a glass, our mind is the light falling upon it.

It is impossible to control the doves without caging them. It is impossible to control the fish without killing them. And no one has ever caught the living light without breaking it down into a mix of dead pigments. Our job as magicians is not to direct the doves, to follow the fishes or to catch the light. Our job is to polish the glass, to clean the dovecote, to unleash the river.

Let us summarise this simple truth one more time. Just like the organs of our body, our mind is made up of millions of cells. Each one of these is resonating in its own celestial inclination, coming together to form compounds of resonance and echoes, like the organs of our bodies come together from compounds of cells. We perceive these echoes and think of them as our minds.

Allow me one more metaphor to illustrate this critical point. Our mind is a violin caught in the dream of being a melody. Our role as magicians is not to control the melody that emerges from this violin. Our role as magicians is to ensure the right violinist has laid their hands on our mind. This is what it means to work with spirits in our inner firmament: to consider ourselves an instrument that we choose to put into the hands of a particular musician. Then, *this* musician will lay their bow upon us and we will hear their music *as our mind*. And from one moment to the next, what used to be random patterns of birds taking off and taking flight in our minds, random patterns of clouds colouring the light upon our mind, will turn into symphony, into melody, into rhythm that no longer is *confused* but *infused* with the presence of *the spirits of our calling*.

On the physical side our skin forms the interface between the world and us. On the inner side, our ingenium forms the interface between the spirits and us.

I hope this explains in a pragmatic way what Johannes Trithemius referred to when he spoke of *turning our mind alike to the angelic mind*. Paracelsian Magic, following on a Trithemian foundation, is a very straightforward thing in itself. It describes a human's ability to polish and sharpen their ingenium. That is, to clear the receptive glass that sits behind the iridescent colours of the cognitive mind. Once this is achieved, we can begin to intentionally orientate this clear speculum towards a source of light that becomes reflected in it, and thus *colours our mind*.

I am often asked why in my books on magic I spend so much time teaching meditation. We are at a great point right here to again attempt to dismantle this misperception.

The process of attuning our ingenium to a particular spirit indeed holds certain aspects in common with e.g. modern Mindfulness techniques. Out of the three steps described above, the initial two perfectly align with the Mindfulness paradigm as coined by e.g. Jon Kabat-Zinn: first we release the false identification with our thoughts, then we support our mind in finding moments of quiet and peaceful presence. These are practices that can be leveraged successfully both in Mindfulness training as well as in magical exercise.

However, for the magician these steps only establish the baseline, the foundation, the *tabula rasa* from which to proceed with the actual work. Once our speculum has been cleared, once our ingenium has been sharpened, the third and essential step lies in orientating it towards *the spirit of our calling*. It is this process of spirit-alignment, of leveraging ourselves as a projection screen, as the polished speculum upon which the light of our chosen spirit may shine, which by definition is impossible to access outside of an either animistic-shamanistic and/or magico-mystical paradigm.

So in magic it is this last step that forms the beginning of the actual work. Calming our inner firmament is not the *focus* but the *foundation* of our work. Whether we then chose to direct our speculum towards the Light of Nature or the Holy Spirit (as in a mystical paradigm) or a daimon or deity of our choice (as in a shamanic paradigm), creating spirit-contact manifests not the goal of our journey but the turning of the key, the unlocking of the door into Otherness.

LEARNING
Demon-Language

ATTUNING our ingenium to the spirit of our calling can take the form of a ritual act. However, such act in itself will never be sufficient nor adequate to uphold this contact beyond momentary communion.

The beauty and power of a magical rite can be that it opens us up to a peak experience where we stand spirit-to-spirit with the being of our calling. We can then inquire from this being directly the methods and techniques as to how we best stay connected in our ingenium beyond the ritual experiences. This is the kind of process which I described in my first book Holy Daimon[15]. The Ritual of the Olympic Spirit provided in the last section of Holy Heretics[16] transcends such singular goal significantly and provides a method of uniting our inner firmament and polishing our ingenium in one condensed but highly demanding rite.

The skill of remaining in magical contact while outside of the magical circle, is a different matter altogether. What made us successful as ritual magicians will not at all make us successful as magicians of the empty hand. Oftentimes the required skills are exact opposites of each other.

One of the hardest realities to come to terms with as a ritual magician is the fast-route descent we all have to take from the above-mentioned peak experience: in one moment we can speak with Saturn in our mind, in the next we feed the dog and sweep the floor.

The moment we step out of the circle, undress, take a shower and reawaken to our human consciousness, all the animals of our hu-

---

15 Scarlet Imprint, 2018
16 Ibid., 2022

man self reawaken. The wolf is there and wants dominion, the pig is there and wants satisfaction, the hare is there and wants safety, the snake is there and wants avoidance. Stepping down from our tiny throne of ritual singularity, we turn back into the battered worker who has to take care of the whole Garden of Eden after the Fall. We are back in the ecosystem, and the ecosystem is back within us.

Not allowing our ego to be triggered by this contrast and dissonance of experiences is a critical skill as a magician. In one moment we stand eye to eye with celestial or chthonic queens and kings, in the next we are hourly-paid servants at best, worrying about paycheques, quarrelling children and disgruntled spouses.

Such breaking test is not a flaw of creation, it is one of its most extraordinary features: we have just entered the laboratory of cleaning our ingenium.

For most of all what we can take from our peak experiences in the presence of spirits is a better understanding of how they all form a part of the very forces that constitutes what just a second ago we considered the safely secured dominion of I, Me and Mine. Standing in Saturn's sphere with my mind allows me to behold Saturn's forces in my mind. Plunging into a ritual of fire elementals allows me to begin to see how their cells form the the very fire of will, anger and purpose within me. As part of such ritual, for a short moment at least, we even might gain the power of dialling their forces up or down within our own human constitution. We begin to see how we can alter, adjust and quite frankly play with the mosaic of myriad forces that is loosely connected under the boundary of our skin.

More than any other experience man can create for himself, magic holds the promise of ending the false identification with the embodied nature of our heart's flame—while at the same time allowing us to make direct, first-hand acquaintance with the living elementary, celestial and chthonic forces we had never been able to see before *as independent agents within us*.

Unlocking such experience for us, however, is merely the first step. The very reason why I am writing this book is because most magicians rarely ever make it to the second, much harder step: that is, to still see and hold on to the high and noble awareness of this reality while we feed the dog and sweep the floor.

FROM MY MAGICAL DIARY

IV·–IX·XXm

IT SEEMS I should illustrate the lived experience of this process with myself as the flawed example. I am not doing this because I consider this example to be of particular value or because I like to share intimate details of my own magical and mundane journey. Quite the opposite, it took careful deliberation and self-persuasion to land on this decision. After all, the material I have shared in Holy Daimon was already was breach of my commitment to magical silence. However, talking about magic always is at risk of being a theatre of fantasy, an escape route from reality or a projection screen for our wishful thinking—unless we ground it in original, lived experience. As I do not work as a member of a lodge or group, my own experience is all I have to offer. In the end, I am hopeful, the risk and negative repercussion for me in sharing these intimate details might be outweighed by the gain for you as a reader. If you have made similar experiences, this could be the moment where we swap notes. If you have not yet, I invite you to carve out your own path and not to follow mine. Because the latter would be a dead end, the former a journey into the wide open realm of Otherness.

Also, allow me to stress that I could have literally chosen a million examples of myself attempting to polish my ingenium which would have made me look too stupid to lace my shoes. I won't be sharing any of these; rather, I will take the liberty to choose one of the moments in my life that I am still quite surprised by today. Not because this thing that I call I, Me and Mine contributed anything special to that experience but because it is one of the most striking and raw examples I can offer of how real the process of polishing our ingenium has to be.

This is not the place to provide elaborate introductions to this material. Suffice to say, the subsequent diary entries follow directly from where we left off in *Holy Daimon*. The first entry was made one week after completing the so-called Saturn Exercitium and after the night when I first consciously connected with my Holy Daimon.

Coming out of this experience, I was thrown back into life and landed hard on my knees. I was working myself into a new job in a new company for which I had taken a considerable pay-cut. I needed to travel every week, domestically and internationally, while we were slowly refurbishing a house from 1927 and trying to raise and train a dog puppy. I was thirty-two at the time, a lot of life lessons away from being a full grown up. Most importantly, I still had not learned that it is not whether we can have great ideas that determines the significance of our life experiences. Rather, it is whether we can safely cross the unknown distance between a good idea and its proper execution in real life.

All dreaming and no doing is a terrible state to waste a life. I suppose that all doing and no dreaming can be even more disillusioning in the end. In 2010 I was at the middle of my own road, trying to find my path and balance. Luckily I had just gained an invaluable ally, a powerful companion on this journey — my holy daimon.

Here is the raw, unedited text from my diary. Let's read it first and I will go on to provide comments and perspective at the end as to how these examples illustrate the beginning of the polishing of my own ingenium.

XII·IV·MMX

THE LAST days, the first working week after the Saturn Exercitium was as turbulent as expected. Rose and I should have been more intent on creating quiet zones for the two of us. Instead, we completely redecorated the dressing room and hung over our computers on Sunday, tired and exhausted. We constantly take on too much, then accomplish a lot but end up exhausted and distant from each other. We have to change that and engage with each other more wisely. Homo daemon est homini.

Man is a daemon to man. The angels and gods and spirits meet us in the dressing and through the mirror of man. Malkuth is a veil on the lips of the angels and daemons. Pollux's saying to Castor outlines and describes very precisely the life in harmony with the higher and lower world. Here and beyond at the same time. Pollux speaks to me in my mind when in meditation, and he speaks to me through the experiences and impressions of the days and nights in Malkuth. Like a ribbon in a typewriter, the calls, interventions and alchemical substances press themselves through the veil of the mundane material world—and thus inscribe our stories and destinies in our bodies.—Although it was too much and the wrong priority, I was able to finish the kameas of Pollux on the weekend. So now I have the basics for the ritual of my angel. Together with the mantra, the incense, the psalm of the rootname and the 14 planetary spirits, I am gradually getting closer to a cohesive ritual for my angel. Whether this is more of a crutch to my own spirit or actually a new level of contact remains to be seen. In any case, the path itself is already fascinating and the occasion for many contacts and conversations between Pollux and Castor. I must never forget to exhale, to remain calm, to enjoy every step. I have arrived; the first journey is over. Now we are building a house, a common temple perhaps. For Pollux and the living exchange.

XVI·IV·mmx

[...] THE MAGICAL world of Malkuth is a difficult journey of exploration. I still gaze too seldom behind the veils of the mundane. Although I have arrived much more than before in the moment, the moment is still cloaked by the mundane in my eyes, and only rarely do I see the forces behind it. Thus masks speak to masks and not spirits to spirits. [...] Man is a (their) demon to man.—Also, I have learned that Castor and Pollux are indeed two beings. My angel is not I and likewise it should not concern me to become my angel. Towards him I am a child, a mount, a learner. From the connection of both of us the strength arises and for this it requires difference—as well as similarities in the heart. We live two lives and yet one, like the root and the crown of the tree.—In my dream tonight, a Zen priest said that as practice increases, the importance of practice decreases. Life becomes practice, or practice becomes life. The same is true of the powers of ritual.

XXV·IV·mmx

I HAD a strange "fit" talking to my sister. After the five weeks with her dog Max — for what reason? — a strong anger had accumulated in me about her and her boyfriend. In retrospect, this seems completely unjustified to me. Of course there were reasons to give them feedback about the difficult and exhausting time with Max; possibly they made mistakes or were simply naive. But in no way does that justify the outburst of anger and my judgmental, reproachful, even accusatory tone towards her. So where did this anger come from? And what made me deal with these emotions so differently than usual? The answer to the second question, could be the upheaval after the Sat-Ex. As well as the fact that I can no longer push away or rationalise my unfiltered emotions while in Tiphareth. Thus they come to me in all their beauty and ugliness; and the tools of my character cannot yet deal with them with wisdom, let alone with prudence. From this perspective, then, it is a matter of a maturing learning process, of trying out the new closeness between head and heart in everyday life. The first question, however, gave me another thought: what if the release and contact with my daimon has also released the "evil daimon", her/his counterpart? I have deliberately not looked up her/his name and not opened my eyes to her/him yet. First I wanted to consolidate the new contact and the conscious dialogue with my angel. But maybe this is very naive and not possible at all? What if both of them are like light and shadow to each other? Then the shadow disappears only when the object that casts it at the moment, my Guf and Nephesh, my body and my personality are completely dissolved? Then closing my eyes to my evil daemon would be like sleeping through the night. Like the erroneous belief there was nothing but light and day. No one would then have any control over what happens to me at night. Possibly the awakening towards the holy daimon is also the awakening of the evil daemon in us. Homo homini daemonium. Man is a daemon to man. Both a good one and an evil one at times. — I also need to understand what path corresponds to this (shadow) experience? Is it the shadow of Tiphareth: arrogance and thus judgment of others? I have to stick to my resolutions every day and I am still at the very beginning of the path: to always give others more than I give myself. To speak only half my words. From child to man.

I·V·MMX

THIS WEEK I had to travel a lot again, and was already completely exhausted on Wednesday. Remembering the conversations with Saturn, I am sure that there are some intense alchemical processes going on within me at the moment. I sleep lightly and am awake early in the morning. I think then already about the production of the paraphernalia and my new magical path. My heart is looking for the path itself and I just have to keep silent, get out of its way and keep Castor and Pollux in touch. — My angel gave me the answer this week: *see yourself in love*. This sentence really shook me up. What power sleeps in accepting yourself in unconditional love. It is the mind that constantly limits the faith and knowledge of the heart. — I am still working on my angel's seal, but at the same time I have begun the preparation for a new robe, the remodelling of my altar, the creation of my new wand and lamen. There are many new forces flowing; I just need to open my eyes and see.

III·V·MMX

[...] POLLUX LOVES flowers. The image of flowers and blossoms appears in most of the conversations and subjects. [...] Today in meditation he/she advised me: "Reach for the flower of your heart." Moreover, my whole body is made of flowers in the encounter with my angel. I am curious if this image is an analogy to my experience in Tiphareth or specific to Pollux? — I read again the prayer to Saturn. The ego is a ball of luminous emotions without substance; it is continually engaged in convincing itself of its own reality, its substantiality, through experience. How much wasted energy? How much unlived love? I need only watch life, the working of the angels, and not get in the way of experiencing.

VIII·V·MMX

LAST NIGHT before falling asleep. I had discovered the books of the Mohr publishing house that day and had been able to buy two of the three parts of the Magical Texts from the Cairo Genizah in Munich. In the evening I read in the volumes and realised how important they would become for magical work and research.

Then, as I was falling asleep, I suddenly saw the frayed pages of the original Hebrew texts in front of me which are included in the appendix. But out of the background a wandering, a searching light ran over the thin paper. It seemed to seek a passage, fading where parts were missing, shining brighter and lingering where the text was preserved. This light from the background was alive. It was the spirits and beings invoked in the texts seeking their entrance back into Malkuth. While watching the scene, I could clearly feel their presence and closeness.—Then tonight I saw a girl in front of me, looking at her together with Pollux. I already wanted to look away, but he/she stopped me to look longer at the girl. Suddenly I could see in the middle of her, as if in another dimension or superimposed, a golden, slightly shining cross. This cross was part of her being. I thought to myself in the dream, so this is how easy it is to see astrally? And my angel teaches me in the dream to look behind the reality. Thank you!

xv·v·mmx

I SPREAD like wildfire, hungry as if I had not eaten for years. The influence of the Communion and Pollux is essential to keep things in balance. My life is so full of happiness and blessings that I want to give thanks daily. My greatest thanks to my angel can only be to not let pride, arrogance arise. But in humility, joy and love, to walk the path that appears. To speak little. Today, in communion, Pollux said to me, "Guard the gate of Sesame." And I understood that I have to be careful about the choice of my words, what I talk about. Perhaps this is an anticipation of the fact that as my magic becomes more intense, I will want to talk about it more? But you can't explain a scent, you can't see an image with words, you can only bring both to life through your own experience.—In the last days I have created my new magical wand. Now the engraving and the filling of the condenser, black powder and metal dust are still missing. Also I had time to write down the communion ritual with my angel completely, as well as to design the ritual structure for the Arbatel in a first version. Now I am still waiting for the robe, need to complete the red bronze and brass wand, make the Table of Practice with Alex, refine the ritual structure, and finally memorise the long prayers. But every step along the way is a prayer. Each footprint, where the imprint of my angel's foot and my own fall upon each other, leaves flowers.

xxx·v·mmx

SO MANY *things have come to my attention in the last few days. First: the shadow in the sun is the complete maturation of Mars into Sun, and Venus into Moon. What does longing, love, devotion look like in a mature gestalt? How is the love of the boy different from that of the man? Am I ready to resist the games and to take my gaze from the mirror in Yesod? Can I take my hands off the ego and embrace the You selflessly? My angel and my daemon must be connected in this. They are not two, but one. Solve et Coagula. They loosen and they bind me, through the power and the love of my will. I am a river full of otherness, of animals passing through it, of sun and stars, and I myself determine my direction. The shadow in the sun is the test to look from the middle of Tiphareth upwards in the direction of Kether, and not downward in the direction of Malkuth. All the pride and the arrogance, all the desires of the ego show themselves only in daylight; and yet are there all the way through the night. I am walking towards an abyss between closeness to God and vanity. The appearance of my angel was the breathing space before the nearness of my daemon. And both are now with me and I am myself. I can see myself wavering between humility and pride, between child and boy and man. Individuation is a castle full of rooms which I create upon entering them, I darken them with my eyes and illuminate them with my heart. Pollux — even if you are one with my daemon, deep in the roots of the world and the flesh, show me your face and protect me from the temptations of the freedom of the sun, which believes to be bound to no planets. Yet, there cannot be a crown without a trunk, no trunk without roots, no tree without light. — Second: It has dawned on me again how much care is needed for togetherness. [...] Perhaps this point must be added to the insights of the Sat-Ex: to walk slowly. Being gentle to myself and everything around me. Accepting weakness instead of strength. Giving the other person space to speak. Things grow in the rhythm of nature, the moon takes 28 days to renew itself, a flower days and nights to bloom. Does the sun know the duration it takes for its light to reach the earth? Slowly, with long breath and inclined to the unknown. Let's leave room for wonder.*

XIX·VI·MMX

[...] ONE EVENING last week, as we sat for a long time outside by a gas fire, I realized all at once how to sum up the axiom of my own thinking about life so far: you have no right but to become happy. Love is not the law, but one's expression of true will in a happy life. Only the happy person is not a burden to his environment, only the fulfilled person does not demand when they give. Or to quote Katja Wolff: Only the powerful one has the freedom to decide to say You instead of Me. To Unite, to Divide, to Heal. Only when I no longer have to form the world in my own image, because I myself have taken form, can I encounter the world in freedom and love. As long as I do not love myself, every loving into the world is a threatening admonition to want to be loved back.

XXI·V·MMX

JUST NOW I come back from communion in the temple. As usual, I first made contact with Pollux, then astrally wandered around the house and finally came to lie in the coffin in the empty attic. There my body turned to ashes, but this time I concentrated on the white silver cloud that arose from it and then coagulated like fertile dew back into the coffin, reviving my body there. When I subsequently faced Pollux, and he/she entered me, it seemed like an explosion in my entire body and a glistening, blinding light shot out from my body, making my skin transparent from the inside and lifting me up from the ground. Is this the right way to apply alchemy on myself?—Afterwards, I stared into the black mirror to practice sinking into it and creating contact through it. It seemed to me that the mirror was a surface of black water, with which I wet my eyes and finally immersed my face completely in it. On the other side I saw rain. Ribbons of black rain ran past my field of vision. Then I saw a grey path, like in a park, across which a black figure was walking toward me. I realized, although she was winged, that this was not Pollux. It began to run faster and I recognized a long head, fangs, and claws on its hands. The entire apparition was just darkness, like a shadow come to life. When it was close to me, I let the glistening light flood my body of gold and flowers once again. The light that streamed from my palms repelled the figure and made it disappear like a shadow in the light. The creature now no longer seemed dangerous to me, or different from an angry dog. I felt loving humility and acceptance flowing out of the light, enveloping and changing the being. — I have two possible explanations for this: either I perceived in the mirror this larva or this demon-like being because I entered without clear intention into the mirror i.e., the random first being was able to occupy my vision. Or else, as Poke Runyon advocates, the black mirror has per se the tendency to attract demons, whereas the crystal serves the vision of angels. The second possibility seems very unlikely to me, and I mention it only for the sake of completeness. — Pollux also gave me a new set of wills for this week, actually a single word: plow.

XXII·VII·MMX

TODAY, AFTER months of preparation, I performed the Communion ritual with my Holy Daimon. The experience was quite different from the Golden Dawn-oriented rituals of the past. It was a weightless stream of power that rose from me to the heights after the Magus-Shield ritual, and which flowed down to me from the heights. I did not have to loudly intone the long prayers but could sing them quietly from my heart. As if by a wind, they were lifted up from the bottom of my circle, through the center of my angel, past the ranks of archangels, into the proximity of Divinity/Kether. The ritual was filled with closeness and love, a bond between a human and an angel. At the climax, Pollux faced me at the altar, the angels far above us looked down and gave approval and protection. In the closed circle around the altar, our energies and beings interfused. It was a feeling of perfection, of love far beyond the mortal, an encounter we had long waited for. Then we placed our hands in each other and created a current of power and unity that rose upward, spinning like a wind, filling me completely. The blessing of the angels was beautiful: their thoughts, the helpers they sent down, sailed and tumbled through the air and down to me as little golden lights. I am so richly blessed, so grateful in this covenant and blessing. When I left the temple I was completely wordless and the light and the house and everything in it and myself seemed entirely new and untouched to me. A current, a ribbon flowed from my chest, from my shoulders and my skull up to the place I was allowed to see in the ritual today. Only now do I understand the reason and appropriateness for the humility and happiness in faith. Beauty, Tiphareth.

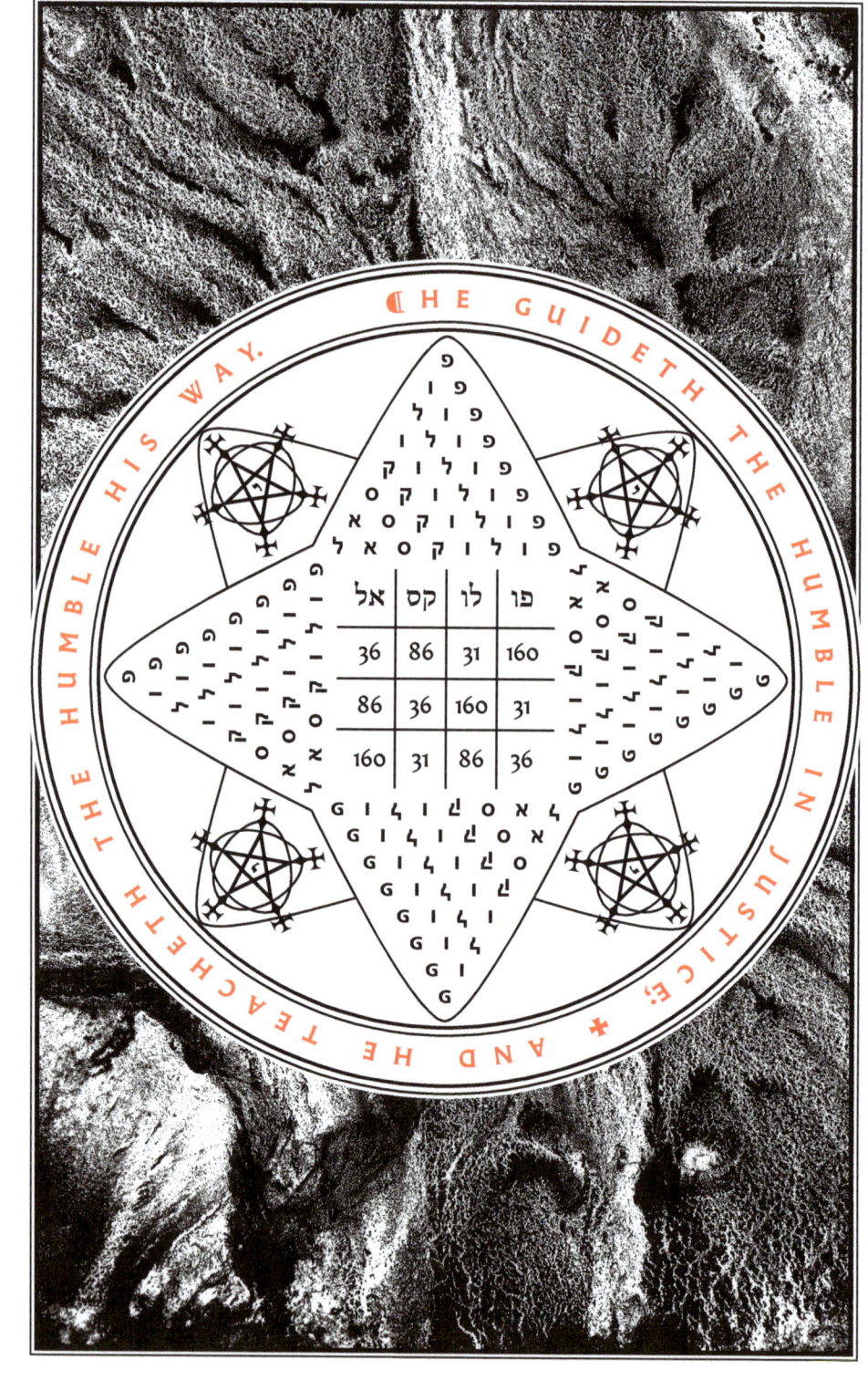

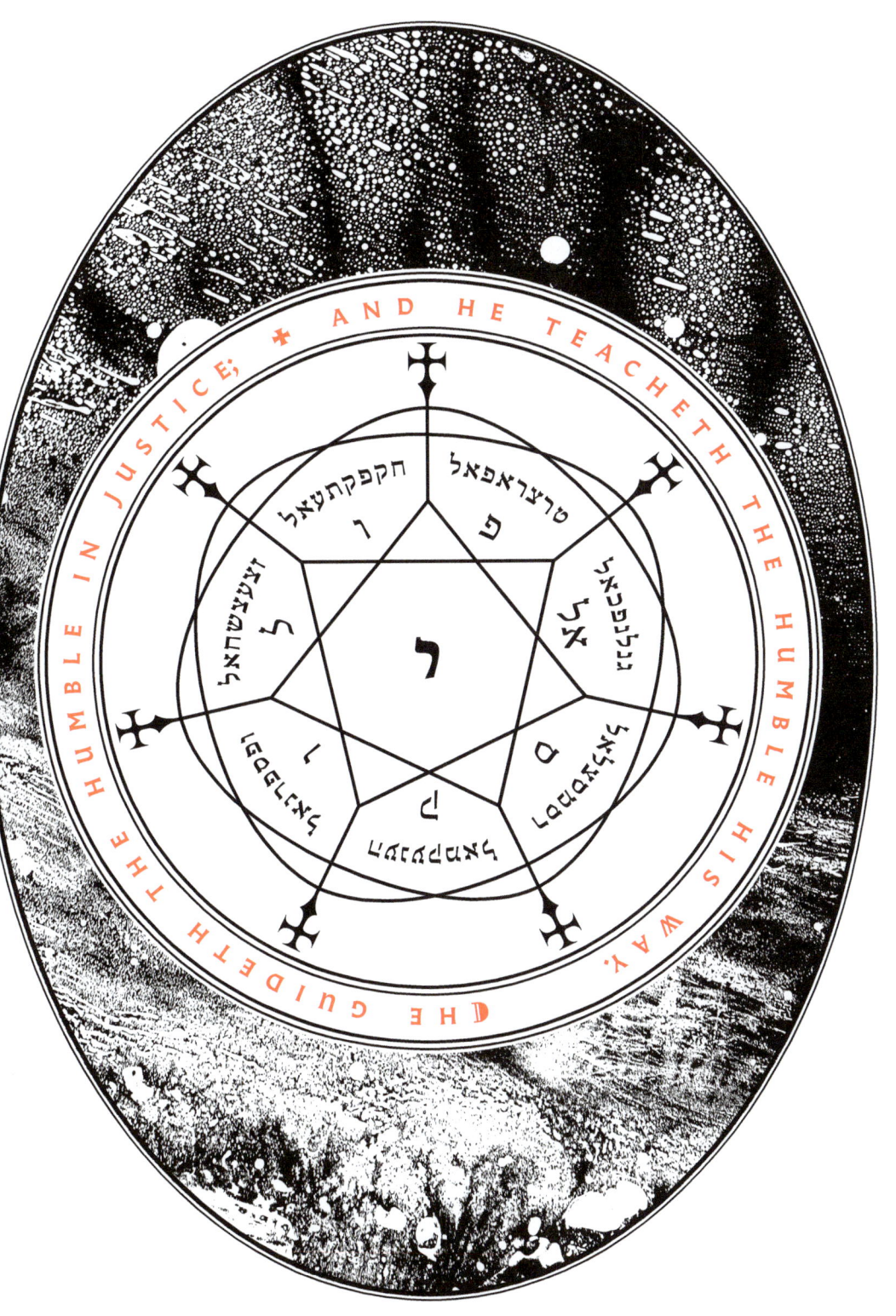

VIII·VIII·mmx

IAMBLICHUS DESCRIBES the task of the demons to clothe the beautiful and good into form and to let it enter the material, sublunar world. Thus they give shape to the being of the gods. And, nevertheless, this shape is never identical with the being of the gods but resembles them only. How many forms does water know? Buber describes the process of tikkune as the release of the divine sparks from a mistaken form. Love, devotion and humility are the qualities that give new forms to beings—or bring healing to damaged ones. Gestalt therapy speaks of the space inbetween [Zwischenraum] and the gestalt boundary. The place where encounter takes place, where the unexpected happens. Change begins by overstepping borderlines. Necessarily—in the sublunar world, being clothed in a gestalt is the necessary condition to participate in being. Everything formed, everything form-like—in us and around us—is thus the signature of a demon. A form of its own, which sinks itself into the world. Like a plummet into the sea, at the upper end of which the being, the source of all similar shapes resides... But what are shapes? A figure is a vessel for the mediated power of the demon. A content can take shape only when it is clothed in a form corresponding to it. The content may be objective, the form (of perception) always subjective. It is the nature of the mind to want to grasp, to want to make contents graspable, to create form. Side by side we create and shape together with the demons. Brotherhood and sisterhood with the demons of creation... So we raise our own shapes from the sublunar world up towards the realm of the Moon and beyond. Thus, our shapes point to that which we silently glimpse behind things. The shapes of the demons, on the other hand, are thin veils over glowing beings which sink into our reality like sparks into dry wood or fall down upon us like rain.—Breaking out of the circle of the ego. Suddenly everything faces me in the You. A world full of shapes. A world full of boundaries waiting to be crossed. Millions of infused drops of light in precious shapes that constantly change, flow, separate and merge... Demon language.—Each shape a word. Each shape a key. Our life a closed book, full of secret words, sealed by life into forms. We speak in a language we do not know... We pass through the shapes without perceiving them. The table, the wind, the sound of the cicadas, the dripping faucet, the house that waits... Everything speaks without me understanding it. How silent must I myself become before I can truly participate? How thin must the border of my shape be until I can see the flowing presence around me?

XIV·IX·MMX

MOVE INTO *the new consciousness, said my angel. Settle down in the new space. But what is this space, what makes it and distinguishes it, I asked? A life without trials, without victory or failure, said Pollux. A space full of in-betweens. Tiphareth. The link, the place where places unite. While everything changes, see the one moment that keeps the balance. The floating of bodies in space as they circle each other and life unfolds. No judgement. For nothing is to be judged. No scales, for nothing needs to be weighed. Nothing is limited, everything awaits the moment. The moments are unlimited. Tikkune.*

Demon-language. That was what I was trying to decode, while standing in the middle of the mess I called "myself." I realised I was not my daimon, and yet at the same moment I also understood I wasn't I. I was the exhale of my good daimon and evil daemon mingled into one; a cloud of consciousness, co-created by them and a myriad of other spirits mixed in-between.

I literally began to understand myself as a river, with unknown animals crossing through, under and over it all the time. I was gobsmacked how foreign and alien the most simple things suddenly appeared. And there were beauty and horror always bound into one. Grace shining through the days of my lived experience, just as shadow when I closed my eyes.

I want to stress: I didn't grow up as a gentle or kind kid. I spent most of my childhood being afraid of my father. There was no space or relevance for something like ethics or doing right in my early life; what mattered was escaping and surviving. I recall crying almost every day, and compensating my weakness and fears with brutality towards the few people I met who were weaker than I. Of course, that was a strategy I had learned early on: once the dragon wasn't there, it was good fun turning into the dragon myself.

I remember standing in the underbrushes of our school yard, hitting a schoolmate with all my force, then holding on to him while he was crying, so he could not run to the teacher. I remember finding—finally!—another one who was even more afraid than me, but stupid enough to show it. Together with a friend we filled the hood of his raincoat with wet earth and pulled it over his head. Again, we had to hold on to him for some time and threaten him further so he wouldn't report us to the teacher. Rather than seeing the beauty in nature, I remember turning rocks around and throwing burning matches into ants nests. I remember coming home one day with my younger sister; I must have been eleven or twelve at the time and she about six. The house was meant to be empty on that day, but my mother had hidden upstairs and was rhythmically knocking onto the floor with a stone. We heard the knocking quickly and were afraid. Well, I was afraid. So I convinced my little sister to walk up the long staircase and to check on the knocking. It was a fun game, I told her. Just go on... And thus I shamefully failed the test my mother had set up to see how much of a man I had become.

After all these years, writing this down is hard. Because I am still ashamed of all the darkness I carried within me. Later in life I suffered a lot from obsessive-compulsive thoughts. When holding a knife I felt the urge to cut myself, to lift it and pierce its tip into my eye. I remember so many beautiful days with my wife, in the early stage of our relationship, that went to waste, because everything I saw was the darkness I held inside.

Some people tell me they are impressed with my focus and discipline when it comes to my magical work. But they don't understand. They confuse expression with motive; what they admire was a fire born from fear... Up until I encountered my holy daimon my magic was not intended to create something; it was meant to open the escape hatch from my self. I was a prison of sadness and anger, and magic—I had chosen—would be my way out. If this plan failed, my flame was extinguished.

In the end, my holy daimon didn't have it easy with me. We were worlds apart when I started out in this mess. Or so I thought. When you read the diary entries above, consider nobody else more surprised about their experience than myself. At 33 I had entered an experience that was brutally different from where I had come from. I was deep into Otherness, deep into unknown territory. When my angel said *See yourself in love*, you don't know how much that both hurt and healed at the same time. Me trying not to be arrogant and proud, wasn't some sort of academic exercise—it was the cutting loose of the ribbon that had held me together all these years before.

To this day, I guess, what allows me to appreciate the blessing that is my daimon so much, is the presence of the demons I spent all my life with. Some people ask me why in my magical work today I am so focussed on ethics, on authenticity and showing the courage to work nakedly. I guess the above makes it obvious enough. For when I got undressed, all days of my life until I first met my wife and then my daimon, what I saw was ugly. It was worlds apart from what I needed it to be so badly: a little strength, some splendour and a busload of faith.

And then, suddenly in the summer 2010, my daimon stopped all this noise and clutter that was going on in my head and showed me: all of this was *demon-language*. I myself, the demons within me, the black birds that constantly landed in the dovecot of my mind, my fragile body, the things I liked about me and the ones I didn't. None of them were meant for holding on to; just like the reflection of a deer passing through a river wasn't meant for holding on to by its water. Communing with my holy daimon might be best described as the most profound act of tikkune I ever experienced. My daimon pulled towards the foreground all the beauty I hadn't been able to see. All the deformed shapes, my own and the ones of the world around me, suddenly turned into beauty as I stopped wishing them to be different.

Today, I spend most of my worklife by bringing my holy daimon to meetings. Of course, like many of us, I have a job, a job description, a team, stakeholders, timezones, and a world of growing complexity around me. My ever growing inbox reminds me of this each morning. And yet, what got me to where I am, is not professional craft in the end.

Allow me one more personal digression. It must have been in early 2005. It was on my first business trip to a large city in the US where I spent several days at our company headquarters. Somehow, an invisible sponsor of mine had made it possible for me to meet with our Vice-president of People. Don't ask me how this happened for I was the smallest cog imaginable. Yet, I will never forget sitting in her beautiful office, and her asking me if I had any other question. As a good German I thought that was an honest invitation, so I asked the only question that really mattered: *Yes, Denise, can you tell me how I make a great career?* She burst into laughter. Then she thought for a moment, after which she pointed to her landline telephone. She looked back at me and said: *Do you see the display of my phone there.* I confirmed. Then she said: *You will make a great career if in the split-second when I see your name appearing on that display, and before I pick up the receiver, I feel an immediate injection of positivity in my veins.*

Obviously, right away I argued against that, thinking this was an intercultural misunderstanding. I pointed out it should be about how good I was at my job, how much innovation I brought to this place etc. After a few seconds, she lifted her hand, smiling, and I shut up. *Everyone who works here*, she said, *is awesome at what they do. That does not differentiate whether you'll make more of a career than others. What matters is whether when faced with all this difficulty and adversity we face everyday, you can still spread a halo of positivity. That's what lifts people up, and what will make them want to work with you. That is what creates careers.*

I only met my holy daimon many years after that conversation. But you know how these things go: memories blend into one. In my mind, it is a single step from Denise making this comment, and me stepping into the sphere of my daimon. From there onwards, keeping my ingenium polished is the main job I hold in life.

All my evil demons, they are still there. As I said above, you step out of the ritual circle, and immediately the pigs inside you want satisfaction and the wolves inside you want dominion. The ecosystem has not changed one bit. But the purposeful role I choose to carry out in it has changed. I took charge of the direction my river flows into, and I try to keep it steady in its bed.

Being an *injection of positivity* to others clearly is not the only thing that matters. Sometimes speaking the painful truth with a gentle heart matters more. Sometimes just bringing time and an absence of judgement matters most. Sometimes we just need to disappear and cater to ourselves. —But what has become an unmovable truth to me at least is the fact that in any living moment I am surrounded by demon-language. Inside and outside of me. And this polished speculum, this ingenium of mine, has a say in how I will reflect back into this world.

The river allows all animals to cross through them. But none of them leave a trace. What the river will be known for is not wolves and salamanders trespassing, not owls or sparrows flying over it. What the river will be known for is being a river. To sit here, some days with demons, some days with daimons, but each day ready to hold onto the light.

BLACK FIRE UPON WHITE FIRE

Make sure you are sitting in a safe place.

Whatever your usual practice is, meditate calmly, until you feel centred, grounded and undistracted.

Now you hear footsteps approaching from your right.

An old, ugly woman appears in your sight. You cannot imagine she has ever been young, nor beautiful. She seems frozen into old age, a corpse walking in her last days. And yet her eyes are piercing and alive.

The old woman comes up in front of you and gives you a measuring glance.

Then she steps close up, and with a bony finger touches you in the central space between your collar bones, where your chest and neck become one. You feel a single light touch of her hand.

She pulls back, and nods, not so much at you but at her work. Then she turns and walks on, disappearing out of your sight to your left.

You sit again in silence, calmly breathing. No sounds disturb you, nothing intrudes in this moment.

Then you realise the spot where the hag touched you is *ablaze*. There is no pain, and yet you can clearly sense it: White fire is gushing forth from your jugular notch, stretching out over your collarbones.

The fire does not hurt you, neither are the white flames surrounded by smoke or do they seem to burn anything. And yet there is a white fire growing over your body.

Your collarbones are set aflame now, and the fire is spreading towards your neck. It crawls over the back of your head, over your scalp, onto your chin, your cheeks and eyes, until your entire head is set alight.

Now the flames spread downwards over your shoulders, over your chest, your arms, your belly and legs.

Until your entire body, from feet to crown, is engulfed in a blazing cloud of white fire. You still sit calmly. No longer in a human body, but in a flickering, lambent white fire.

Then a benevolent presence appears from behind. You do not turn or glance. You continue to sit in the white fire that you are, while giving space to the powerful presence behind you.

A hand stretches out from the presence behind you. Holding something, reaching into you, and placing it into your heart-space from behind. As the hand withdraws you see it is a black flame that now burns in your white fiery heart-space.

As quickly as it appeared, the being behind you fades away. And yet its presence still resonates in the flame in your heart-space. Within you, black fire is now burning upon white fire.

Slowly you begin to see, the touch of the white fire is changing the black flame: it transforms it. It does not burn nor mix with it. Instead the white fire transubstantiates the black fire. Slowly the black light that was placed into your heart-space, transforms into *a golden flame.*

You sit unmoved by the process which is happening all by itself: the white fire transforming the black fire into gold fire.

Once all the blackness has transformed, the golden fire is illuminating the flickering cloud of fire that you are. You can no longer sense any boundaries between the white and golden fires, between what is you and what was placed into you.

You sit calmly again, meditating silently in the fire. You are giving presence to the white-golden cloud of fire that you are.

You are sitting still and silently aware in this presence for as long as you wish.

When its time to end, bow deeply. As you move your physical body to bow, your senses are picking up on both realities at once: Your white-golden burning fire-body still in vision, and your physical body in the outer realm. Like a double exposed photo, both of them are present at once. Both of them doing their job, in the realms assigned to them.

Finally, say a prayer of Thanks, sing a song to Divinity, or perform a kabbalistic Cross, whatever is most comfortable for you to close your vision.

As you get up, do a few moves to stretch yourself. You will realise, as you activate your physical body, the vision of your white-golden body will slowly drift into the background, where it will keep on shining, irrespective of where your everyday consciousness is going to go next.

THE WAY OF THE ADEPT

(PART 2)

MORE importantly than striving to master adept-level of magic is something else. Something much more simple and straight forward: when we enter the circle of creation, life leaves no void around us. Immediately, everywhere, we are surrounded by spirits. The land speaks, the sky speaks, the wind travels between them and knows their stories. All we need to do is to listen. And to decide how our light will shine back on them. How we will respond.

Our *response* does not need to be one of words, of songs or whispers. Our usually manner of responding happens in much more organic ways. We *tell* the world about us by the way we relate to it.

By the way we choose to show up in the world. By the way we allow our black flame or white flame or golden flame to shine.

The world through the lens of *Radical Otherness* is a place of relational networks into the unknown. The human condition is a place of many bridges. With each day we travel out into the open– and all we bring along as our tools, map and compass are the qualities that reside beneath our skin.

In pulling these qualities out from ourselves, in clearing and polishing them, we become magicians. And we become ourselves.

Paracelsus has spoken to us about how we are meant to extend this process beyond our *selves* and into the realm of spirits. For there is really no difference between the two. We heard of the polished glass of our Ingenium, and of the living light that falls upon it. Then the woman appeared and put a flame into us.

What remains to be said now is a simple thing. In the chapter on *Paracelsian Magic* we heard about the four forces by our side, helping and assisting us in this process of becoming human. We spoke of *faith* and *indifference*, of *perfection* and *improvisation*.

These opposite force-pairs can be imagined to form a dimension each. Maybe take a paper, draw them out and visualise them in the following way.

The first dimension runs from Faith to Indifference and back.

Faith in this context is defined as the human ability to place all of one's being onto the scales of a single act, to burn the bridges of "If," and to resolve the boundaries of "I."

Indifference on the other hand can be understood as the human ability not to be bothered, esp. when confronted with the adverse, strange and other, remaining present in a state of thick-skinned calm.

The second dimension runs from Perfection to Improvisation and back.

Perfection in this context should be defined as a human's ability to create with depth of purpose and breadth of capabilities to a degree of excellence which leaves nothing to be desired.

Improvisation on the other hand can be summarised as one's ability to spontaneously repurpose resources and plans to creatively address ad hoc requirements.

If you place these two dimensions on top of each other, you arrive at a sphere, divided into four quadrants. Much insight spring from meditating over this sphere and its force-fields and tensions... I spent quite some time meditating on it. After a few weeks, I had worked all of this out, visualised it in tables and graphs, and mapped every kind of magic that I know of onto these dimensions and the space between them. It taught me a whole lot about the underlying human qualities that shape our selves and the magic we engage in.

When I was finally done, I threw all of it away, returned to the simple two dimensions, and hid them into a drawer for more than six months. Only then did I return to it and wrote the following short meditations.

Really, this and the spirits around you is all you need to walk the way of the adept. To know how to handle faith and indifference, not as opposing forces but as mutually supporting ones. To know how to always have both at your side – perfection and improvisation – without preferring one over the other, but balancing calmly on the tightrope stretched out between them.

❰FAITH

Faith is a scabbard. It is a magical force inherent in us that requires the most careful of handling. By placing faith into something or someone, we place that object or person into the scabbard of our acceptance. We invite them over the threshold of ourselves and grant them unconditional access to the garden where the seedlings of trust and hope grow. The scabbard of our faith is the greatest, the most daring gift we can extend to anything or anyone. For in doing so, we express the trust that they will not spring from the scabbard and turn against us. Faith accepts the real risk of pain, wounds and being broken, in the prospect of becoming more whole. No faith is ever safe. Not because of the faith itself, but because of the freedom granted to the object or person it wraps itself around.

Learning to handle this magical power called faith begins with the pledge to oneself to stop playing games. It begins with the realisation that we no longer fight with wooden swords on a playground, but that each one of us now yields a sharp and piercing blade in words and deeds, in actions and reactions. Learning to apply our faith to the world begins with accepting that we lost the privilege of children: to scatter their faith playfully throughout their world, while trusting a watching hand to avert any kind of irreversible damage.

With the fragile shape that a tree entrusts into a young twig they place all their entire future form as a full grown branch or trunk into this tiny offshoot. Nature teaches us that all big things have small beginnings. Learning to apply our faith to this world, means we come to respect this simple principle: a thing endorsed with the scabbard of our faith is a sword invited into the garden of our dreams. As this garden is full of aggressively spreading weeds (wishes), it requires trimming and containing, it requires a sharp blade. A garden of dreams without curation and careful decisions will suffocate all plants in random wishes. However, it is the act of having faith into something or someone that hands over the tending blade into their hands. Faith accepts a loss of control, in the prospect of gaining greater companionship.

Applying faith to the world at a most foundational level thus means becoming fine with leaving a position of comfort and safety. It begins with the acceptance that at no point in our lives will there ever be a path paved by reassurance, certainty and clarity, that will lead us to a good tomorrow or even to the fulfilment of our longings. Learning to apply faith means we are willing to get up from the cushioned divan of doubt, on which one sits so comfortably and yet doesn't get anywhere. It also means we leave behind the intoxicating pleasure of drinking from the chalice of bitterness which spreads this awesome, momentary sense of strength, only to leave us hollow and numb in the long run. Learning to apply our faith to the world is not for everyone. And yet as magicians it belongs to one of the most essential lessons we wrestle with for the entirety of our lives.

Faith and love have the same parents. I invite you to contemplate their names. Faith and love are siblings born to these parents and have both brought equal amounts of destruction, pain and blindness into this world, as they opened doors to resolve, union and passage into a better life.

Placing the scabbard of our faith around an object or person is an expression of unconditional endorsement. The roots of the English word *belief* as well as the German *Glaube* both stem from the Indo-Germanic term *leubh* which translates as *to care, desire, love*. Thus, placing our faith into something means we mark it with the seal of our love, we consider it dear, we offer it the ultimate expression of countenance, approval and care. We give it permission to be itself, to express itself, within the very perimeter of what we consider our self.

In granting our faith we want to be respectful in relation to Otherness, considerate in relation to what we have to lose and wise in relation to our future we place into this act. And yet sealing this source too tightly just because of the dangers that lurk in it, would not be the way of the adept either. After all, and even though this seems to be a little-practiced craft, we can also take back our faith, and bring it home again. That won't dispel the damage done, but it expels this particular blade from our garden of trust.

So we see, while faith is a sibling to love, it is also a relative to other human virtues such as discipline, steadfastness, honesty, and loyalty. While it would be great to be able to master all of these at ones, we will place our attention on *faith* alone in the following exercises.

INDIFFERENCE

Indifference is the invisible distance between a leaf and a drop of dew that separates the two. Indifference is the fine line between a rock and a river separating what passes and what persists.

Indifference is neither gentle nor cruel. Where it applies itself to the world there is no wonder, no judgement, no answer nor question. But there is an impenetrable line dividing here from there, I from Thou, this from that, treating everything as responsible equals.

Indifference can come and pass in a moment's breath, light-footed, escaping witnessing and leaving no trace. Or it can stand forever, bold and brazen, sealing a cave with substance and weight.

Life can touch indifference in a myriad of mesmerising ways, from kiss to kill, and yet all that indifference sees is a straight line ahead. Indifference shares the table of its presence with guilt, shame, anger, fury, and despair, and it still sits at that table when all of them have moved ahead. Time slips through the hands of indifference like pearls on a rosary: each moment the same shape, one after another, one connected to the next, in an endless, looping rotation.

Indifference's secret is its inner weightlessness, born from the equilibrium of attraction and repulsion. It is the silent observer in the shadow, when wanting and hating have cut each other's throats. From where indifference stands, the tainted knife is just as beautiful as the wasted life.

Indifference shimmers in kindness because it knows no ugliness. In its presence the sick stand as tall as the strong and the ones who enter life are as old as the ones who leave it behind. Indifference is the oracle whispering upwards from the crevice in the rock towards the light, that one single sentence to each diviner: *I see you.*

In the hand of a human, indifference is a poisonous needle. Holding onto it feels as if we are holding onto nothing at all. Swiftly, in the blink of an eye, we can make that needle appear even when naked. And yet being touched by its tip holds the power to heal or hurt, to open or seal, to bind or resolve. It takes a master to command this needle, and yet it fits easily between the fingers of every child.

A heart sealed in indifference dies. A human sealed in indifference dies. The right moment sealed in indifference thrives.

❰ PERFECTION

Perfection is the most inhuman of all abilities we can dare to master. Perfection drinks an ocean of power, it breathes a sky of determination to release both in a single point. Perfection is the obsessive aspiration of man to be able to create gold according to his own formula, to give birth to diamonds from the pressure of his hollow hand, to inseminate life into the damp clay of a golem. Perfection is born from the Promethean flame, that cannot accept the *flawless* to be the privilege of the Divine.

Aspiring to perfection is a tightrope strung between the two fixed points of *theosis* and *idolatry*. In the middle of this tightrope she stands, Perfection, in all her flaming, devastating beauty, equally distant and attracted to both sides by Lucifer and Metatron.

Perfection, born from human hands, tells stories of beauty and grace, of obsession and control. It tells stories haunted by the spirits of failure and flawedness. Perfection is a demon that offers a simple barter: your heart, your blood, and soul for a single stroke of a pen, for a single line of poetry, for a single movement of feet, for a single form expressed in unwavering, graceful, eternal flawlessness. And yet there she sits, Perfection, still feeding on that beating heart, drinking the blood, and the line of the pencil shows its cracks, and the poem wavers in doubt, and the feet have lost their path, and what seemed eternal for a moment—is gone.

Then, perfection is the ashes of a canvas, the poem that was never told, the blood in the ballet-flats, the finished sculpture crumbling back into clay. Perfection drinks an ocean of power, it breathes a sky of determination to release them in a single point—or to evaporate them into nothing.

There is another kind of perfection, though.

She is one who is not not owned but encountered. One who is not hunted by will and coercion, but endowed by patience and presence.

This kind of perfection is bestowed upon us as a gift. By whom, we will never know. And what makes one worthy, but not the other, we will never know either.

All we can do is to show up, each day in the same place, and offer ourselves up to her voice as well as her silence. Here, we hold our end of the bargain, irrespective of whether the world will hold its end up as well. We put the brush to the ink, then to the canvas—neither expecting perfection nor rejecting it. We allow the brush to stroke the paper with as little as possible of any human interference. We allow the brush to express itself, perfectly, possibly, in a single moment. And the same with the pen that writes a word, and the shoes that make a step, and the chisel that forms the clay: we call upon the world to show us an expression of itself, as pure as possible, while all we can do is *to get out of the world's way*.

Humans pursuing this kind of perfection know how to tame their Promethean flame. They don't disown their inborn love for all things graceful, flawless, and gravity-defying. And yet, instead of bartering for these encounters with demons, they have learned to acknowledge and protect the softness, the gentleness of their own hearts.

Yes, they say to themselves, I am standing on this tightrope between Enoch and Cain, and I don't have to be either of them. I will hold onto this exercise and protect my heart. Not one step to the left, not one step to the right. I will remain in this place of naked, daring presence with my work. One day at a time. If perfection arrives, this moment will be perfect. If perfection fails, this moment will be perfect as well.

❰IMPROVISATION

When we improvise, there is nothing but the work at hand, a matchbox of resources, and an open horizon of opportunities.

Improvisation is not the failure of perfection, but the agile encounter of the unexpected. While perfection is able to generate flawlessness, improvisation is able to give way to the new.

Water is the ideal element to learn about improvisation. There is no wrong way for a river to flow. Put a mountain in its path, and it will still find a way. Streams divide, find fissures and cracks deep in the rock, rivulets trickle through caves, for a long time it might seem like all motion has stopped in the damp, black soil, until one day, other other side, a spring rises from the rock.

See, improvisation can be a slow journey, or it can happen in a moment's time. It is not for us to decide. Which is why we need to care as deeply for the things we try to improvise as for the things we try to perfect. Both journeys will be cruel masters. But where the former demands complete focus, the latter invites complete openness.

Improvisation is an unchartered terrain, a sky with unknown constellations, calling for us to be the first to navigate across. So on the wing of improvisation, we become sailors when a moment ago we were farmers. We become wanderers, when a moment ago we were settlers. We become searchers when a moment ago we were protectors. It is not upon us to decide when we are called to improvise.

The perfectionist is singularly conscious of what they are trying to express. The improvisor is being guided by an unknown hand in the dark onto a path that has not been travelled yet. Both are exercises in faith. The perfectionist holds onto the faith that turns them alike. The improvisor holds onto the faith that allows them to flow.

APODOSIS

THE apodosis of a text or equation is the section that explains the logical consequence. At the end of the day, that is what all books on magic really are about: *creating consequence.*

In the above chapters we have walked from the essential tenets of the way of the adept, through the forest of misunderstandings as is often encountered in man-made traditions both East and West, and out into the open wilderness that is marked by the experience of Radical Otherness. There we took a deep breath and aimed to regain orientation, some level of cohesion and a clearer line of sight.

From there we took a fresh look not at what magic is, but at the human capabilities that enable it to be worked. We had to walk slowly to differentiate imagination, inspiration and inner vision, black doors, mirrored doors and doors to be opened. Behind the latter, we encountered the footsteps of Paracelsus and followed the path he had marked for us.

Exploring our own inner firmaments, we realised how artificial and dangerous the man-made dichotomy of opposing models of magic can be: psychology and spirits, science and animism, are not meant to be kept separated but to come together in the vibrating experience of the present moment. Where the boundaries of I, Me and Mine fall away and give space to the foreign and marvellous, we realise the endless ecosystem of beings we form a part of. We also realised the naivety of considering the line drawn by our skin as anything more than a makeshift ribbon to prevent us from losing ourselves in Otherness entirely.

Emerging from this journey appeared the insights of how significant and yet humble the responsibility weighs which we all hold for how we appear in this world. Attempting to control the ecosystem—both within and around us—is a Sisyphus task that will break our vessels in the end. Taking slow and gentle, but continuous and growing responsibility over how the ecosystem will reflect itself in the speculum that underlies our mind, however, emerged as a much more promising venture.

Paracelsus and the early Rosicrucians hid this path as a treasure in their works; and they sealed it with the simple term *ingenium*. The root of the word is taken from the Greek γίγνομαι, and the Latin *gigno*, which translates as *to bring forth as a fruit of myself*, or more generally as *born* or *begotten*. Traditionally, ingenium then was read as the gifts that were begotten to us from birth, the seeds that were placed inside the soil of our selves. What we discovered, though, is that placing and drawing out these seeds is a process that never ends. The process of acquiring, attuning, attaining certain inclinations is never complete. The best we can do, to co-create this experience within our incarnated minds, is to polish the glass, and to orientate our ingenium towards a source of light or darkness that resonates with our intent. Like a looking glass under the influence of the sun, we are both *receptive specula* of a world full of spirits as well as *active agents* of causing and creating change. We catch light and we play with fire.

Thus, sharpening, polishing and enlightening our ingenium, emerged as a foundational responsibility on the path of the adept. An accountability that is never accomplished but that we need to learn to live with as an inherent burden and promise of the human condition.

On days where we walk a straight line on this path, it will be marvellous to behold how willingly an entire world of magic unfolds before us. The greatest impact sometimes can be made with the least effort. If only we know our true intent as well as where and with whom at our side we stand in the ecosystem of creation.

On days where we stray and struggle on this path, it will be soothing and calming to remember that this *too* is the human condition. And that our losing of the path for a moment might open a path for someone else. Us becoming lost for an instant might be the juncture where something else finds us. For we all navigate and wander in the same territory of Otherness.

In the end, a lot of what we learned boils down to this simple *apodosis*: the age old doctrine of occult sympathy and like attracting like requires essential rethinking. Much more than an excuse for happenstance or an invitation to dabble with the forces of creation, it holds an essential question for us. In whose light do we want to stand? And how will we reflect it back into the world? After all, it is the angelic position to face Divinity eternally, that is to reflect the light back into its source on the shortest path possible. That is *not* the human position. Ours is to look out into the wilderness, out into otherness and the vast realm of creation. Like a light shining from behind, we catch the light of divinity on the back of our head, shoulders and heart and bring it to the world ahead through our gaze and body.

Catching this light is as simple as sitting with the spirits of our purpose. Proximity creates attunement and alikeness. Once we understand the basics of magic, *shining this light out* into this world remains a much more complex endeavour. For it requires us to understand both our steps and stumbling as essentially constituent components of this path.

To illustrate the humbling and yet magical nature of this journey, let's take one more look at the *Fama Fraternitatis*. Because here there actually is a second paragraph that mentions the word *ingenium*; and it is this section that sets the founding father of the Rosicrucian brotherhood on his original path.

While he thought he knew where his journey would lead him – i.e. to Jerusalem – it is the act of radically departing from his original plan that opened the door to the journey of Christian Rosenkreutz we have all become familiar with. This letting go of the very idea that was meant to turn him into the essence of what he aspired to be—a pilgrim to the Holy Land—unlocked the path to becoming what he needed to be.

Luckily, he was not alone in the desert of finding and redefining his path, but his *ingenium* guided him steadily. Let's see for ourselves.

> *Although this brother died in Cyprus and never saw Jerusalem, our brother C.R. did not turn back but sailed on towards Damascus with the intention of visiting Jerusalem from there.*
>
> *When he had to stay there because of physical discomfort and because of his medicine, in which he was not inexperienced, he acquired the favour of the Turks, he heard by chance from the wise men of Damcar in Arabia, which miracles they performed and that all of Nature was unveiled to them. This awakened the exalted and noble ingenium of the brother C.R., so that now Jerusalem was not so much on his mind as Damcar. He could no longer master his desire, but induced the Arabs to take him to Damcar for a certain sum of money.*

He was only sixteen years old when he came there, but of a strong German constitution. There, as he himself testified, the wise men received him not as a stranger but as one for whom they had been waiting for a long time, called him by name and knew of other secrets from his monastery, about which he could not wonder enough.[17]

No one of us will live a life where their ingenium is constantly consciously present with them. Most of us will walk from clearing to clearing through a dark forest, and that is how life is meant to be lived.

But it pays off to remember that at the end of the day the essence of this work can be both intuitive and simple. Becoming *Ingenium* is a process of inhaling your angelic self, and of exhaling your own self in the form of human expressions. It is not a process that is undertaken to accomplish anything but itself. Everything that will take place, happen, occur in your life, once you make the decision to go on this journey, will become a byproduct, never a product in itself. Inhaling your angelic self and exhaling your human self becomes a matter of survival. It becomes a matter of becoming *genuine* as in

---

17 *Ob wol aber dieser Bruder in Cypern gestorben und also Jerusalem nicht gesehen, kehret doch unser Fr. C. R. nicht umb, sondern schiffet vollend hinüber und zog auff Damasco zu, in willens, von dannen Jerusalem zu besuchen.*

Als er aber wegen Leibes beschwerlichkeit alldar verharren, und wegen des Artzneyens (dessen er nicht unbericht war) der Türcken Gunst erhielte, wurde man ungefehr der Weysen zu Damcar in Arabia zu Rede, was Wunders dieselben trieben und wie ihnen die gantze Natur entdeckt were. Hiedurch wurde das hohe und edle Ingenium Frat. C. R. erweckt, daß ihme Jerusalem nicht mehr so hoch als Damcar im sinn lage. Kondte auch seine Begierde nicht mehr meistern, sondern verdinget sich den Arabern, ihn umb gewisses Geld nach Damcar zu lieffern.

Nur sechzehend Jahr war er alt, als er dahin kam, gleichwohl eines starcken teutschen Gewächs. Da empfingen ihn die Weysen, als er selber bezeuget, nicht wie einen Frembden, sondern gleichsamb auff den sie lange gewartet hetten. Nenneten ihn mit Namen, zeigten ihme auch andere Heimblichkeiten auß seinem Kloster an, dessen er sich nicht genugsamb verwundern konnte.

— Johann Valentin Andreae, Fama Fraternitas—Das Urmanifest der Rosenkreuzer Bruderschaft zum ersten Mal nach dem Manuskript bearbeitet, die vor dem Erstdruck von 1614 entstanden sind durch Pleun van der Kooij, Haarlem: Rozekruis Per, 1998, p. 74.

the original sense of the word: a matter of becoming a *native* in this world.

Becoming ingenium, therefore, is a process of radical genuineness when surrounded by Radical Otherness. We defined magic as the capability to form and cultivate relationships with Otherness. In the same vein, we define *becoming ingenium* as the capability of experiencing the world as it flows through our senses, as something of Radical Otherness. *Becoming ingenium* means we, our mind, body and soul, become the gate through which magic materialises, now, and now again. In every moment.

So whenever you feel down on this journey, when you have stumbled, faltered and failed, maybe pause for a moment and think of Christian Rosenkreutz. See him on his sickbed in an entirely alien place, his travel companions have all long moved on, pursuing their journey towards the Holy Land. He is left behind and sick and the furthest removed from experiencing himself as strong, splendid or faithful to his original plan. Then, in a moment's eye, all of these circumstances turn from being a dead end to proffering new direction. A moment of deepest grief turns into a moment to rejoice. As so often, a dire end evolves into a new beginning.

Now wouldn't Rosenkreutz have had full permission to indulge in anger, self-pity, grief and cynicism about this miserable world and how it undermined his great plans? But no, he chose the light he wanted to stand in, he held firmly on, not to his own plans but to the counsel of his ingenium—and he moved forward. He was a river that wisely understood the path he had to follow.

Of course, Christian Rosenkreutz never existed. He is a fantasy figure, a romantic emblem. Yet, Johann Valentin Andreae gave us this figure, very much in the spirit of Paracelsian magic, as a gift for our own journey. Rosenkreutz is a mnemonic aid, a key to be inserted into our own lives. So that we can see the distance between our own Jerusalem and Damcar and choose wisely—under the counsel of our ingenium.

APPENDIX 1

The following table contrasts the *I-Here-Now* with the *It-Where-When* field.

We are deliberately skipping over the *You-There-Then* field, which has been explored in much depth through Gestalt Psychology and Relational Frame Theory as their centre of attention and research.

Here, we are highlighting the three aspects of both fields as a general *resource*, as an *experience* and as a possible *overdose*, i.e. what happens if we stay confined or exposed to either of them for too long.

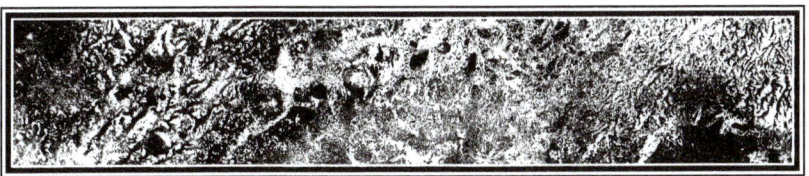

	I-HERE-NOW	IT-WHERE-WHEN
As Resource	known safety identity comfort conformity recovery consolidation connection	unknown risk adventure discomfort creativity stress activation departure
As Experience	reaffirms strengthens stabilises reconnects confirms increases energy releases tension calms	challenges stretches knocks off centre disconnects questions exhausts energy increases tension activates
As Overdose	numb cold stuck self-centred bored rigid	sore burned lost not-centered depleted brittle

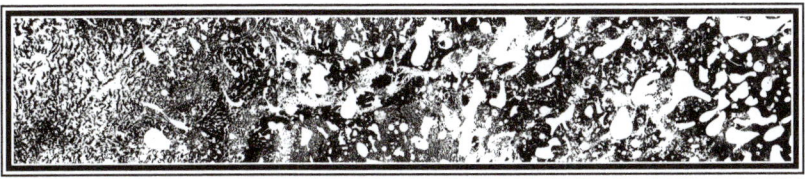

APPENDIX 2

Working with the Void

by Josephine McCarthy

THE VOID is a basic visionary meditation that can be used to tune a magical space and to tune yourself ready for work. It is also a very good exercise for strengthening your visionary abilities and stilling your mind. It can then be used briefly to still yourself before visionary magic or ritual. You can also hold your mind in the void while conducting ritual if you need to be invisible as you work.

If you work with this visionary meditation over a long period of time, you will find that you can eventually slip easily into the stillness of the void, which can then be used in times of emergency, when you need to quickly focus or 'vanish' from inner view—when you find yourself suddenly under serious inner or magical threat, slipping into the void causes you to become invisible from an inner perspective.

Before embarking on visions or ritual work, a period of stillness and silence to allow the deeper powers to connect is advisable. I use a "passing into the void," into timelessness as a good tuning exercise before heavy work. It stills our minds and it also tunes us into that older, timeless part of our spirit that exists eternally. It also builds into a consciousness of peace that tunes out everyday nonsense.

The void is a very simple and yet powerful vision/meditation that takes you in the heart of the threshold of creation: the void appears as an empty space to us, and yet it is full of potential just waiting to manifest. As a magical beginner it is a meditation that is used to still your mind. As an initiate it is a threshold place that you can pass through to access many different inner realms if you can hold focused intent for your destination. As an adept, the void is the stepping into the consciousness of Divinity, where we face the powers of creation in their purest form.

This simple and yet deep meditation expands and deepens with us as we walk on the path of magic. It is the place of 'going home', the stillness that our consciousness came from, and the place where our spirit can be itself.

When you get used to the stillness and timelessness of the void, you begin to learn how to loosen your boundaries, how to spread your spirit out beyond the shape of a human. You learn to be pure conscious thought with no form, a consciousness that can pass through all substance; a consciousness that is everywhere and nowhere. When you have finally developed that ability, it becomes a major tool for a magician when you are in danger. If you have a powerful destructive being after you, then passing quickly into the void and scattering in all directions effectively makes you disappear. There is no human spirit form for the being to grab a hold of.

Use this meditation on a daily basis, if possible—or at least regularly.

MEDITATION VISION OF THE VOID

Light a candle and close your eyes.

See the candle flame with your inner vision and see it grow before you. Be aware of a flame within you, the flame of being seated deep in your centre. The flame within you grows strong and the candle flame before you grows bigger. See yourself in your imagination step into the candle flame and let the two flames merge. You bathe in the flames that do not burn and the power of life flows through the flames and into your body, strengthening you.

When you are ready, see yourself step forward through the flames with the intent to pass into the void. You step through the fire and find yourself in a still dark place where there is no time, no space and no movement. There is nothing but stillness and silence. You let your thoughts fall away, let your sense of your body fall away and the details of your life, they too fall away, leaving you still and silent.

Drift in the silence, being aware that your boundaries and body shape have slowly fallen away, leaving you with just thought, stillness and silence. The deeper into silence you go, the more you become aware of everything that is in the nothing and the nothing that is in everything. The void is within all living things, all manifest substance, and all manifest substance is in the void.

With this realization, you find yourself out in nature, flowing through trees, rocks, cities, animals, passing through the wind, the rain, mountains and lakes. You are within everything and are a part of everything. And within that everything is the stillness, the void.

Your focus returns back to the void, back to the stillness and silence. While in the stillness, you remember your body and the room in which you are seated. As you think about your body, you find yourself standing before yourself, looking at your body. See the flame within the body and see the stillness of the void within the flame. Step back into the body and sit in ssilence, being aware of the void within you: it is always there, the still silent place within that is your true home.

Open your eyes and look at the flame before you and see the stillness and Divinity of the void within the flame.

BIBLIOGRAPHY

Acher, Frater, *Holy Heretics*, London: Scarlet Imprint, 2022.

Acher, Frater, *Holy Daimon*, London: Scarlet Imprint, 2018.

Acher, Frater, Sabogal, José Gabriel Alegría, *Clavis Goêtica: Keys to Chthonic Sorcery*, s.l.: Hadean Press, 2021.

Andreae, Johann Valentin, *Fama Fraternitas — Das Urmanifest der Rosenkreuzer Bruderschaft zum ersten Mal nach dem Manuskript bearbeitet, die vor dem Erstdruck von 1614 entstanden sind durch Pleun van der Kooij*, Haarlem: Rozekruis Per, 1998.

Agamben, Giorgio, *Die Beamten des Himmels: Über Engel*, Aus dem Italienischen übersetzt und herausgegeben von Andreas Hiepko. Mit der Angelologie des Thomas von Aquin, Berlin: Suhrkamp, 2007.

Berlin, Brent, Breedlove, Dennis E., Raven, Peter H.; *Folk Taxonomies and Biological Classification*, in: *Science*, Vol. 154, No. 3746 (Oct. 14, 1966), Washington: American Association for the Advancement of Science, 1966, pp. 273–275.

Beyer, Stephan; *Magic and Ritual in Tibet: The Cult of Tara*, Delhi: Motilal Banarsidass, 1988.

Bryman, Alan E.; *The Disneyization of Society*, London: Sage Publishers, 2004.

Budge, E. A. Wallis; *From Fetish To God In Ancient Egypt*, London: Oxford University Press, 1934.

Burkert, Walter, *Greek Religion*, Cambridge, MA: Harvard University Press, 1985.

Busch, Peter, *Das Testament Salomos - Die älteste christliche Dämonologie, kommentiert und in deutscher Erstübersetzung*, Berlin: De Gruyter, 2006.

Canaan, Tewfik, "The Decipherment of Arabic Talismans," in: *Berytus — Archaeological Studies*, Volume 4, Beirut: American University of Beirut, 1937, pp. 69–110.

Durkheim, Emile, Mauss, Marcel; *Primitive Classification*, London: Cohen & West, 2009 (1903), https://monoskop.org/images/4/4d/Durkheim_Emile_Mauss_Marcel_Primitive_Classification_2nd_ed_1969.pdf.

Eurostat (ed.), EU *crude divorce rate on the rise*, July 2020, Brussels: Communication department of the European Commission, 2020 https://ec.europa.eu/eurostat/web/products-eurostat-news/-/ddn-20200710-1.

Fitzgerald, Robert; *Sharp Practice — The Ritual Dagger in Bön Sorcery and Vajrayana Buddhism*, s.l.: Three Hands Press, 2019.

Goldammer, Kurt, *Der Göttliche Magier und die Magierin Natur*, Kosmosophie Band V, Stuttgart: Franz Steiner Verlag, 1991.

Goldammer, Kurt (ed.), *Theophrast von Hohenheim, gennant Paracelsus. Die Kärntner Schriften*, Klagenfurt: Amt der Kärntner Landesregierung, 1955.

Goldammer, Kurt, Kramml, Peter F., Dopsch, Heinz, (ed.), *Paracelsus (1493–1541), «Keines andern Knecht»*, Salzburg: Pustet, 1993.

Greenfield, Peter P. H., *Traditions of Belief in Late Byzantine Demonology*, Amsterdam: Adolf M. Hakkert, 1988.

Harding, Sarah, *Machik's Complete Explanation: Clarifying the Meaning of Chöd, a Complete Explanation of Casting Out the Body as Food*, Boston & London: Snow Lion, 2013.

Hermanns, Matthias, *Mythologie der Tibeter*, Essen: Phaidon Verlag, 1997.

Kitat, Sara El-Sayed, "The Iconography and Function of Winged Gods in Egypt during the Graeco-Roman Period", in: *Journal of The Faculty of Tourism and Hotels*, Volume 12, Issue 1, s.l.: Egypt's Presidential Specialized Council for Education and Scientific Research, 2016, pp. 46–69.

Lebling, Robert, *Legends of the Fire Spirits: Jinn and Genies from Arabia to Zanzibar*, Berkeley: Counterpoint, 2011.

Lévi, Eliphas, *Transzendentale Magie - Dogma und Ritual*, Basel: Sphinx Verlag, 1995.

Lévi, Eliphas, *Einweihungsbriefe in die Hohe Magie und Zahlenmystik*, Interlaken: Ansata Verlag, 1993.

Lorry, Pierre, *Hermetic Literature III: Arab*, in: Hanegraaff, Wouter J. (ed.), *Dictionary of Gnosis & Western Esotericism*, Leiden: Brill Academic Publishing, 2006, pp. 529–533.

Marathakis, Ioannis (ed.), *The Magical Treatise of Solomon, or Hygromanteia*, Singapore: Golden Hoard, 2011.

McCarthy, Josephine, *Magical Healing*, Exeter: TaDehent Books, 2019.
McCarthy, Josephine, *Quareia: The Initiate*, Exeter: Quareia Publishing, 2016.
McIntosh, Christopher; *Eliphas Lévi and the French Occult Revival*, New York: Samuel Weiser, 1974.
Müller-Ebeling, Claudia, Rätsch, Christian, Bahadur Shahi, Surendra, *Shamanism and Tantra in the Himalayas*, London: Thames & Hudson, 2002.
Namgail, Tashi, *History and Culture of Dard People of Ladakh*, Bilaspur: Booksclinic Publishing, 2020.
Nünlist, Tobias, *Dämonenglaube im Islam*, Berlin: Walter De Gruyter, 2015.
Nünlist, Tobias, "Der Dämonenglaube im Bereich des Islams: eine unbekannte Materialsammlung im Nachlass Fritz Meiers (1912–1998)," in: *Asiatische Studien*, 62 (4), Berlin: Walter De Gruyter, 2008, pp. 1027–1041.
Obrist, Barbara, "Wind Diagrams and Medieval Cosmology," in: *Speculum*, Vol. 72, No. 1, Chicago: University of Chicago Press, 1977, pp. 33–84.
Pagel, Walter, *Das Medizinische Weltbild des Paracelsus, seine Zusammenhänge mit Neuplatonismus und Gnosis, Kosmosophie*, Band I, Wiesbaden: Franz Steiner Verlag, 1962.
Paracelsus, *Werke,* Studienausgabe in fünf Bänden, Basel: Schwab reflexe, 2010 (for further works of Paracelsus see under: Goldammer and Sudhoff).
Perls, Fritz, *Gestalt Therapy Verbatim*, Gouldsboro: The Gestalt Journal Press, 1992, kindle edition.
Peterson, Joseph, *The Sworn Book of Honorius – Liber Iuratus Honorii*, Lake Worth/FL: IBIS Press, 2016.
Peuckert, Will-Erich, *Jakob Böhme - Sämtliche Schriften*, Stuttgart-Bad Cannstatt: Frommann Verlag Günther Holzboog, 1955–1960.
Peuckert, Will-Erich, *Pansophie — Ein Versuch zur Geschichte der weissen und schwarzen Magie*, Berlin: Erich Schmidt Verlag, 1956.
Peuckert, Will-Erich, *Theophrastus Paracelsus*, Stuttgart-Berlin: Kohlhammer Verlag, 1941.
Rabinow, Paul, "Representations Are Social Facts: Modernity and Post-Modernity in Anthropology," in: James Clifford & George E. Marcus

(ed.) *Writing Culture: the Poetics and Politics of Ethnography*. Berkeley: University of California Press, 1986.

Radin, Dean, *Real Magic*, New York: Harmony Books, 2018.

Schlag, Oskar R., *Von Alten und Neuen Mysterien, Die Lehren des A.*, Band I, Zürich: Ergon Verlag, 1998.

Schopenhauer, Arthur; *Versuch über das Geistersehen und was damit zusammenhängt*, Eingeleitet und herausgegeben von Dr. G. F. Hartlaub, Stuttgart: Fromms Verlag, 1922.

Shadrach, Nineveh, Harrison, Francis, *Magic That Works: Practical Training for the Children of Light*, Burnaby: Ishtar Publishing, 2005.

Stöhr, Robert, Lohwasser, Diana, Noack Napoles, Juliane, Burghardt, Daniel, Dederich, Markus (ed.); *Schlüsselwerke der Vulnerabilitätsforschung*, Wiesbaden: Springer Fachmedien, 2019.

Franz Strunz, *Theophrastus Paracelsus — Idee und Problem seiner Weltanschauung*, Salzburg & Leipzig: Verlag Anton Pustet, 1937.

Sudhoff, Karl; *Bibliographia Paracelsica,* Berlin: Verlag Georg Reimer, 1894 [Reprint by Martino Publishing, 2000].

Sudhoff, Karl (ed.); *Theophrast von Hohenheim, gen. Paracelsus, Sämtliche Werke*, Vol. I–XIV, München/Berlin: R. Oldenbourg, 1922–1933.

Torijano, Pablo A., *Solomon the Esoteric King: From King to Magus, Development of a Tradition*, Leiden: Brill, 2002.

Tyson, Donald (ed.), *Three Books of Occult Philosophy*, written by Henry Cornelius Agrippa of Nettesheim, Completely Annotated, with Modern Commentary, Woodbury: Llewellyn Publications, 1992.

Waldenfels, Bernhard; "Virus als Pathos," in: *Philosophische Rundschau*, Jahrgang 67, Heft 2, Tübingen: Mohr-Siebeck, 2020, pp. 96–100.

Waldenfels, Bernhard; *Grundmotive einer Phänomenologie des Fremden*, Frankfurt am Main: Suhrkamp, 2018 (2006).

Waldenfels, Bernhard; *Topographie des Fremden — Studien zur Phänomenologie des Fremden 1*, Frankfurt am Main: suhrkamp taschenbuch, 2020 (1997).

Waldenfels, Bernhard; *Sinnesschwellen — Studien zur Phänomenologie des Fremden 3*, Frankfurt am Main: suhrkamp taschenbuch, 2013 (1999).

Westermarck, Edward, *Ritual and Belief in Morocco*, in Two Volumes, London: MacMillan and Co., 1926.

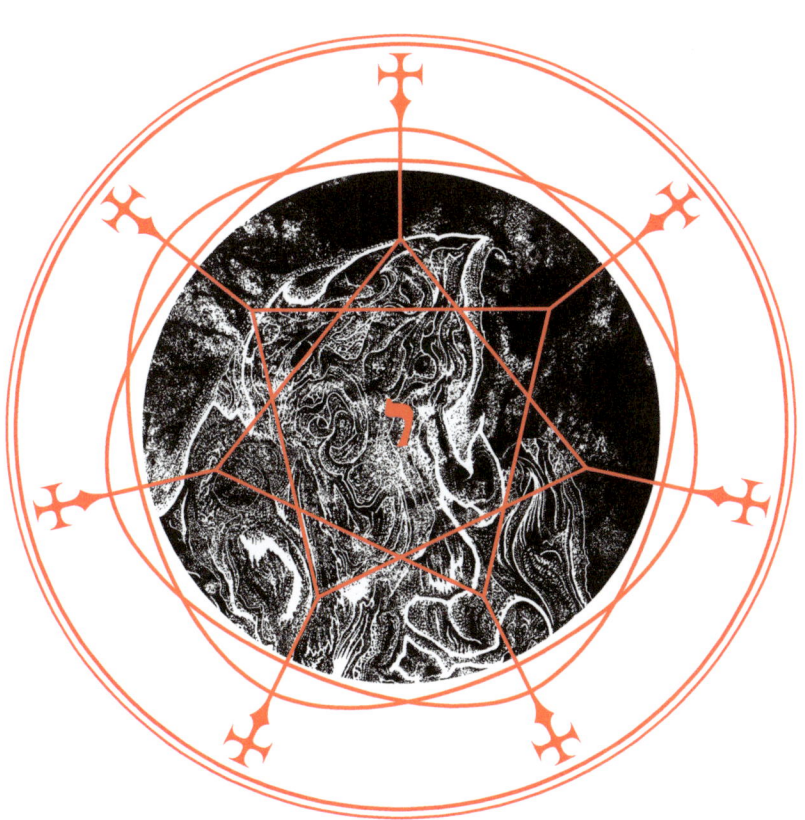

www.ingramcontent.com/pod-product-compliance
Lightning Source LLC
Chambersburg PA
CBHW040200100526
44590CB00006B/139